Job Bias

Job Bias

Edited by Lester A. Sobel

Contributing editors: Joseph Fickes, Stephen
 Orlofsky, Gerry Satterwhite, Barry
 Youngerman

Indexer: Grace M. Ferrara

FACTS ON FILE, INC.   NEW YORK, N.Y.

Job Bias

Library of Congress Cataloging in Publication data:
Job bias.

Includes index.
1. Discrimination in employment—United States.
I. Sobel, Lester A.   II. Facts on File, Inc., New York.
HD4903.5.U58J6   331.1'33'0973   76-41984
ISBN 0-87196-244-6

9 8 7 6 5 4 3 2 1
PRINTED IN
THE UNITED STATES OF AMERICA

Contents

1935454

*   *   *

GRAPHS, TABLES & OTHER ILLUSTRATIVE MATTER

Employment Discrimination in American

E QUALITY OF OPPORTUNITY HAS BECOME a basic economic ideal of the United States. Americans appear to be in general agreement that merit should be the only criterion for getting a job or for advancing in one. Yet it is widely acknowledged that women and blacks and members of various other racial, ethnic and religious minorities in this country are seriously handicapped by their sex or origin rather than merely by any lack of ability when they seek employment or job advancement.

The roots of employment discrimination against black and other minority workers and women (regardless of race) are embedded to a great extent in the struggle for economic survival.

In the case of the black worker, this motive goes back to the days when most black Americans were slaves. As E. Franklin Frazier pointed out in *The Negro in the United States* (1957), "the utilization of slave labor in manufacture . . . [in the South] brought to the surface the competition between Negroes and the poor whites. There was agitation against the hiring out of slaves as competitors of white mechanics and artisans. In Georgia the white laboring class succeeded in getting the legislature to pass a law in 1845 prohibiting contracts with slave and free Negro mechanics. On the whole, however, the slaveholders were able to prevent any serious restriction upon the employment of slaves in industrial occupations." In the industrial North, the emancipation of the slaves was opposed by white workers, many of them immigrants, for fear that many former slaves would move North, compete for "white" jobs and cause wage rates to fall.

An influx of white women into industry took place in the South

1974-75 Unemployment Rates by Sex & Race

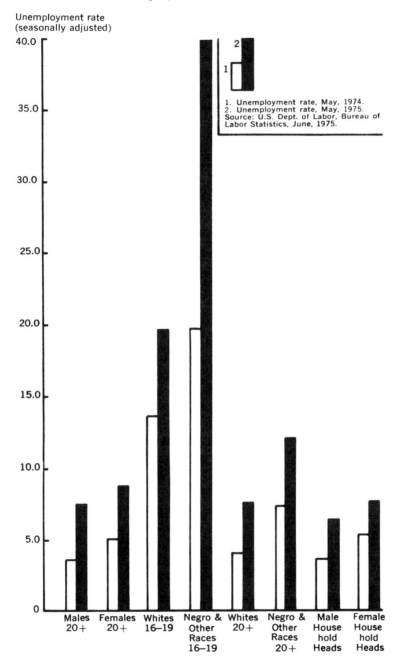

Unemployment rate
(seasonally adjusted)

1. Unemployment rate, May, 1974.
2. Unemployment rate, May, 1975.
Source: U.S. Dept. of Labor, Bureau of
Labor Statistics, June, 1975.

From Congressional Budget Office, "Inflation & Unemployment: A Report on the Economy." June 30, 1975 in the decades after the close of the Civil War. Gunnar Myrdal noted in *An American Dilemma* (1944) that this new competition for jobs provoked fresh discrimination against black workers, both because of the Southern code that barred white women and black men from working together and because of the basic rivalry over employment advantage.

Fluctuations in the economic climate in the century following emancipation alternately eased and tightened restrictions on black and women workers. The needs of industry, especially during World Wars I and II and the Korean War, brought an influx of black workers to the North, Middle West and West and opened cracks in the employment barriers erected against women. But blacks and women were the first to suffer when economic depression caused lay-offs.

The 1960s appeared to be a period of promise for minority workers. But the economic downturn of the early 1970s brought reverses for almost all wage-earners, with black workers, as usual, faring the worst.

Barbara Becnel reported in the July 1976 issue of the AFL-CIO *American Federationist* that the stage had apparently been "set for growing opportunities within the black community by events of the 1960s—an advancing national economy, a rising level of social awareness and such vital pieces of legislation as the 1964 Civil Rights Act and the manpower and economic opportunity programs of that same era. Consequently, many blacks were able to benefit from the opening of doors that were once closed. The rapid advances of the 1960s were shortlived. . . . Although most Americans have felt the adverse effects of back-to-back recessions, black workers have suffered more severely. . . . When unemployment among all Americans rose to 8.9% in 1975, it was 13.9% for nonwhites. . . . As unemployment rates began to increase, layoffs loomed ahead for many of the blacks who had just begun to acquire new and higher paying jobs."

According to Becnel, "much of the income gains registered by blacks [in the 1960s] was a direct result of increased educational opportunities, vocational training and occupational upgrading. The number of blacks age 20 to 24 completing four years of high school or more rose dramatically—up to 65% in 1970 from 42% in 1960. Similarly, the proportion of blacks 25 to 34 years old who completed four years of college or more also rose, from 4.1% to 6.1% over the 10-year period, 1960 to 1970. . . .[A]s more blacks man-

Unemployment Totals & Rates by Sex & Race (Annual Averages)

	Number unemployed (thousands)									Unemployment rate								
				White			Negro and other races						White			Negro and other races		
Year	Total	Male	Female	Total	Male	Female	Total	Male	Female	Total	Male	Female	Total	Male	Female	Total	Male	Female
1947	2,311	1,692	619	(1)	(1)	(1)	(1)	(1)	(1)	3.9	4.0	3.7	(1)	(1)	(1)	(1)	(1)	(1)
1948	2,276	1,559	717	(1)	(1)	(1)	(1)	(1)	(1)	3.8	3.6	4.1	3.5	3.4	3.8	5.9	5.8	6.1
1949	3,637	2,572	1,065	(1)	(1)	(1)	(1)	(1)	(1)	5.9	5.9	6.0	5.6	5.6	5.7	8.9	9.6	7.9
1950	3,288	2,239	1,049	(1)	(1)	(1)	(1)	(1)	(1)	5.3	5.1	5.7	4.9	4.7	5.3	9.0	9.4	8.4
1951	2,055	1,221	834	(1)	(1)	(1)	(1)	(1)	(1)	3.3	2.8	4.4	3.1	2.6	4.2	5.3	4.9	6.1
1952	1,883	1,185	698	(1)	(1)	(1)	(1)	(1)	(1)	3.0	2.8	3.6	2.8	2.5	3.1	5.4	5.2	5.7
1953	1,834	1,202	632	(1)	(1)	(1)	(1)	(1)	(1)	2.9	2.8	3.3	2.7	2.5	3.1	4.5	4.8	4.1
1954	3,532	2,344	1,188	2,860	1,913	947	674	431	243	5.5	5.3	6.0	5.0	4.8	5.6	9.9	10.3	9.3
1955	2,852	1,854	998	2,248	1,475	773	601	376	225	4.4	4.2	4.9	3.9	3.7	4.3	8.7	8.8	8.4
1956	2,750	1,711	1,039	2,162	1,368	794	592	345	247	4.1	3.8	4.8	3.6	3.4	4.2	8.3	7.9	8.9
1957	2,859	1,841	1,018	2,289	1,478	811	569	363	206	4.3	4.1	4.7	3.8	3.6	4.3	7.9	8.3	7.3
1958	4,602	3,098	1,504	3,679	2,488	1,191	925	611	314	6.8	6.8	6.8	6.1	6.1	6.2	12.6	13.8	10.8
1959	3,740	2,420	1,320	2,947	1,904	1,044	794	518	276	5.5	5.3	5.9	4.8	4.6	5.3	10.7	11.5	9.4
1960	3,852	2,486	1,366	3,063	1,987	1,076	787	497	290	5.5	5.4	5.9	4.9	4.8	5.3	10.2	10.7	9.4
1961	4,714	2,997	1,717	3,742	2,398	1,344	970	599	371	6.7	6.4	7.2	6.0	5.7	6.5	12.4	12.8	11.8
1962	3,911	2,423	1,488	3,052	1,915	1,137	859	508	351	5.5	5.2	6.2	4.9	4.6	5.5	10.9	10.9	11.0
1963	4,070	2,472	1,598	3,208	1,976	1,232	864	496	368	5.7	5.2	6.5	5.0	4.7	5.8	10.8	10.5	11.2
1964	3,786	2,205	1,581	2,999	1,779	1,220	786	426	360	5.2	4.6	6.2	4.6	4.1	5.5	9.6	8.9	10.6
1965	3,366	1,914	1,452	2,691	1,556	1,135	676	359	317	4.5	4.0	5.5	4.1	3.6	5.0	8.1	7.4	9.2
1966	2,875	1,551	1,324	2,253	1,240	1,013	621	311	310	3.8	3.2	4.8	3.3	2.8	4.3	7.3	6.3	8.6
1967	2,975	1,508	1,468	2,338	1,208	1,130	638	299	338	3.8	3.1	5.2	3.4	2.7	4.6	7.4	6.0	9.1
1968	2,817	1,419	1,397	2,226	1,142	1,084	590	277	313	3.6	2.9	4.8	3.2	2.6	4.3	6.7	5.6	8.3
1969	2,831	1,403	1,428	2,261	1,137	1,124	570	266	304	3.5	2.8	4.7	3.1	2.5	4.2	6.4	5.3	7.8
1970	4,088	2,235	1,853	3,337	1,856	1,480	752	379	373	4.9	4.4	5.9	4.5	4.0	5.4	8.2	7.3	9.3
1971	4,993	2,776	2,217	4,074	2,302	1,772	919	474	445	5.9	5.3	6.9	5.4	4.9	6.3	9.9	9.1	10.8
1972	4,840	2,635	2,205	3,884	2,160	1,724	956	475	482	5.6	4.9	6.6	5.0	4.5	5.9	10.0	8.9	11.3
1973	4,304	2,240	2,064	3,411	1,818	1,593	894	423	471	4.9	4.1	6.0	4.3	3.7	5.3	8.9	7.6	10.5
1974	5,076	2,668	2,408	4,057	2,146	1,911	1,018	521	497	5.6	4.8	6.7	5.0	4.3	6.1	9.9	9.1	10.7
1975	7,830	4,385	3,445	6,371	3,597	2,774	1,459	787	671	8.5	7.9	9.3	7.8	7.2	8.6	13.9	13.7	14.0

1 Absolute numbers by color are not available prior to 1954 because of the absence of population controls by color, and rates by color are not available for 1947.

From "Employment and Training Report of the President," submitted by President Ford to Congress June 1976

aged to stay in school longer, the types of jobs held by blacks began to improve. In 1964, for example, the proportion of nonwhite males employed as white-collar workers was only 16%, but by 1970 that figure was up to 22%. An even more dramatic change during the same period saw the percentage of females employed as white-collar workers advance from 22% to 36%. . . .''

The recession and inflation that followed the 1960s, however, idled about one-third of the nation's industrial plant and equipment by 1975. Unemployment ''among nonwhites jumped from 8.9% in 1973 to 13.9% in 1975,'' Becnel said, ''and many of the gains made by blacks during the 1960s abruptly began to vanish. . . . [W]orker attitudes have grown more and more negative in the face of high and continued levels of unemployment. One by-product has been the decrease in labor force participation—the proportion of the civilian, non-institutional population that is actively seeking work and therefore officially counted as part of the labor force. For nonwhite adult males, participation rates have dropped in almost all age categories. From 1970 to 1974, labor force participation rates for nonwhite men, age 16 years and over, dropped to 73.3%, down from 76.5% in 1970. . . . By 1975, obtaining or holding on to a job became difficult or impossible for large numbers of workers. Older blacks, black teenagers and adult black women have been particularly hard hit. Not possessing the level of skills, education or experience enjoyed by others in the labor force, these workers faced an impossible situation in securing employment and many gave up the search, joining the ranks of discouraged workers—workers who after trying for many months and sometimes years to obtain employment, finally give up because they know no jobs are available. Of the 1.1 million persons officially reported by the Bureau of Labor Statistics as being discouraged workers in 1975, nonwhites accounted for approximately 28%, or slightly over 300,000, while blacks made up only 11.4% of the total civilian labor force at that same time. . . . For blacks in 1975, there were an average of 1.5 million workers without jobs, 13.9% of the 10.5 million blacks in the civilian labor force. Adding in the average 300,000 black discouraged workers and one-half of the 664,000 blacks working part-time involuntarily—and one-half of them should be counted as unemployed—brings the black jobless total in 1975 to 2.1 million, or 19.4% of the adjusted black civilian labor force of 10.8 million. That's decidedly more than the 'official black unemployment of 13.9%.''

'Meanings' of the Bias Problem

The National Manpower Policy Task Force pointed out in a 1975 report that discrimination has "various meanings." "Some interpret racial discrimination only as specific overt acts against people because of their race," the report said. But "in a broader and more important sense," it continued, ". . . [racial] discrimination designates racism or institutionalized discrimination which permeates social and economic institutions and therefore does not require conscious or overt acts or decisions. Institutionalized discrimination leads to segregated housing, schools, jobs, training and health care. These disadvantages produce unequal job opportunities and income whether or not specific individuals are prejudiced against blacks or make specific decisions adversely affecting them. . . ."

"Discrimination apparently is based to a significant degree on status considerations; people regarded as 'inferior' are the object of discrimination because the 'status' of the discriminators is damaged by the hiring or upgrading of those discriminated against," the report said. "Employers discriminate partly because of racial prejudices and partly for economic reasons. Although employers ordinarily make employment decisions aimed at maximizing profits, management employment decisions often reflect fears of adverse reactions from biased employees, supervisors or customers. Managers also have biases, largely based on status considerations, which modify their economic motives. While management apparently will accept minorities or women in blue-collar occupations, the main biases affecting those occupations are probably those of employees. However, management's status biases will have stronger direct influences on the hiring of women or minorities into managerial positions. White workers may resist the entry of blacks into jobs because of emotional bias and bigotry as well as the more rational quest for job control. White incumbents in particular jobs will try to monopolize those jobs for themselves and will attempt to resist the hiring of people regarded to be of lower status. . . ."

The task force report related the developments of the 1960s and early 1970s to the "status" situation. During the 1960s, the report said, "nonwhites (of whom over 90% are black) increased their proportions of higher status and better paying white-collar jobs while they reduced their proportion in the service and laborer categories. Blacks in the 25-44 age group improved their employment patterns relative to whites and relative to blacks in other age groups. Despite these gains, however, blacks have a long way to go to gain equality with whites. The steady progress made by blacks during the 1960s has been seriously interrupted during the 1970s. Blacks still account for over half of all private household workers and over a fifth of all laundry and dry-cleaning operatives, laborers, hospital attendants, janitors, maids and cleaners. At the other end of the employment scale, blacks represent only 2.8% of managers, administrators and proprietors; 3% of sales workers; and very low proportions of many professional and technical workers. Entry into these occupations remains difficult.''

The task force found that ''blacks experienced dramatic percentage increases in some professional-technical jobs, but within these occupations they continue to be heavily concentrated among the lower-paid classifications, including social and recreation workers, registered nurses, medical and dental technicians, and elementary and high school teachers. Similarly, in the craft occupations, blacks are underrepresented in the electrical, plumbing and printing crafts and overrepresented among brick masons, cement and concrete finishers, cranemen, derrick operators, painters, and roofers and slaters. Black males earn less than whites even after adjusting for years of schooling, regularity of work and occupational differentials. After adjusting their incomes for education, intermittent work, and occupation, black males in the 25-34 age group still earn only 82% as much as whites. On the other hand, adjusting relative female incomes for education, regularity of work, and occupation brings black females to parity with whites in the 25-34 age group. The dramatic shift in the relative economic status of black women (as measured by ratios of black/white median incomes) is due partly to the restrictions placed on the upward mobility of white women. Black women, particularly heads of families, however, remained at the bottom of the income pyramid.''

''Blacks also suffer more from unemployment that whites,'' the task force report said. But it cited the incidence of unemployment as ''only one measure of the problem of joblessness. Blacks not only have a higher rate of unemployment than their white counterparts, but the mean duration of their unemployment is longer. In addition, the number of spells of unemployment during the year is greater for blacks than for whites. . . . Because of these work interruptions and the fact that they have more recently entered many nonagricultural jobs, blacks tend to have less tenure on the job than whites. Since seniority is an important determinant of job security, occupational upgrading and other benefits, work interruptions and relatively short job tenure have long-run consequences. . . . An important factor in

1974–75 Employment Status by Race, Spanish Origin, Sex & Age (Annual Averages)

Employment status, sex, and age	Total		White		Negro [1]		Spanish origin [2]	
	1975	1974	1975	1974	1975	1974	1975	1974
MALE, 20 YEARS AND OVER								
Civilian noninstitutional population	63,357	62,149	56,501	55,497	5,954	5,803	2,664	2,618
Civilian labor force	50,855	50,363	45,617	45,195	4,514	4,495	2,278	2,253
Percent of population	80.3	81.0	80.7	81.4	75.8	77.5	85.5	86.1
Employment	47,427	48,445	42,801	43,630	3,955	4,168	2,057	2,117
Agriculture	2,422	2,523	2,216	2,297	178	191	150	192
Nonagricultural industries	45,005	45,921	40,585	41,332	3,777	3,978	1,907	1,925
Unemployment	3,428	1,918	2,816	1,565	559	326	220	135
Unemployment rate	6.7	3.8	6.2	3.5	12.4	7.3	9.7	6.0
Not in labor force	12,502	11,786	10,884	10,302	1,440	1,308	386	365
FEMALE, 20 YEARS AND OVER								
Civilian noninstitutional population	71,650	70,396	63,145	62,163	7,427	7,244	3,083	2,896
Civilian labor force	32,959	31,836	28,609	27,616	3,786	3,720	1,345	1,233
Percent of population	46.0	45.2	45.3	44.4	51.0	51.4	43.6	42.6
Employment	30,310	30,088	26,459	26,222	3,328	3,397	1,189	1,138
Agriculture	505	520	467	479	30	33	19	27
Nonagricultural industries	29,805	29,568	25,993	25,743	3,299	3,365	1,171	1,111
Unemployment	2,649	1,748	2,149	1,394	458	322	156	95
Unemployment rate	8.0	5.5	7.5	5.0	12.1	8.7	11.6	7.7
Not in labor force	38,691	38,560	34,537	34,547	3,641	3,525	1,738	1,663

[1] Data relate to Negro workers only.
[2] Data on persons of Spanish origin are tabulated separately, without regard to race/color, which means that they are also included in the data for white and Negro workers. According to the 1970 census, approximately 98 percent of their population is white.

From "Employment and Training Report of the President," submitted by President Ford to Congress June 1976

explaining the higher unemployment rate of blacks is that they are concentrated in occupations where unemployment tends to be high such as nonfarm laborers, operatives, and service workers. Blacks also suffer relatively high unemployment rates because they are more likely than whites to be concentrated in 'secondary labor markets,' where seniority means very little and where wages and working conditions are barely preferable to street life and welfare. On the average, in 1972, non-white workers were two-thirds more likely than whites to have lost and quit their jobs and 2.2 times more likely to be experiencing reentry or first-entry problems."

According to the task force, "unemployment rates are imperfect indicators of nonwhite labor market disadvantages, however, because these rates reflect only those who are willing and able to work and actively seeking jobs. The unemployment data exclude those working part-time who would like full-time jobs, those working but not earning enough to raise them above the poverty level, or those who have become discouraged and ceased looking for jobs. Consequently, there is reason to be concerned about the fact that relative to whites, the labor force participation rates for nonwhite males over 16 years of age declined from 83% in 1960 to 74% in 1973 (when the white rate was 80%). Although rising school attendance may have accounted for some of the decline in young nonwhite male participation, the decline in the labor force participation of black males in the prime working age group, 25 to 54 years, has been sharp. Among nonwhite females, there was a slight increase in participation from 48% in 1960 to 49% in 1973, but over the same period, the white female rate rose substantially, from 37% to 44%. . . ."

The task force reported that "many of the changes in black employment patterns were apparently due more to the indirect effects of antidiscrimination laws than to their enforcement. As noted earlier, many employers were motivated by business reasons to hire blacks but were reluctant to do so for fear of adverse reactions from white employees or, probably, to a lesser degree, white customers. One of the most significant aspects of legislation is that it represents the attitudes of a majority of voters and consequently carries considerable moral force. Many employers who faced limited opposition to change therefore probably responded to legislation by adopting anti-discrimination policies. Even those employers who faced opposition from white communities and employees used the law to 'neutralize' this opposition where they were inclined for profit or moral reasons to hire or upgrade blacks. We suspect, however, that the hiring or upgrading of blacks in many relatively low-wage industries in the South can be attributed to the fact that these employers were having trouble locating an adequate supply of whites who met their hiring standards. Qualified blacks, whose employment opportunities have been more restricted because of discrimination, formed more dependable supplies of labor for these jobs. . . ."

Federal Action Against Job Bias

The original federal fair employment practices regulation was issued by President Franklin D. Roosevelt June 25, 1941 as a war measure almost as much as a matter of economic justice. This Executive Order 8802 created a Committee on Fair Employment Practices and required that defense contracts ban employment bias because of race, creed, color or national origin.

Since the expiration of this wartime order, the federal government has attacked employment discrimination through a variety of legislative and executive actions. The following are among significant federal actions in this area:
• The Civil Rights Act of 1964 (as amended) requires a wide degree of "equal employment opportunity" under Title VII. This title prohibits discrimination based on race, color, religion, sex and national origin in all terms, conditions and privileges of employment by: (a) employers who have 15 or more employes; (b) employment agencies that regularly procure employes for an employer who is covered by Title VII (covered employment agencies include the U.S. Employment Service and the system of state and local employment services receiving federal assistance); (c) most labor unions.

Title VII established the Equal Employment Opportunity Commission (EEOC) to administer the act.

Title VII covers the entire range of the employe/employer/ employment agency/union relationship. Thus, employes are entitled to be free of unlawful discrimination with regard to recruitment; classified advertising; job classification; hire; utilization of physical facilities; transfer; promotion; discharge; wages and salaries; seniority lines; testing; insurance coverage; pension and retirement benefits; referral to jobs; and union membership. It is unlawful for an employer, employment agency or labor union to discharge, discipline, harass or otherwise retaliate against any person for filing a charge; for participating in an EEOC investigation, proceeding or hearing; or for opposing any employment practice prohibited by Title VII. Where there is a pattern or practice of employment discrimination, not only the charging party but also the U.S. attorney general was originally given the power to bring suit in the appropriate federal district court. At the discretion of the court, the attorney general, moreover, was given authority to intervene in suits brought by charging parties if he certified that the case was of general public importance. The EEOC since 1972 has had the power to institute court proceedings to seek enforcement of rulings against employment discrimination as well as to intervene in the court actions brought by aggrieved persons.

According to the Labor Department, "some of the EEOC's most significant contributions to the understanding and elimination of employment discrimination have occurred not in the context of case processing but in the performance of its broader obligations under the act. In meeting its responsibilities for dealing with employment discrimination on a 'wholesale' basis, the EEOC has conducted and financed research and held hearings on significant occupational categories and major industries in areas where such occupations and industries are concentrated. Thus, the EEOC financed a report on the rubber industry in Ohio issued in September 1967; and conducted hearings on the textile industry in North and South Carolina in January 1967, in white-collar employment in New York City in January 1968, in the aerospace and communications industries in Los Angeles in March 1969, and in a number of industries, such as petroleum and chemicals, in Houston in June 1970."

Beginning in 1966 for employers and 1967 for labor unions and joint labor-management apprenticeship committees, the EEOC has required annual reports on the employment of members of minority groups and women, with information on the types of jobs they hold, their union membership, their participation in job referral systems and apprenticeship programs, etc. The research activities of the EEOC are designed to improve the patterns of minority groups and women's employment. For this reason, the commission makes available, within the confidentiality restrictions of the act, the information gained through research. Thus, a large number of state and local fair employment practices agencies have access to the reports filed with the commission through data-sharing agreements. The relationship between the EEOC and state and local anti-discrimination agencies goes far beyond the sharing of research information. Title VII gives the EEOC both the authority and the duty to work closely with and through these agencies to accomplish the common goal of eliminating employment discrimination. In this connection, the commission plans and administers a program of grants and contracts to such agencies for services rendered to assist the EEOC in carrying out its responsibilities. The commission focuses on "affirmative action" grants, whose purpose is to place minority group members and women in jobs previously unavailable to them.

The act provides that the EEOC may furnish to those subject to the act such "technical assistance" as they may request to further their compliance with Title VII. Accordingly, employers, employment agencies and labor unions may call on the resources and personnel of the commission to assist them in voluntarily ending past patterns of discrimination, instituting fair employment practices and developing "affirmative action programs" designed to increase opportunities for minorities and women. In addition to responding to requests for aid, the EEOC takes the initiative in developing key programs to eliminate discrimination. Some of these programs are directed at specific industries and unions, some concentrate on a particular geographical area, and some operate across the board with regard to one or more aspects of the employment process. Thus, commission personnel have met with representatives of the drug and utilities industries; have worked with unions in expanding the "Operation Outreach" program, which seeks to provide opportunities for apprenticeship training for minority group youth; and have developed the "New Plants" program, designed to ensure the establishment of fair employment practices when a new plant is opened.

Title VI of the Civil Rights Act of 1964 stipulates that "no person in the United States shall, on ground of race, color, or national origin be excluded from participation in, be denied the benefits of, or be subjected to discrimination under any program or activity receiving federal financial assistance." In essence, Title VI forbids discrimination on the basis of race, color, or national origin in any federal or federally funded program. The continuation of such discrimination is considered justification for suspending, terminating or refusing to grant federal financial assistance to the offending program. Each federal agency sets up its own procedures and regulations to govern the implementation of these nondiscriminatory provisions. Title 29, Part 31 of the Labor Department Rules & Regulations sets up the provisions for the department's enforcement of Title VI. The Office of Equal Opportunity oversees the efforts of the department in the enforcement of these regulations.

• Executive Order 11246, issued Sept. 28, 1965 and later amended by Executive Order 11375, gave the Secretary of Labor the responsibility for administering a program for the promotion and insurance of equal employment opportunity on government contracts and federally-assisted construction contracts for all persons without regard to race, creed, color, sex or national origin. The prohibition against sex discrimination was added by Executive Order 11375, which became effective in October 1968. The Secretary of Labor delegated responsibility for the program to the director of the Office of Federal Contract Compliance. Executive Order 11246 and the rules and regulations of the Office of Federal Contract Compliance require that federal contractors not discriminate and that they take "affirmative action" to insure nondiscrimination. Sanctions such as disbarment and contract termination are provided in the event of noncompliance.

• The Equal Pay Act of 1963 amended the Fair Labor Standards Act of 1938 to prohibit employers from discriminating on the basis of sex in the payment of wages for equal work. The equal-pay standard, however, applied only to employes subject to the statutory minimum-wage requirements. The Equal Pay Act required an employer to pay equal wages within the same establishment to men and women doing equal work on jobs requiring equal skill, effort and responsibility and which are performed under similar working conditions. The act did not prohibit the payment of wages at lower rates to one sex than the other for equal work where the wage differential is based on a seniority system, a merit system, a system measuring earnings by quantity or quality of production or on any other factor other than sex. The law prohibited any labor organization, or its agents, representing employes of an employer having employes subject to the minimum-wage provisions of the act, from causing or attempting to cause the employer to discriminate against an employe in violation of the equal-pay provisions.

(The equal-pay issue first achieved wide public attention during World War I when it became necessary to employ many women in war industries on the same jobs as men. To help attract woman workers, the National War Labor Board enforced a policy of "no wage discrimination against women on the grounds of sex." After the war, equal-pay laws were adopted in 1919 by Michigan and Montana. No other state enacted similar laws until late in World War II, when state legislation began to follow the practices of many companies, unions and government agencies in banning wage discrimination.

(The Women's Bureau was created by Congress in 1920 to formulate standards and policies to promote the welfare of wage-earning women, improve their working conditions, increase their ef-

ficiency and advance their opportunities for profitable employment. . . . As the only agency in the federal government designated to assume responsibility and concern for the welfare of wom-
en, the Women's Bureau serves as the center of informed concern,
policy advice, and leadership within the federal government on
questions relating to the utilization of womanpower and the
economic, legal and civil status of women. The overall program of
the bureau focuses on enlarging the contribution and participation of
women in economic and community life as jobholders, homemakers, and citizens.)

• The Age Discrimination in Employment Act, which became law
Dec. 15, 1967 (its provisions took effect June 12, 1968), was
adopted to promote the employment of the older worker based on
ability rather than age. It prohibits arbitrary age discrimination in
employment. It protects most individuals who are at least 40 but
less than 65 years of age from discrimination in employment based
on age in matters of hiring, discharge, compensation or other terms,
conditions, or privileges of employment. Responsibility for administration and enforcement of this act rests with the Wage & Hour Division of the Department of Labor. The act applied to: most
employers of 20 or more persons, public and private employment
agencies serving such employers, and labor organizations with 25 or
more members, or which refer persons for employment to covered
employers, or which represent employes of employers covered by
the act. The prohibitions of the act do not apply: (1) where age is a
bona fide occupational qualification reasonably necessary to the
normal operations of the particular business; (2) where the differentiation is based on reasonable factors other than age; (3) where the
differentiation is caused by observing the terms of a bona fide
seniority system or any bona fide employe benefit plan that is not a
subterfuge to evade the purposes of the act; (4) where the discharge
of an individual is for good cause.

• The Equal Employment Opportunity Act of 1972 and the earlier
Executive Order 11478 (signed Aug. 8, 1969) prohibited discrimination against federal employes and applicants for federal jobs on the
basis of race, color, religion, sex or national origin. The 1972 law
made Title VII of the Civil Rights Act of 1964 apply to federal
agencies and employers. Legislation signed April 8, 1974 extended
coverage of the Age Discrimination in Employment Act of 1967 to
include the federal government.

• The Education Amendments of 1972, under Title IX, barred sex bias against employes and students in most educational programs receiving federal financial aid. Regulations that became effective July 21, 1975 required some 16,000 school systems and 2,700 colleges and universities to end discrimination against women in employment, vocational counseling and various educational services or face a loss of federal money. Employment bias is banned under Title IX in recruitment, advertising, application, promotion, tenure, upgrading, transfer, demotion, layoff, compensation, assignment, classification, fringe benefits, marital or parental status and selection and financial aid for training.

THIS VOLUME IS A RECORD OF EVENTS in the struggle against job discrimination in the United States since the end of the 1960s. The material that follows consist largely of the developments chronicled by FACTS ON FILE in its weekly reports on current history. As in all FACTS ON FILE works, a conscientious effort was made to keep this volume free of editorial bias and to make it a balanced and reliable reference tool.

LESTER A. SOBEL

New York, N.Y.
October, 1976

Nixon Adminstration

Nixon at Odds With Blacks

Richard Milhous Nixon became the 37th President of the United States Jan. 20, 1969. Nixon had promised before his inauguration that he would take concrete steps to improve the economic situation of the nation's black citizens. But many black leaders indicated unhappiness with Nixon's early performance, especially in contrast to the efforts of the recently departed administration of Lyndon B. Johnson.

Nixon pledges aid to blacks. President-elect Nixon had met with six black leaders Jan. 13 and pledged, according to one of those attending, "to do more for the underprivileged and more for the Negro than any President has ever done." The pledge was reported to newsmen after the meeting by Hobson Reynolds, grand exalted ruler of the Improved Benevolent & Protective Order of Elks of the World (the Negro Elks). Reynolds reported that Mr. Nixon had told the Negro group "that in the next week he'd have some high-level appointments we'd be happy with." The failure of Mr. Nixon to name a Negro to his cabinet had drawn criticism from Negro leaders, who reported it to be a source of discontent in the Negro community.

In addition to Reynolds, other Negro leaders attending the meeting with Mr. Nixon were John Murphy, president of the National Newspaper Publishers Association; Sandy Ray, first vice president of the National Baptist Convention; the Rev. Ralph David Abernathy, head of the Southern Christian Leadership Conference; Dr. Nathan Wright, chairman of the Black Power Conference; John Johnson, president of the Johnson Publishing Co. (publisher of Ebony and Jet magazines).

Murphy told reporters after the meeting that "we were quite satisfied."

Also attending the conference as Nixon aides were Robert J. Brown and Daniel Patrick Moynihan, whom the President-elect had designated to be his urban affairs adviser. During the talk with newsmen after the meeting, Wright objected to Moynihan's presence at the conference on the ground that Moynihan, a white, had a "white mind-set." Wright warned that Moynihan misunderstood the urban crisis and that his presence as a Nixon adviser "does add to the possibility of disorder in the streets."

In his inaugural address Jan. 20, Nixon asserted that "no man can be fully free while his neighbor is not. To go forward at all is to go forward together. This means black and white together, as one nation, not two. The laws have caught up with our conscience. What remains is to give life to what is in the law: to insure at last that as all are born equal in dignity before God, all are born equal in dignity before man. . . ."

Black 'distrust.' President Nixon expressed concern at his news conference Feb. 6 about the "distrust," as a newsman worded it, of the Negro community toward him.

The President said: He was aware, from a report of his task force on education, that he was not considered "a friend by many of our black citizens." He was "concerned about this problem" and could only say "that by my actions as President I hope to rectify that." "The President is the counsel for all the people of this country," and he hoped to "gain the respect and . . . eventually, the friendship of black citizens and other Americans."

Roy Wilkins, executive secretary of the NAACP, met with Mr. Nixon Feb. 7 and then said that he believed the President intended to "rectify" the problem of Negro disaffection. "He must be judged on what his Administration does," Wilkins said.

NAACP Convention. The 60th national convention of the National Association for the Advancement of Colored People (NAACP) opened June 30 in Jackson, Miss., with delegates and officials assailing the Nixon Administration's recent civil rights policies. In the keynote address, Bishop Stephen G. Spottswood, chairman of the NAACP Board of Directors, said that "the clear message from Washington is: if you are black, stay back." Spottswood told the 2,000 delegates that the Administration's civil rights policies were impediments to Negro progress.

Alexander quits as EEOC chief. Clifford L. Alexander Jr., 35, resigned as chairman of the Equal Employment Opportunity Commission April 9, 1969 because of what he called "a crippling lack of Administration support."

Alexander, a Negro and a Democrat, said in his letter of resignation that the timing of a March 28 White House announcement indicating he would be replaced as EEOC head had suggested to the public that "vigorous efforts to enforce the laws on employment discrimination are not among the goals of this Administration." Ronald L. Ziegler, White House press secretary, had made the announcement cited by Alexander a day after Senate Republican Leader Everett McKinley Dirksen had threatened to "get somebody fired" because of businessmen's complaints that "they've been harassed by [Anderson's] operation."

Dirksen's remark, made during Alexander's testimony March 27 at a Senate Judiciary subcommittee investigation of Nixon Administration civil rights policies, provoked a heated rebuke from Sen. Edward M. Kennedy (D, Mass.), chairman of the subcommittee. Kennedy said: "I hope no one has been threatened in here today because he is trying to do the job he is expected to do." He said to Alexander that "those who threaten your job" would find "they have as much trouble getting rid of you as they would anybody else."

Assistant Attorney General Jerris Leonard, head of the Justice Department civil rights division, said April 22 that the commission had been ineffective under Alexander and, without naming him directly, called for his resignation. (Alexander had retained his seat on the commission while resigning the chairmanship.) Alexander, in response, said: "No threats from any source will silence me from speaking out on what I believe to be correct—equal employment opportunity for all Americans." The White House said the next day that Leonard's remarks did not represent an Administration statement on the issue.

Dirksen and Kennedy again clashed over the role of the EEOC May 5 during Senate confirmation of a newly nominated member of the commission, William H. Brown 3d. Dirksen said that he would watch Brown's actions on the commission to prevent "continued harassment of businessmen" by "over-zealous staff people." Kennedy accused Dirksen of "demagoguery." Dirksen replied that Kennedy "does not know what he is talking about."

Immediately after Brown was sworn in as a member of the EEOC May 6, Mr. Nixon appointed him chairman of the commission. Brown promised that he would be "equally vigorous" as Alexander in enforcing laws against job discrimination. The commission, established under the 1964 Civil Rights Act, had no enforcement authority. It could act only to persuade employers to stop discriminatory practices. Brown, however, said he would seek commission power to issue cease-and-desist orders against firms violating the law.

Delay on complaints—EEOC Chairman Brown said July 20 that limited funds had caused an 18-month delay in the EEOC's task of processing complaints of alleged job discrimination. Brown said that by the time the commission delivered a decision, many of those who had lodged the complaint "have lost interest; many have moved away."

Brown said the shortage of funds limited the effectiveness of the commission to do the job it should be doing under a section of the 1964 Civil Rights Act barring discrimination in employment because of age, sex, religion, national origin, race or color.

Moynihan proposes 'benign neglect.' Daniel P. Moynihan, domestic adviser to President Nixon, proposed in a private 1970 memo to the White House that "the time may have come when the issue of race could benefit from a period of 'benign neglect'." The 1,650-word "Memorandum for the President" was leaked to the press Feb. 28 and later confirmed by Moynihan at the White House.

Moynihan, the leading liberal Democrat within the Nixon Administration, explained March 2 that all he meant was that Negroes could fare better if extremists on both sides of the political spectrum would lower their voices. He said that "what I was saying was that the more we discuss the issue of race as an issue, the more people get polarized, the more crazy racists on the left and maybe crazy racists on the right shout and yell and make things seem so much worse than they are, when in fact the 1960s have been a period of enormous progress."

Moynihan said that the phrase "benign neglect" was used in an 1839 report to Queen Victoria on Canada by the British Earl of Durham. According to Moynihan, the report described Canada as having grown more competent of governing herself "through many years of benign neglect" by Great Britain, and recommended full self-government for the provinces. Moynihan indicated that the same might also apply to the nation's blacks.

In the memorandum to the President, Moynihan urged the Administration to avoid building up "extremists of either race" and to ignore "provocations" from black militants, particularly the Black Panthers. The White House counselor asserted that the problems of America's blacks had been "too much talked about" and "too much taken over by hysterics, paranoids and boodlers on all sides."

In a White House press briefing March 2, Moynihan asserted that his memorandum had been written with a twofold purpose: to bring the President up to date on the "quite extraordinary" progress of the Negro in the last decade, and to suggest ways in which these gains could be "consolidated" in the future.

Moynihan said one of the principal efforts of the document was to convey his fears to Nixon that the Negroes' gains of the 60s were becoming, and would continue to become, increasingly vulnerable to "a new racial rhetoric" inspired by "demagogues of the left and right." He said therefore the memorandum had been used in part to suggest to the President that a "lowering of voices" on the issue of race could be beneficial to the Negro and society at large.

The memo included a section on "employment and income," in which Moynihan said: "The 1960s saw the great breakthrough for the blacks. A third (32%) of all families of Negro and other races earned $8,000 or more in 1968 compared, in constant dollars, with 15% in

1960. . . . Young Negro families are achieving income parity with young white families. Outside the South, young husband-wife Negro families have 99% of the income of whites! . . . Income reflects employment, and this changed dramatically in the 1960s. Blacks continued to have twice the unemployment rates of whites, but these were down for both groups. . . . Black occupations improved dramatically. The number of professional and technical employes doubled in the period 1960–68. This was 2½ times the increase for whites. In 1969, Negro and other races provided 10% of the other-than-college teachers. This is roughly their proportion of the population (11%)."

Civil rights leaders protest—Twenty-one civil rights leaders, including authors, leading black educators and a U.S. congressman, charged March 5 that Moynihan's memorandum was "symptomatic of a calculated, aggressive and systematic" effort by the Nixon Administration to "wipe out" nearly two decades of civil rights gains.

The statement was dispatched from the National Urban League's New York City offices and was signed by individuals with widely disparate viewpoints, such as Dr. Nathan Hare, an outspoken black militant, and Rep. John Conyers Jr. (D, Mich.).

The rights leaders rejected Moynihan's assertions that the Negro had made "extraordinary" gains and instead said that the gains made by America's blacks "have been significant, but they have not been monumental." "Nor have they brought equality to black people," the statement said.

Others who signed the statement included: Bayard Rustin, director of the A. Phillip Randolph Institute; Herman Badillo, former borough president of the Bronx, N.Y.; California State Sen. Mervyn Dymally, National Conference of Black Elected officials co-chairman, and Dr. Andrew Billingsley, assistant chancellor, academic affairs, University of California at Berkeley.

2nd Moynihan memo—The New York Times reported March 10 that two weeks before Nixon's inauguration, Moynihan had told him in a memo that "the Negro

lower class must be dissolved" by turning it "into a stable working class population."

According to the Times, Moynihan acknowledged in his report to Nixon that the transformation of what he estimated at "almost half the total Negro population" would be the "work of a generation."

Moynihan said, however, that it was essential to social stability and elemental justice "that the low income, marginally employed, poorly educated, disorganized slum dwellers" should have the chance to become "truck drivers, mail carriers, assembly line workers—people with dignity, purpose, and, in the U.S., a very good standard of living indeed."

Brooke scores Nixon's policy. Sen. Edward W. Brooke (R, Mass.) the Senate's only black member, charged in Washington March 12, 1970 that the Nixon Administration has made a "calculated political decision" to shun the needs of blacks in America in favor of pursuing a Southern strategy to win re-election in 1972.

Brooke said he and other Republicans who worked for President Nixon's election in 1968 because he had promised to "bring us together" were now "deeply concerned about the lack of commitment to equal opportunities for all people." Brooke charged that the so-called Southern strategy "is to appeal to the same voters that the Administration appealed to in 1968 election and this is generally suburbia, white middle-class America."

Brooke accused the Administration of following this same course in preparing for the 1972 election.

Job drive relaxation denied. The White House Feb. 28, 1970 denied published reports that the Nixon Administration had decided to relax its pressure on federal agencies to step up employment of minority group members. The allegations had been made by Robert E. Hampton, chairman of the Civil Service Commission, who said Feb. 26 that the Nixon Administration had ended the drive because it believed the pressures to increase minority employment amounted to discrimination in reverse.

(Hampton told newsmen Feb. 27 that his remarks had been misunderstood. "I want to make it clear," he said, "that there has been no lessening of the efforts to achieve true equal opportunity for minorities and women.")

Ronald L. Ziegler, Nixon's press secretary, restated Hampton's claim that the civil service chief's remarks had been misunderstood. Ziegler said the Nixon Administration "has taken no steps whatsoever to ease minority hiring opportunities."

NAACP head scores Administration. Chairman Stephen G. Spottswood of the NAACP Board of Directors, keynoting the 61st annual NAACP convention in Cincinnati June 29, 1970, charged the Administration with a "calculated policy to work against the needs and aspirations of the largest minority of its citizens."

Spottswood detailed his contention that the Administration "can rightly be characterized as anti-Negro." He cited the "signing of defense contracts with textile companies long in violation of contract requirements" instead of canceling them as the NAACP had suggested.

He cited the nominations of Judges Clement F. Haynsworth Jr. and G. Harrold Carswell to the Supreme Court as evidence that the Administration was anti-Negro.

As his final point, Spottswood cited President Nixon's description of the ideal federal judge: "someone who believes in the strict construction of the Constitution—a judge who will not use the power of the court to seek social change by freely interpreting the law or constitutional clauses." Spottswood called this "the Adminstration's expressed opposition to the equal protection clauses of the 14th Amendment."

The White House's June 30 response was in the form of a long telegram to Spottswood by Leonard Garment, Nixon's chief liaison with civil rights groups. Garment said Spottswood's charges painted a false picture, rallied every fear, reinforced every anxiety and made a just society more difficult to achieve.

The telegram declared that "the President and the Administration are committed to achieving equal opportunity for every American, and are determined to maintain their efforts to reach that goal."

Garment said the specific grievances leveled at the Administration by Spottswood "misstate and misrepresent the record of the the Administration so as to present it in a highly distorting light."

Commission finds enforcement breakdown. The U.S. Commission on Civil Rights reported Oct. 12, 1970 that there had been a "major breakdown" in the enforcement of the nation's legal mandates forbidding racial discrimination.

The commission urged President Nixon to exercise "courageous moral leadership" and to establish within the White House machinery committees to oversee enforcement of court decrees, executive orders and legislation relating to civil rights.

The commission's findings were announced by the Rev. Theodore M. Hesburgh, the panel's chairman and president of the University of Notre Dame. Hesburgh said the findings, based on a six-month study of the executive departments and agencies charged with enforcing the nation's civil rights laws, showed that "the credibility of the government's total civil rights effort has been seriously undermined."

The 1,115-page report was entitled "The Federal Civil Rights Enforcement Effort." Hesburgh called it one of the most important documents "the commission has issued in its 13-year history."

Hesburgh indicated, in response to newsmen's questions, that the White House had sought to delay release of the report until after the November Congressional elections. Hesburgh said that the panel, however, did not view its report as a political document. A spokesman for the White House confirmed that a delay had been sought, but not out of concern for the elections. He said that the findings would have been better received by conservatives within the Administration if presented outside the context of the elections.

At the news conference, Hesburgh emphasized that the breakdown in enforcement of the civil rights laws "did not originate in the current Administration, nor was there any substantial period in the past when civil rights enforcement was at a uniformly high level of effectiveness."

Hesburgh said the commission had noted that in the past decade and a half an impressive number of laws had been passed seeking to eliminate racial discrimination.

"Each civil rights law that has been passed, each executive order that has been issued, and each court decision favorable to the cause of civil rights has been viewed as another step along the road to full equality for all Americans," Hesburgh said.

"But perhaps," he added, "what has been lost sight of is that these legal mandates in and of themselves cannot bring about a truly open society, that they must be implemented—and it is at this point that we have found a major breakdown."

Hesburgh said the report found that some of the laws had worked, notably in the areas of voting rights, public accommodations and school integration, but that these were found to be exceptions. The rights panel said it found government-wide failure in enforcement in such areas as employment, housing and use of federal grants.

The commission also said that the absence of pressures from the White House had contributed to the general breakdown in enforcement of the laws. The rights unit said federal departments and agencies had inadequate staffs for civil rights, top leaders were unconcerned with enforcement and those assigned to enforce the laws were given secondary positions with little contact with top department officials. The commission also said it found a tendency of many U.S. agencies to regard civil rights enforcement as an impediment to their primary function.

NAACP sees improvement. By the time of the 1971 NAACP convention, held in Minneapolis July 5-9, NAACP leaders agreed that the Nixon Administration had made strides to dispel its "anti-Negro" image. NAACP Board Chairman Stephen G. Spottswood, in his keynote

address, reported "the racial sky ...not as murky and dark as it was a year ago."

"The answer in 1971," Spottswood said, "has to be that the Nixon Administration has taken certain steps and has announced policies in certain phases of the civil rights issue which have earned cautious and limited approval among black Americans."

Dr. Andrew F. Brimmer, the sole black on the Federal Reserve System's board of governors, said July 6 that the job outlook for black Americans was so bleak that some had "given up" and no longer even entered the nation's labor force. He said it would be "quite some time" before the situation improved.

A former U.S. appeals court judge said July 7 that the current trend towards racial separatism could lead only to an "even more inferior status than black Americans now experience." William H. Hastie, who recently retired as the chief judge of the 3rd U.S. Circuit Court of Appeals, said that the trend had to be halted and reversed. He said he was deeply concerned at the "alarming number of Negroes" who have accepted and encouraged racial separatism as a "desirable and potentially rewarding" way of life.

Despite the NAACP's more moderate view of Administration policies, Herbert Hill, the group's labor director, expressed strong criticism of the Administration's racial posture, Hill said July 8 that what he saw as the Administration's policy of "benign neglect" has "become criminal negligence." Hill accused the government of having failed to enforce laws forbidding discrimination by federal contractors. He said the government failure had contributed to the high unemployment rate among blacks.

NAACP Executive Director Roy Wilkins said July 9 that President Nixon could win a sizeable share of the black vote in 1972 if he made more jobs available for blacks. Wilkins made his remarks to newsmen at the closing session. Wilkins said that there had been some improvement in the Administration's posture toward blacks, but that he found it hard to cite the specific strides made.

Philadelphia Plan
& Construction Jobs

A Labor Department order June 27, 1969 set in operation a pilot program to increase black employment in Philadelphia-area construction trades. The order directed contractors on federally assisted construction exceeding $500,000 to hire a specified number of minority workers. This (revised) Philadelphia Plan was issued to implement a Sept. 24, 1965 Presidential order (Executive Order 11246) requiring "affirmative action" to prevent job bias on federal contracts and federally aided construction. The plan was delayed, however, until the attorney general Sept. 22 finally issued an opinion overruling a decision of the comptroller general that the plan's requirement of specific goals for minority participation violated the Civil Rights Act of 1964 and therefore was illegal. Meanwhile, Philadelphia-Plan arrangements for minority employment in construction were being made (and often opposed) in other areas.

Dispute in Philadelphia. Implementation of the pilot Philadelphia Plan in the Philadelphia area was delayed after Republican Senate leader Everett M. Dirksen (Ill.) asked President Nixon July 8, 1969 to hold it up as possibly in violation of the 1964 Civil Rights Act.

Labor Department Solicitor Laurence H. Silberman held in a letter to Comptroller General Elmer B. Staats July 16 that the plan did not violate existing federal laws.

Secretary of Labor George P. Shultz had declared July 3 that the plan was a "fair and realistic approach" toward eliminating racial discrimination in the construction industry. Shultz said, however, that no contractor who failed to meet the standards set by the Labor Department would lose a federal contract if the contractor showed he had "made a good faith effort" to recruit the required number of minority workers.

The comptroller general had to confirm the agreement before it could go into effect.

Under the plan, federal contractors

bidding on construction jobs in the Philadelphia area would be required to employ a fixed number of minority workers before they could obtain a contract. The plan called for the Labor Department to establish the number of workers to be hired. This approach would be expanded to other cities if it succeeded in Philadelphia.

Staats rejects plan—Comptroller General Staats ruled Aug. 5 that the Philadelphia Plan was illegal because it established a quota system. His ruling was made in a letter to Labor Secretary Shultz.

Staats said that the 1964 Civil Rights Act prohibited contractors from considering race or national origin in their hiring practices and argued that the plan violated this ban.

Shultz Aug. 6 rejected Staats' ruling. The labor secretary said the Justice Department "had approved the plan as consistent with the Civil Rights Act."

Mitchell approves plan—Attorney General John N. Mitchell held in a letter to Labor Secretary Shultz Sept. 22 that the Philadelphia Plan was legal. Mitchell said:

The requirements which the Plan would impose on contractors may be briefly summarized. The contractor must—

(a) In his proposal set specific goals for minority group hiring within certain skilled trades, which goals must be within the range previously determined to be appropriate by the Secretary;

(b) He must make "every good faith effort" to meet these goals;

(c) But he may not, in so doing, discriminate against any qualified applicant or employee on grounds of race, color, religion, sex or national origin.

If a plan such as this conflicts with Title VII of the Civil Rights Act, its validity concededly cannot be sustained. But in my view no such conflict exists. Section 703(a) of the Civil Rights Act makes it an unlawful employment practice for an employer—

"(1) To fail or refuse to hire or to discharge any individual, or otherwise to discriminate against any individual with respect to his compensation, terms, conditions, or privileges of employment, because of such individual's race, color, religion, sex, or national origin; or

"(2) To limit, segregate, or classify his employees in any way which would deprive or tend to deprive any individual of employment opporutnities or otherwise adversely affect his status as an employee, because of such individual's race, color, religion, sex, or national origin."

Nothing in the Philadelphia Plan requires an employer to violate section 703(a). The employer's obligation is to make every good faith effort to meet his goals. A good faith effort does not include any action which would violate section 703(a) or any other provision of Title VII. If the provisions of the Plan were ambiguous on this point, its interpretation would be governed by the principle that "where two constructions of a written contract are possible, preference will be given to that which does not result in violation of law," *Great Northern Ry. Co. v. Delmar Co.*, 283 U.S. 686, 691 (1931). However, to remove any doubt the Plan specifies that the contractor's commitment shall not be used to discriminate against any qualified applicant or employee.

Nevertheless, it might be argued—and the Comptroller General appears to take this position—that the obligation to make good faith efforts to achieve particular goals is meaningless if it does not contemplate deliberate efforts on the part of the contractor to affect the racial composition of his work force, that this necessarily involves a commitment "to making race or national origin a factor for consideration in obtaining [his] employees," and that any such action would violate Title VII.

It is not correct to say that Title VII prohibits employers from making race or national origin a factor for consideration at any stage in the process of obtaining employees. The legal definition of discrimination is an evolving one, but it is now well recognized in judicial opinions that the obligation of non-discrimination, whether imposed by statute or by the Constitution, does not require and, in some circumstances, may not permit obliviousness or indifference to the racial consequences of alternative courses of action which involve the application of outwardly neutral criteria.

Plan ordered into effect—Labor Secretary Shultz Sept. 23 ordered the Philadelphia Plan into effect in the Philadelphia area.

Under the Philadelphia Plan, contractors holding federally-assisted contracts would be required to establish hiring guidelines for minority groups. The six crafts were ironworkers, steamfitters, sheetmetal workers, plumbers and pipefitters, elevator constructors and electrical workers.

Employers would be expected to show "good faith efforts" in meeting the new guidelines. The 1969 goal for minority group employment was 4%, rising to 26% by 1973.

The Department of Labor announced Sept. 29 that it planned to extend the Philadelphia Plan to nine other cities—New York, Boston, Chicago, Detroit, Los Angeles, Pittsburgh, St. Louis, San Francisco and Seattle.

Assistant Labor Secretary Arthur A. Fletcher, who made the announcement, said that officials or organized community groups in the nine cities had asked the government to implement the same program that was ordered into effect in Philadelphia.

Philadelphia Plan disputed. Nixon Administration aides appeared before a Senate subcommittee Oct. 28, 1969 to assure Congress that the government's Philadelphia Plan did not require a contractor to increase minority employment on federal construction projects but only called on the employer to make a "good faith effort" to do so.

Despite the Administration's contention that the job plan did not force an employer to enforce minority employment quotas, Sen. Sam J. Ervin Jr. (D., N.C.) and others on the Senate Judiciary Subcommittee on Separation of Powers expressed some doubts.

Sen. Ervin asserted that the plan "required quotas that were based on race in violation of Title VII of the Civil Rights Act of 1964."

Sen. Ervin attacked the testimony of Jerris Leonard, assistant attorney general for civil rights, who defended Labor Secretary George P. Shultz' statement to the committee. Shultz had asserted earlier that "all that was required was a good faith effort" to meet the required goals of the Philadelphia plan.

Sen. Ervin replied that the job plan violated the 1964 Civil Rights Act. Ervin quoted a passage from Title VII of the law: "nothing contained in this title shall be interpreted to require" employment on account of "race, color, religion, sex or national origin."

Plan's death blocked. Congress adjourned Dec. 23, 1969 after agreeing not to kill the Philadelphia Plan. The controversy involved a fiscal 1970 supplemental appropriations bill to which the Senate Dec. 18 added an amendment to kill the plan. The amendment granted the comptroller general authority to withhold funds for any program he deemed unlaw-ful.

Prior to the House's consideration Dec. 22 of the conference version of the bill, which retained the Senate amendment to kill the plan, President Nixon issued a statement urging removal of the amend-ment and warning of a possible veto of the bill if it were retained. The House then re-jected the amendment by 208–156 vote and, by voice vote, signaled its intention to insist on the deletion. In the Senate later Dec. 22, the Senate agreed, 208 to 156, on a motion by majority leader Mike Mansfield (D, Mont.), to drop the amend-ment.

Court upholds plan. The Supreme Court Oct. 12, 1971 rejected a challenge to the Philadelphia Plan by the Contractors Association of Eastern Pennsylvania.

The contractors had argued that the plan violated 1964 Civil Rights Act equal employment provisions by setting up racial "quotas." Lower courts had ruled that the plan established "goals" stated in percentage ranges rather than absolute quotas.

Similar plans had been instituted in Washington, D.C., San Francisco, St. Louis and Atlanta. Other programs were scheduled for New York, Buffalo, Cin-cinnati, Detroit, Houston, Indianapolis, Kansas City, Mo., Miami, Milwaukee, Newark, N.J., New Orleans, Denver, Boston, Los Angeles and Seattle.

The court Jan. 12, 1970 had declined to review an Ohio state court ruling that declared valid an equal-employment plan similar to the Philadelphia Plan. The case involved an Ohio contractor who had been denied a contract for a federally-sub-sidized college building even though he had been low bidder. The contractor had refused to give assurances, required by the federal government, that he would attempt to employ a specified number of Negro workers.

Plan misses early goals. The Philadel-phia Plan was falling short of its initial minority hiring goals, according to progress reports disclosed May 2, 1970. Citizen organizations in Philadelphia, where the plan was first set into motion, had reported to the department's Office of Federal Contract Compliance that

contractors were abusing and disregard-ing the plan by not taking on additional minority group employes.

The preliminary reports were still being received by Benjamin Stanley, head of the Compliance office. Stanley said that an official count of minorities on construction job payrolls had not been completed, but that initial reports had shown that "there is no question, com-pliance is lagging."

Stanley said his office was "taking steps now to determine what is wrong and do something about the situation, such as get the federal agencies in-volved to get after the contractors."

Plumbing union plan. The Department of Labor announced Jan. 27, 1970 that the United Association of Plumbers and Pipefitters had agreed to assist 500 Ne-gro apprentices in finding jobs in areas where there was a manpower shortage. Labor Secretary George P. Shultz de-scribed the accord as an important breakthrough in federal efforts to find new jobs for Negroes and other minori-ties.

The agreement was in the form of a contract signed by the union, the Na-tional Constructors Association and the Labor Department. Under its terms, the 500 apprentices would be able to bypass the union's apprenticeship requirements so long as they had passed the appren-ticeship age and had some experience to take jobs as soon as they were available. They would take the jobs as apprentices with guarantees that they would become journeymen when fully qualified. Jour-neyman status represented higher wages and more union fringe benefits.

Navy to enforce job accord. The direc-tor of the Defense Department's equal employment opportunities office an-nounced April 14, 1970 that the Navy would require all contractors who were planning to bid for $2 million worth of new construction projects to comply with the minority-hiring provisions of the Labor Department's Philadelphia Plan.

Stuart Broad, the Defense Depart-ment's officer for equal employment op-portunities, said the job plan was "a matter of first importance with the De-fense Department."

Job bias action threatened. Labor Secretary James D. Hodgson warned July 9, 1970 that unless the building industry opened up more jobs for black workers during the summer, the government might begin to enforce federal hiring quotas in 73 cities. The labor secretary said "there has been too much of a lag in this work and the big push is on."

Hodgson said the 73 cities would be given an opportunity to develop voluntary plans to increase black employment in the construction trades, but unless it was done soon the Labor Department would impose quotas as it had already done in Philadelphia and Washington.

The 73 cities were in addition to 18 already targeted. Hodgson said he was not satisfied with progress under existing voluntary agreements but added that he was pleased that some larger cities (Boston, Los Angeles and St. Louis) had developed effective antibias job plans.

U.S. terminates contract. The Nixon Administration announced Aug. 19, 1970 that it was canceling a contract with a Pennsylvania company due to its failure to comply with the Philadelphia Plan.

It was the government's first enforcement action against a contractor charged with violating the job agreement.

Secretary of Health, Education and Welfare (HEW) Elliot L. Richardson said that Edgely Air Products, Inc., of Levittown, Pa., had been notified by HEW's Office for Civil Rights that the office intended to cancel a contract and bar the concern from future federal contracts on the ground of noncompliance with the job accord ordered into effect by President Nixon.

The government's contract with the Edgely concern was for sheet metal work on a building at the University of Pennsylvania. Edgely was entitled to 10 days to ask HEW for an administrative hearing.

Leonard Nucero, Edgely's president, denied "that we practice discrimination in any fashion. We believe that the news release which has been given to the news media is premature and grossly unfair."

Unions vow to fight job quotas. The nation's building and construction unions Feb. 10, 1971 rejected charges that they practiced racial discrimination as "reckless rhetorical and political pandering," and vowed to resist proposed federal job quotas for nonwhite workers.

A statement issued by the Building and Construction Trades Department of the AFL-CIO said the group rejected "quotas under any name."

The government's proposed quota rules had been published in the Federal Register Jan. 29, attracting little public attention at the time. They were promulgated by Labor Secretary James D. Hodgson. According to the apprenticeship rules as published, unions with federally registered trainee programs would be required to adopt "affirmative action plans" to bring more nonwhites into the programs.

In rejecting the proposed job quotas the unions maintained that "the goal of equal employment opportunity in apprenticeship has generally been achieved under existing regulations."

Although the proposed rules would give the craft unions some flexibility in drawing up programs to carry out "affirmative action," basically they required the unions to place a specified quota of nonwhites in the apprenticeship programs.

The federal quotas were reportedly designed to do on a national scale what various job programs had accomplished in local areas—bringing more blacks into the building and construction trades.

Construction Jobs in Other Areas

Pittsburgh protests end of job pact. Mass protests against racial bias in construction jobs in Pittsburgh, Pa. in the summer of 1969 resulted the following year in an agreement to increase the hiring of black workers.

Black civil rights groups had joined hundreds of black construction workers and their white supporters to shut down $200 million worth of construction projects in Pittsburgh Aug. 25-29, 1969 after trade unions refused to increase Negro employment on construction jobs.

The Black Construction Coalition (BCC), a loosely organized alliance of several Negro groups, called for the work stoppage in protest against what it called discriminatory hiring practices for construction jobs. The BCC said Negroes had been denied the jobs because they were not admitted to white-controlled labor unions. The BCC pledged to continue the shutdown at 10 construction sites unless the pace of job integration was "substantially increased."

Five of the sites were shut down Aug. 25 after more than 1,000 demonstrators surged into downtown Pittsburgh, snarled traffic and caused massive tie-ups throughout the city. The project sites were closed on the recommendation of Pittsburgh police, who sought to avert violence between the demonstrators and white construction workers. Work was halted at the other five sites by the presence of a five-block line of protesters, about half of them white.

Police and demonstrators clashed Aug. 26 near the $31.9 million Three Rivers Stadium, being built near downtown Pittsburgh. One hundred and eighty persons were arrested during the skirmish. Forty-five, including 12 policemen, were injured.

The stadium had been the focal point of BCC demands. (A study by the Mayor's Commission on Human Relations showed that of the 30,000 members of building and trade unions in Pittsburgh, only 2 per cent were Negroes.)

Police Superintendent James W. Slusser said the stadium scuffle began after some of the demonstrators disrupted traffic. The police moved in with riot clubs, and the demonstrators retreated into downtown Pittsburgh, tying up traffic. The police then cordoned off the marchers and moved in to make the arrests. Byrd Brown, chairman of the Pittsburgh chapter of the National Association for the Advancement of Colored People (NAACP), told the demonstrators to disperse but asked them to return to the stadium site Aug. 27.

About 700 Negroes and white protesters gathered Aug. 27 across the street from the site of the $100 million, 64-story building scheduled to become the headquarters of the U.S. Steel Co.

to press their demands. White construction workers perched atop the steel structure dropped objects on the demonstrators, and the demonstrators hurled bottles at the workers.

The protesters had gone to the construction site after meeting with U.S. Steel officials at the company's temporary headquarters in downtown Pittsburgh. Following the hour-long meeting, a spokesman for U.S. Steel announced that the company "sympathized completely with their position that all persons should have the same privilege of union membership." But the company said it would not comply with the demonstrators' demand that work on the building be halted until more jobs were made available to Negroes.

Pittsburgh Mayor Joseph M. Barr announced Aug. 27 that the owners of the 10 halted construction projects had agreed to stop further operations to permit negotiations. The demonstrators responded by announcing that they would suspend further demonstrations. The leaders of the demonstrators sought a black-controlled job-training program, for 500 Negroes, that would guarantee graduates journeyman status in Pittsburgh's trade unions. The Master Builders Association, which represented the contractors, had refused to accept a Negro-run program.

Angry white construction workers staged demonstrations Aug. 28–29, denouncing the decision to suspend all major building projects in Pittsburgh.

At a 10-hour negotiation session in Barr's office Aug. 29, Negroes rejected an offer under which up to 100 Negroes would be trained in the construction trades.

Construction work was halted on a building project at Carnegie-Mellon University Sept. 22 after several campus groups threatened to boycott classes in a show of support for Negroes demanding more jobs in the construction industry.

The BCC announced Jan. 30, 1970, after a continuation of demonstrations and shutdowns, that an agreement had been reached to employ 1,250 Negroes as workers with journeyman status in Allegheny County, Pa., during the next four years. The accord was reached by the coalition, representatives of 15 contractor associations and the Pittsburgh Trades and Construction Council, who represented Pittsburgh's craft unions.

W. J. Usery Jr., assistant secretary of labor, who sat in on the negotiations, said the Labor Department supported the agreement. He said legal action would be instituted against any union that failed to enroll the new workers.

The agreement was officially accepted by the federal government Oct. 24, 1970.

The government's decision to accept the plan marked the end of its freeze on $100,000 for federally assisted projects in the Pittsburgh area. The government had frozen the funds to force unions to comply with minority hiring guidelines.

The agreement called for 1,250 blacks to be employed as workers with journeyman status in the Pittsburgh area during the next four years.

Chicago situation. Efforts to increase black hiring in construction jobs in Chicago produced controversy and several job plans, but early results were termed disappointing.

More than 4,000 Negroes and their white supporters had staged their first "black Monday" demonstration in downtown Chicago Sept. 22, 1969 to protest discrimination in Chicago's building trades. Spokesmen for the demonstrators said rallies would be held every Monday until more skilled jobs in the construction industry were made available to Negroes.

The Chicago Coalition for United Community Action, an amalgamation of 61 national black organizations, had organized the rally to press their demands for at least 9,000-on-the-job training positions leading to membership status in the trade unions.

Negotiations between the coalition and the Building Employers Association, which represented the construction trades, had halted Sept. 18 after black leaders turned down the association's offer to train 1,000 qualified Negroes and to seek positions for 3,000 apprentices. The Rev. Jesse Jackson, director of

Operation Breadbasket, the economic branch of the Southern Christian Leadership Conference, said the Association's plan was "like no jobs at all."

White construction workers demonstrated Sept. 24–26 against a Labor Department decision to withhold funds from federally sponsored projects in the area unless contractors agreed to hire a minimum number of black workers.

Fighting with police erupted Sept. 26 when the white construction workers attempted to block Negro leaders from entering the U.S. Customs House, where the Labor Department was conducting hearings on alleged discrimination in the building trade unions.

The workers had packed the conference room Sept. 25 and refused to permit the meeting to begin. Assistant Secretary of Labor Arthur Fletcher adjourned the meeting until Sept. 26.

The whites jammed the streets around the Customs House Sept. 26, preventing Fletcher and other Negro leaders from entering the building. Police escorted Fletcher into the building and two other Negroes were whisked out of the area by police who reported at least nine arrests.

An anti-bias plan was accepted in Chicago Jan. 12, 1970. After months of negotiations, black community leaders announced they had agreed upon a program designed to train Negroes for skilled construction jobs.

The agreement called for 4,000 Negroes to be trained as skilled construction workers and admitted to the Chicago unions.

Under the agreement, 1,000 Negroes who could qualify as apprentices or journeymen would be put to work immediately.

A second 1,000 would start on-the-job training as soon as possible, and another 1,000 would be slated to begin journeyman training leading to full status as skilled workers.

The other 1,000 would be given a specialized pre-apprentice training program for rudimentary construction skills.

Chicago's voluntary plan collapsed after 18 months. Known as the Chicago Plan for Equal Opportunity, the program was acknowledged to be a failure. By June

4, 1971, only 885 blacks and Spanish-Americans had been taken on for apprentice training and only a few had obtained membership in Chicago's construction unions.

More than $824,000 had been provided by the federal government to finance the city's "hometown" job plan.

The Labor Department announced June 4, 1971 that it was withdrawing its support for the city plan and would impose mandatory racial quotas on federally-assisted projects throughout the city. Assistant Labor Secretary Fletcher said the federal plan would be similar to the Philadelphia Plan.

"It's not a question of whether we'll impose a plan on Chicago, but a question of how," Fletcher said.

The Labor Department announced Oct. 18, 1972 that nine Chicago construction contractor associations and fifteen building trades unions had signed a voluntary agreement to employ 2,820 more minority workers by 1976, with specific yearly hiring goals for each trade.

The Chicago Urban League would run a $1.7 million recruitment and training program with funds supplied by the Labor Department's Manpower Administration. But no minority representatives actually signed the agreement, a reflection of disputes in some of the 52 minority hiring plans in the country over who would represent minority groups.

Donald M. Irwin, Chicago regional director for the Labor Department, called the plan "the most extensive" ever signed. The participating unions had current memberships of 41,000. Irwin said locals of roofers and ironworkers, which had not signed the plan, would be restricted in bidding for federal contracts.

The new agreement collapsed Oct. 18, 1973, and the Labor Department announced that it was withdrawing its support because of poor performance.

Conceding that Chicago was "just not susceptible to a voluntary solution," the department noted that only about 200 minority workers had been hired under a first-year federal grant of $1.7 million, compared with a goal of training and qualifying 1,700 such workers. The Chicago Urban League accused both unions and contractors of intransigence.

The Labor Department's announcement that it would impose its own hiring plan was greeted with skepticism by Herbert Hill, labor director of the National Association for the Advancement of Colored People, who said compulsory plans in other cities had "invariably" been based on "less than what the law requires."

The Labor Department announced Dec. 20 that it had imposed a mandatory minority-jobs plan on the Chicago-area construction industry.

The plan set "goals and timetables" and provided penalties of contract cancellations and ineligibility for future contracts if companies failed to demonstrate "good faith" efforts to comply.

Los Angeles decree. The Justice Department said Sept. 24, 1969 that the U.S. District Court at Los Angeles, Calif., had approved consent decrees forbidding discrimination against Negroes in the steamfitting and pipe-fitting trades in the Los Angeles area. The Justice Department said the court-approved decrees were against Steamfitters Local Union 250 of the United Association, and the Joint Apprentice Committee, Steamfitters and Industrial Pipefitters.

The court's ruling concluded a civil suit filed by the Justice Department in February 1968, charging the union and the committee with discriminating against Negroes in membership, apprenticeship training and work referral in violation of the 1964 Civil Rights Act. The suit had charged that only one Negro was a member of Local 250's 2,800-man union.

The court's consent decree with the union required the union to process all membership applications on a nondiscriminatory basis, forbade denial of Negro applicants for lack of union sponsorship and provided that for the next three years Negro journeymen with acceptable credentials would receive priority work referrals.

New York developments. A plan for increasing the number of minority workers employed by the New York City construction industry also failed.

Labor and management leaders in the city's construction industry March 21,

1970 had announced a pilot New York Plan for recruiting and training minority-group members. The city's program was devised after the Labor Department said it would extend its job plan, the Philadelphia Plan, to 18 other cities unless they designed their own arrangements for increasing minority group employment in the construction trades.

Peter J. Brennan, president of the Building and Construction Trades Council of Greater New York, said the plan would go into effect as soon as the funds become available. He said New York Gov. Nelson Rockefeller had committed an unspecified amount of money for financing the New York Plan.

Under the terms of the arrangement, trainees would be selected by community screening committees for on-the-job training at participating projects. The Workers Defense League, an organization which had aided other groups in selecting and preparing blacks and other minority group members for construction trades apprenticeship programs, said March 21 that it would assist the community committees in screening potential candidates for the New York Plan. In addition to on-the-job assignments, the apprentices would be given craft training, guidance and counseling until additional on-the-job assignments could be secured.

Brennan said the plan "will combine periods of instruction, counseling and remedial education at a central training facility with periods of on-the-job training. The result will be a comprehensive work-learn program with a continuity of training, a completion of training and a reasonable assurance of entry into the industry as a qualified craftsman."

Gov. Rockefeller, Mayor John Lindsey and union and management representatives signed the New York Plan Dec. 10.

After two years, however, the city announced Jan. 12, 1973 that it was withdrawing from participation in the plan because it was "very disappointed" in the poor results. Only 537 trainees had been placed by June 1972.

The city asked the U.S. Labor Department to impose minority job goals and timetables, as mandated by federal law in the absence of a local voluntary plan, on all federally aided construction in New York. The city said it would also seek city and state legislation requiring affirmative action plans from all city- or state-aided contractors.

Thomas J. Broidrick, a construction company executive and head of the New York Plan, said the city's charges were unfair, since the city had not supplied its $100,000 share of the costs until June 1972, and the federal government had decided not to fund a central training facility.

Broidrick said 620 trainees were currently in the plan, of whom 480 were actually in jobs and 34 were journeymen. He said the record, along with other city training programs, was "the best in the country in numerical terms," which the city's announcement had not disputed.

The city later formulated a new plan to replace the New York Plan. The new plan, with mandatory provisions to increase minority hiring in construction, was opposed by the Labor Department. U.S. District Court Judge Morris E. Lasker overruled the department's objections July 25, 1974 and approved the plan. But in a decision reported Aug. 10, a state supreme court justice ruled that the city had exceeded its authority in imposing mandatory standards.

The city's new program required that contractors working on federally-aided municipal projects hire one minority on-the-job trainee for every four experienced workers on each project. In addition, long-term goals would require that the number of minority workers be increased so that their representation in the industry equaled their proportion of the city's population by July 1, 1978.

The Labor Department had withheld federal construction funds from the city on the ground that the city had implemented the new plan without federal approval. The city's suit to have the funds released led to Lasker's decision. The conflicting state court decision came in another suit filed by the industry and unions.

According to the Lasker ruling, the city had the authority to impose anti-discrimination rules more stringent than those approved in advance by the federal government. The ruling would also empower the city to require that contractors bidding on government-financed projects meet the same hiring standards on other operations, including private projects, during the life of the government contract.

Lasker ruled Nov. 8 that neither the federal nor the state government had the right to interfere with local minority-jobs plans. The Labor Department said Nov. 13 that it would not appeal.

Upgrading of apprentices—New York City Steamfitters Union Local 638 was ordered in federal court Jan. 3, 1972 to upgrade 169 black and Puerto Rican apprentices to journeyman status.

The ruling involved the largest number of reclassifications ordered in a suit brought by the federal government. The court reserved the right to rule on individual cases if the union tried to downgrade any of the 169 workers on grounds of incompetence.

Action re Washington. The Department of Transportation April 13, 1970 ordered a freeze on new roadway and airport construction contracts in the Washington, D.C. metropolitan area as part of a drive to bring more high salaried jobs to black and other minority group workers.

The director of the department's civil rights division, Richard F. Lally, reported that the suspension of funds had been ordered after three days of hearings during which contractors had been warned that if they did not implement their own job plan, the Labor Department "would be ready to impose" a mandatory job plan on the contractors. The freeze prohibited any contracts to be financed by Transportation Department funds until a regional employment and job-training program was adopted.

The freeze order also applied to projects scheduled for Virginia and Maryland, as well as Washington, D.C.

Labor Secretary George Shultz June 1 imposed a department-devised Washington Plan requiring all contractors with federal jobs of $500,000 or more in Washington, D.C. to make "good faith" attempts to increase minority hiring on all their projects. Under the plan, 3,500 minority group workers had to be hired in 11 skilled construction trades on such federal jobs as construction of the metropolitan subway system, highway building and federally subsidized housing projects.

The plan was ordered into effect after Washington area contractors and labor unions had failed to come up with a voluntary hiring practice agreement by May 25, a deadline set by Shultz after bargaining sessions between the participants had failed.

The Washington Area Construction Industry Task Force, a coalition of 25 black organizations, June 4 denounced the Washington Plan as "devoid of promise" and "wholly unacceptable." The group sent a letter to Shultz demanding that 70%–80% of jobs in all crafts go to minority group workers. The federal plan called for unions to have from 25% to 43% black membership, depending on the trade, by May 31, 1974 for the Washington, D.C. metropolitan area.

The task force accused the Labor Department of diluting the plan by incorporating into it the construction sites in Virginia and Maryland. The task force's chairman, R. H. Booker, said "it serves little purpose" to offer a black construction worker a job in Virginia or some "other remote construction site when in his own city (Washington, D.C.) the overwhelming majority of jobs will continue to go to whites."

East St. Louis ban lifted. Secretary of Transportation John A. Volpe announced June 6, 1970 that a 23-month federal freeze of federal construction funds for two counties in East St. Louis, Ill. that had been imposed because of discrimination charges against blacks had been lifted. It was reported the ban had fallen short of its desired objectives to increase minority group employment in the East St. Louis area.

The freeze for St. Clair and Madison Counties was imposed July 1, 1968 after civil rights groups had lodged complaints with various federal agencies that the construction companies were discriminating against black workers. The freeze of federal funds was then ordered by the Bureau of Public Roads.

The freeze was in effect at the same

time that the Labor Department ordered a pilot job training program to increase minority group hiring in the building trades in the city.

Volpe said he was lifting the freeze after receiving assurances from Illinois Gov. Richard B. Ogilvie that efforts would be made to increase black employment in the area. Volpe said he was also prompted to lift the ban after a federal court handed down consent decrees requiring three East St. Louis union locals to operate nondiscriminatively.

Ogilvie's assurances included a pledge that he would see to it that a new employment arrangement was implemented in the city. The Ogilvie plan called for the establishment of a six-member local opportunity committee to oversee recruitment, training and placement of blacks in jobs in the construction projects now under way in East St. Louis. Six training programs would be established with 300 persons enrolled in 1970 and 600 in 1971.

Job accord in New Orleans. New Orleans city officials joined local representatives of the construction industry, craft unions, and a coalition of area chapters of the National Association for the Advancement of Colored People (NAACP) and the Urban League to announce July 26, 1970 that they had accepted a plan to increase minority hiring and open the unions' rank-and-file membership to Negroes.

The New Orleans Plan was designed to place more members of minority groups, mainly blacks, in the construction industry labor pool in the New Orleans area. One official said, however, that the plan was put together to prevent the federal government from implementing more stringent racial hiring guidelines in the New Orleans area.

A similar plan had been designed for Atlanta by local groups in July but it was rejected by the NAACP and Urban League representatives, who had quit a meeting with local industry representatives on the ground that the Atlanta plan was "weak and pallid."

A spokesman for the New Orleans NAACP-Urban League coalition said the Atlanta plan had been rejected because it did not mention a minority group quota for union membership. The plan agreed to by NAACP-Urban League officials in New Orleans contained a provision calling for a 20% minority group membership in all New Orleans construction trades and crafts unions.

San Francisco plan. The Labor Department announced June 3, 1971 that it was imposing a mandatory racial hiring plan for federally-assisted construction projects in San Francisco. Labor Secretary James D. Hodgson said the plan went into effect at once.

Hodgson said the San Francisco plan was aimed at opening nearly 1,100 jobs for minority workers in the various construction trades.

Like the Philadelphia and Washington plans, the San Francisco program would affect only federal construction projects costing over $500,000.

The Justice Department June 24, 1969 had filed suit against a San Francisco iron workers local and two joint committees that administered an apprenticeship training program, charging employment discrimination. The suit alleged that Local 377 of the International Association of Bridge, Structural and Ornamental Iron Workers and the two committees discriminated against Negroes in recruiting and work referrals.

U.S. job quotas set for Seattle. The Labor Department ordered federal minority-group hiring quotas for U.S.-assisted construction work in Seattle June 17, 1971, effective immediately. It rejected the city's own plan as ineffective.

The Seattle plan required all contractors to submit minority-hiring goals and job training quotas with their project bids. The goals would be required to fit within federal guidelines that sought to have each contractors' work force show a 9.7 to 13% increase in minority-group employes by 1973. Labor Secretary James D. Hodgson said the Seattle plan would affect all construction crafts except four —iron workers, sheet metal workers, plumbers and pipefitters and electricians —that were covered by a minority-hiring plan ordered by federal courts.

The department had sued in U.S. District Court in Seattle Oct. 31, 1969, charging five Seattle construction unions with bias against blacks. In a complaint endorsed by Attorney General John N. Mitchell, the department asked the court to enjoin the unions "from failing and refusal to recruit, refer for employment and accept Negroes for membership on the same basis as white persons."

The suit named as defendants the ironworkers, electrical workers, plumbers and pipefitters, sheet metal workers, and operating engineers union locals.

(White construction workers had protested against what they called the government's insistence on accelerating Negro membership in craft unions and more jobs for minority workers by demonstrating in Seattle and Olympia.)

Atlanta gets U.S. jobs plan. Atlanta June 18, 1971 became the fifth U.S. city to get a federal jobs plan as the Labor Department announced immediate implementation of a plan to bring more black workers into the higher-paying construction trades in the city.

The terms of the Atlanta plan were announced by Arthur A. Fletcher, assistant secretary of labor. Fletcher said he expected that "compliance would come even easier" in Atlanta than it had in other cities. He said his investigation of labor practices in metropolitan Atlanta had indicated that leaders of the higher paid craft unions would turn to the heavily black laborers unions where men had worked as skilled laborers for many years and invite them into their unions.

Private Job Bias & the Government

Federal government accused. The U.S. Civil Rights Commission charged May 1, 1969 that the U.S. government had subsidized racial discrimination in employment by cooperating with private firms that defied the 1964 Civil Rights law prohibiting job bias. The charge was included in the commission's release of a Brookings Institute report calling on the government to take disciplinary action against firms whose employment practices reflected racial discrimination.

The report also recommended that the government transfer all federal functions relating to employment discrimination from the Labor Department to a strengthened Equal Employment Opportunity Commission (EEOC). The Nixon Administration had been criticized by civil rights leaders for what they said was a Presidential plan to dilute the powers of the EEOC.

Howard A. Glickstein, acting staff director of the Civil Rights Commission, leveled the sternest accusation. In a separate letter attached to the Brookings Report, Glickstein wrote that enforcement of an executive order banning job bias by federal contractors "has been seriously deficient." Glickstein also accused the government of "spending public funds to subsidize such discrimination."

Federal contracts. Deputy Defense Secretary David Packard Feb. 7, 1969 announced the award of $9.4 million in Defense Department contracts to three textile companies that had been found in violation of federal regulations against job discrimination. Packard said he had approved the contracts after receiving oral "assurances of affirmative action" by the three firms to eliminate discrimination. The Office of Federal Contract Compliance (OFCC) had recommended in January that the companies be barred from federal contracts because of noncompliance with equal employment policy. The three firms were Dan River Mills, J. P. Stevens Co. and Burlington Industries.

In Senate Judiciary subcommittee hearings on equal employment opportunity under federal contracts March 27, Sen. Walter F. Mondale (D, Minn.) charged that Packard had "totally bypassed the OFCC" and "personally accepted oral, nonspecific assurances despite the regulations' requirements for written, specific assurances." Packard told the subcommittee March 28 that he had intervened personally because compliance negotiations with the companies had been "virtually dead-locked." Sen. Edward M. Kennedy (D, Mass.), chairman of the subcommittee, described

Packard's oral agreement as an "unfortunate precedent."

The subcommittee also heard testimony on a March 17 order by Transportation Secretary John A. Volpe that contractors would not have to meet equal employment requirements before bidding on highway contracts as previously required. Volpe had said that the department instead would include non-discrimination clauses in its contracts. In testimony March 28, Volpe said that the old policy had "undermined the competitive bidding system" and had been unevenly applied.

Bias suits. The Justice Department April 8, 1969 filed its first anti-discrimination suit against a major Southern textile company. The suit, filed in U.S. District Court in Greensboro, N.C., charged the Cannon Mills Co. of Kannapolis, N.C. with racial discrimination in employment and the rental of housing to employes, alleging that Negroes were given "menial and low-paying" jobs and inferior housing as compared with white employes.

The department filed suit against the International Longshoremen's Association (ILA) and two of its Baltimore, Md. locals April 22, charging that the locals were operating on a segregated basis. The suit, filed in U.S. District Court in Baltimore, alleged that Local 829 was 99% white and Local 858 was 99% Negro although members of both did substantially the same work. The department said that the Negro workers got fewer and less desirable jobs than the white workers as a result of the alleged discrimination. The department had filed a similar suit against Texas ILA locals in January.

The department filed suit April 24 in U.S. District Court in Kansas City, Kan. seeking a court order to end alleged discrimination by a Kansas insulating material manufacturer and Teamsters Union Local 41 in Kansas City. The suit charged that the Gustin-Bacon Division of Certain-Teed Products Corp. discriminated against Negroes and other nonwhites in hiring, job assignment and promotion. It also charged that the collective bargaining agreement between the company and Local 41 perpetuated

the effects of the firm's alleged discrimination.

In a suit filed in U.S. District Court in Newark, N.J. April 25, the department sought to end alleged discriminary practices by Local 10 of the Sheet Metal Workers International Association in Newark and a labor-management apprentice training committee for Essex and Passaic counties in New Jersey. The suit charged that the union did not give equal employment opportunity to Negroes and Puerto Ricans and that the committee applied more stringent requirements to non-white apprentice applicants.

The department filed a consent order June 13, barring discrimination against Negroes and Spanish-Americans and ending a March 1968 suit against Sinclair Refining Division of Atlantic Richfield Co. and the Oil, Chemical, and Atomic Workers Union. Under the order, entered in U.S. District Court in Houston, Tex., Sinclair, the union and its Local 4-227 agreed to halt discriminatory practices at the company's Houston refinery. Sinclair had merged with Atlantic Richfield after the suit was filed.

Alabama suit. Four black women sued in federal court in Birmingham, Ala. March 20, 1970 on charges that black applicants were being denied available jobs by the Alabama State Employment Service.

The women also charged that blacks were being systematically steered into ineffective training programs. The suit alleged that whites received better training and better jobs than blacks. In addition to the State Employment Office, the suit named as co-defendants the Alabama Department of Industrial Relations, the State Department of Education, the Department of Vocational Education, the Jefferson County Committee for Economic Opportunity and the Birmingham Skill Center, Inc.

The suit alleged that 250 Negroes enrolled in an employment program had received no training or training allowance and had been unable to secure employment, although they had been through several employment training programs. The defendants were accused of violating the 1964 Civil Rights Act's equal employment provision and the 14th Amendment, guaranteeing Negroes equal rights. The defendants were said to have conspired "to place Negroes in inferior training leading to no employment or no better employment than that previously available to Negroes."

N.Y. job pledges. The head of New York City's Office of Contract Compliance announced March 21, 1970 that seven elevator companies had pledged to "employ immediately a significant number" of Negroes and Puerto Ricans after the city had withheld millions of dollars in payments to the companies because of alleged job discrimination. The seven companies were Otis, Armor, Westinghouse, Staley, Serge, Haughton and Burlington.

Director James D. Norton said $6.5 million in payments to the seven firms would be delayed for several more weeks while his office checked the firms' compliance with their pledge.

Norton said the firms had promised to hire at least 50 minority group members immediately, to redouble "their efforts to hire minority workers;" and to re-examine those requirements now in existence as they related to employment.

Shipyard job plan. A spokesman for the Maritime Administration announced April 9, 1970 that the Newport News, Va. shipyard, largest in the U.S., had agreed to end racial discrimination among its 20,000 workers by implementing a pilot job plan. Maritime Administrator Andrew E. Gibson, the chief negotiator for the government during talks between the yard's officials and black workers, called the plan "a milestone" and "one of the most forward looking of any major industry."

The agreement removed the yard, the Newport News Shipbuilding and Dry Dock Co., from the government's black list, which had prohibited the company from signing contracts with federal agencies. (The yard had been placed on the black list March 12 when the Maritime Administration ordered the company to

"produce an affirmative action plan" to meet the equal job opportunities provision of the 1964 Civil Rights Act.)

Under the plan, the yard would open up more skilled jobs for black workers. The plan also set a numerical target for the number of blacks to be employed in the yard's executive offices. About 5,600, or 28% of the yard's workers were black.

Order to D.C. utility. The Washington (D.C.) Public Service Commission April 15, 1970 ordered the Potomac Electric Power Co., which served the D.C. area, to hire more black workers and other minority group members on a preferential basis. Under the order, the utilities concern must specifically request "all minority group persons contacting the company . . . to file an application for employment regardless of whether vacancies exist."

The order also provided that the firm maintain a file of applications from the minority applicants and "before consulting other sources for applicants . . . give every consideration to the hiring of applicants from this file."

Farm agency scored. The Labor Department reported April 22, 1972 that its 10-month probe of the Rural Manpower Service (RMS) had disclosed widespread evidence of discrimination against blacks, Chicanos and women, and cooperation by the RMS in exploitation of migrant workers.

The probe was begun after 16 civil rights and farm labor groups filed a complaint against the RMS, formerly the Farm Labor Service, asking migrant worker takeover of RMS functions.

Secretary of Labor James D. Hodgson said April 22 that the RMS would be consolidated at the local level with the Department's non-agricultural Employment Service, and that efforts would be made to allow non-college graduates to obtain posts in the new offices. He pledged immediate action to enforce the laws, admitting that past reforms had been ineffective.

The probe uncovered a pattern of discrimination in the industry, frequently abetted by the Employment Service and the RMS, in job referrals, housing and transportation. Violations of minimum wage and child labor laws were also found, as well as substandard living facilities.

The report said the RMS consistently erred "in favor of the employer to the detriment of the worker."

Seventeen farm worker and civil rights groups filed a federal suit in Washington Oct. 6 to prevent Labor Secretary Hodgson from further financing of the RMS' state rural manpower programs.

The suit charged that the state migrant worker referral offices, financed by the federal Rural Manpower Service, had favored white, Anglo and male applicants in recruitment, counseling, training and job referral, to the detriment of blacks and Spanish-surnamed workers.

According to the suit, workers were regularly referred to employers who violated minimum wage and child labor laws, who frequently failed to make Social Security payments to workers' accounts and who maintained worker housing that was racially segregated and below legal health standards. Workers who complained about conditions were ignored or blacklisted, the plaintiffs charged.

Lawrence J. Sherman, executive director of Migrant Legal Action Program, Inc., which filed the suit, charged that the reforms Hodgson promised in April had been "just promises." He said all the state agencies had been funded again for the current fiscal year at a $23 million level without any assurances of change. A Labor Department spokesman said Oct. 6 "implementation of the reforms has begun but everything can't be done overnight."

A $20 million program to improve working and living conditions for migrant workers, and to train 6,000 of them for better jobs had been announced by the Labor Department in June 1971, after 16 migrant and civil rights groups had filed an administrative complaint against the department. A department spokesman said Oct. 6 that $15.7 million had been spent so far, but only 1,200 workers had completed training. The program was funded at $10 million for the current fiscal year. Florida Rural Legal Services, Inc. had filed suit against Florida state agencies in September, charging that a $3.5 million grant to the Florida Department of Commerce under the program had not alleviated any of the abuses.

The plaintiffs in the latest suit included the western region of the National Association for the Advancement of Colored People, the Mexican-American Legal Defense and Education Fund, migrant groups from California, Texas, Oregon, Idaho, Michigan, Indiana and Ohio, and 88 individual workers.

Houston job bias charges. William H. Brown 3d, chairman of the Equal Employment Opportunity Commission (EEOC), announced June 4, 1970 that he had filed charges of racial and sex discrimination against four companies and 15 labor unions in Houston on behalf of two EEOC Houston staffers. Brown accused the companies and the unions of discriminating in recruiting, hiring and upgrading of blacks, Mexican-Americans and women, in violation of the 1964 Civil Rights Act.

The action came as the EEOC ended three days of public hearings June 2–4 into employment discrimination in Texas's second largest city.

The complaints were lodged against a tool company, a chemical firm, an oil company and a local utility company. By law, the EEOC did not disclose the names of the concerns. The commission also declined to identify the 15 local unions named in the complaint.

Biased job tests barred. The Supreme Court decided, 8–0, March 8, 1971 that employers could not use job tests that had the effect of screening out Negroes if the tests were not related to ability to do the work. The court held that the employment bias section of the 1964 Civil Rights Act involved the consequences of employment practices, not simply whether the practices were motivated by racial bias.

The court limited the use of general educational and aptitude tests and said that "any tests used must measure the person for the job and not the person in the abstract." Writing for the court, Chief Justice Warren E. Burger said, "If an employment practice which operates to exclude Negroes cannot be shown to be related to job performance, the practice is prohibited."

The case grew out of applications for promotion by 13 black laborers at the Duke Power Co. generating plant at Dan River in Draper, N.C. Jack Greenberg of the NAACP Legal Defense Fund Inc. contended that the plaintiffs could challenge employment practices on the basis of discriminatory impact and need not prove bad motive on the part of the employer. The Justice Department and the Equal Employment Opportunity Commission had sought the ruling.

Pennsylvania sues union. In the first suit by a state against job discrimination by unions, the Commonwealth of Pennsylvania Nov. 8, 1971 charged Local 542, International Union of Operating Engineers, and three contractor associations with bias against blacks.

The suit, filed in U.S. district court in Philadelphia, said the union had failed to provide sufficient memberships or jobs for blacks despite spending almost $1 million provided by the state for job training of blacks. The court was asked to supervise the union's apprenticeship and referral practices until discrimination ceased.

Utilities accused. The Equal Employment Opportunity Commission (EEOC), after three days of hearings, charged the nation's gas and electric utilities Nov. 17, 1971 with "rampant discrimination" in hiring and promoting minority group members and women. EEOC Chairman William H. Brown III promised to use his largely advisory powers to help "break the grip of Anglo males on virtually every good job in this industry."

The EEOC reported that only 6% of the industry's work force was black, the lowest percentage among the 23 largest industries, and 1.6% had Spanish surnames compared with 3.6% of all major industry workers.

The commission contended that some utilities used "culturally biased" general hiring tests unfair to non-Anglos, despite court rulings barring tests not directly related to job openings.

Women, who constituted 34% of the major industry work force, held only 15% of the utility jobs, the report noted, and were traditionally relegated to clerical jobs with little management opportunity and relatively low pay.

Industry spokesmen claimed that efforts to upgrade blacks had uncovered few qualified for better positions, although black workers for Detroit Edison and Southern California Edison Co. offered evidence of under-utilization of blacks.

Low employe turnover and promotion from the ranks in the highly unionized industry were also cited by company executives and independent experts as major causes of continuing inequality.

FPC denies role. The Federal Power Commission (FPC) July 11, 1972 issued a ruling that it had no power under federal law or the "public interest" concept to enforce fair employment practices by utilities.

The ruling came after 12 civil rights groups petitioned the FPC June 23 to take such action, charging "rampant discrimination against blacks, women and Spanish-surnamed Americans" by gas and electric utilities. They cited a September 1971 letter to the FPC from David L. Norman, assistant attorney general for the Justice Department's Civil Rights Division, who said the agency could exercise such powers.

But the FPC said Congress had relegated fair employment powers to the Equal Employment Opportunities Commission, and said its "public interest" regulatory functions no more covered employment practices than it covered securities, taxes, wages or advertising, all of which were regulated by other agencies.

Trucking cases. The Justice Department announced Sept. 1, 1970 that a U.S. judge in Cleveland had entered a consent decree requiring the nation's third

largest trucking concern to implement
an equal employment program. The order
brought to a close the department's first
suit seeking to enjoin job discrimination
throughout a company's nationwide operation.

The court order entered by Judge
Thomas D. Lambros against Roadway
Express Inc., of Akron, Ohio, enjoined
the firm from engaging in any act or
practice that had the purpose of denying
Negroes equal employment opportunities in hiring, upgrading and promotions.
The decree also ordered Roadway, which
had freight terminals in 28 states, to
offer job opportunities on a first available vacancy basis to nearly 105 individuals, with seniority and other benefits
for 45 of them.

The department had filed the suit
against Roadway in May 1968, charging
that Negroes had been discriminated
against in job placement and opportunities.

The department Aug. 12, 1969 had
filed a similar suit against a North
Carolina trucking company and three
locals of the International Brotherhood of
Teamsters. The suit, filed in U.S. District
Court in Asheville, N.C., charged that
Central Motor Lines, Inc., of Charlotte
N.C. and union Locals 71, 391 and 701
had discriminated against Negroes in
employment practices.

The Equal Employment Opportunity
Commission (EEOC) Dec. 3, 1971 asked
the Interstate Commerce Commission
(ICC) to ban job bias by 15,000 interstate
trucking firms employing over 1 million workers, charging the trucking industry with discriminating against wom-
en, blacks and Spanish-Americans by
giving them only the lowest-paying
jobs. The EEOC said the ICC's "life-and-
death power to license truckers" could
be used to end bias, but the American
Trucking Association claimed "no lawful
basis" for such ICC action.

The Justice Department notified 514
trucking firms, their collective bargaining association and the Teamsters
union Oct. 30, 1973 that an investigation of the industry had found a pattern
of illegal employment practices discriminating against blacks and Spanish-

surnamed Americans. It said the industry had assigned most minority members to lower-paying jobs and had refused
transfers or promotions on an equal basis
with whites. The discrimination was perpetuated by the national freight contract
with the Teamsters, which required that
employes transferring to higher-paying
jobs give up accrued seniority rights.

The department March 20, 1974 won a
consent decree under which seven large
trucking companies would adopt percentage hiring goals for blacks and
Spanish-surnamed persons.

The legal basis for the agreement was a
discrimination suit filed the same day
against the seven companies, 342 smaller
truckers, the International Brotherhood
of Teamsters, the International Association of Machinists, and Trucking Employers Inc., the industry's collective
bargaining organization.

The accord provided that 50% of
vacancies would be filled by black and
Spanish-surnamed applicants in communities where the groups made up more
than 25% of the work force. In areas
where the groups made up less than 25%
of the work force, the hiring goal would be
33 1/3%. The quotas would be subject to
the availability of qualified applicants in
any locality.

The agreement could be modified to include Indians or Asian-Americans in
certain areas.

The seven companies were Arkansas-
Best Freight System Inc., of Fort Smith,
Ark.; Branch Motor Express Co. of New
York City; Consolidated Freightways
Inc., of Menlo Park, Calif.; I.M.L.
Freight Inc., of Salt Lake City; Mason
and Dixon Lines Inc., of Kingsport,
Tenn.; Pacific Intermountain Express
Co., of Oakland, Calif.; and Smith's
Transfer Corp., of Staunton, Va.

Action on AT&T job charges. The
Equal Employment Opportunity Commission (EEOC) recommended Dec. 10,
1970 that a request by the American Tel-
phone and Telegraph Company (AT&T)
for a telephone rate increase be rejected
because of the company's gross discrimination against women, blacks and
Spanish-Americans.

H. I. Romnes, the board chairman of AT&T, Dec. 11 described as "outrageous" the commission's attempt to block the company's request for a rate rise on the ground that it engaged in discriminatory practices. Romnes told newsmen that "in the field of equal employment we have been leaders, not followers." He said the EEOC report was "completely distorted" and unsupported by fact.

The EEOC's recommendation was forwarded to the Federal Communications Commission (FCC), where AT&T's request for the rate increase was being considered. The EEOC asked the FCC to block the company's request, to hold hearings and declare the proposed increase illegal until AT&T's operating companies end what the EEOC said was "pervasive, system-wide and blatantly unlawful" discriminatory practices.

In its 48-page memorandum to the FCC, the EEOC said that AT&T, the world's largest corporate enterprise, was in violation of both statutory and constitutional laws. The rights agency petitioned the FCC to establish an independent investigatory panel to identify all persons who had been victims of the company's alleged discrimination and determine what relief should be granted to them. The EEOC also asked the FCC to request that the attorney general file civil action against the Bell System and criminal action against those in the company responsible for the alleged discriminatory job practices.

Included in the report was a request that the FCC seek a court order to compel the company to end immediately the alleged discrimination. The EEOC memorandum cited the alleged violations:

■ Job classification based on sex and race.

■ Refusal to hire women, blacks and Spanish-Americans because they lacked high school diplomas or had criminal records.

■ Retirement plans that were discriminatory because they were based on sex.

■ Seniority systems that were discriminatory because they were based on race and sex.

■ Denial of promotional and advancement opportunities because of discriminatory practices fostered by the company's original policies.

Romnes said AT&T would present its side to the FCC even though "we don't think this is the place to resolve this kind of thing—in a rate case."

Documenting its charges in a report to the FCC, the EEOC Dec. 1, 1971 charged AT&T and its operating subsidiaries with systematic job bias against blacks and Spanish-Americans, and called AT&T, with nearly a million employes, "the largest oppressor of women workers in the United States."

AT&T denied the charges Nov. 30 in a statement prepared before the report was released. Executive Vice President Robert D. Lilley claimed that nonwhites or persons with Spanish surnames constituted 13% of all employes and one quarter of those hired within the last four years, and that minority employment had risen 265% since 1963.

Lilley admitted that the 7,500 minority people in management jobs were "not enough," but said the number had doubled in three years. He said 55% of all AT&T workers were women, including one third, or 57,000 of those in management positions.

The EEOC contended that most of the female and minority workers were underpaid and denied advancement opportunity. Blacks were said to be "largely relegated to the lowest-paying, least desirable jobs in the companies," and were subject to unfair hiring standards and tests. Southern AT&T affiliates lagged behind "even the minimal efforts" made elsewhere, and most black employes nationally were female, and "suffer from a dual handicap of race and sex." Spanish-surnamed Americans were systematically excluded from jobs, the report charged, and denied equality once hired.

As for women, the EEOC claimed that the phone company maintained recruitment and promotion policies that in effect created men-only and women-only categories. Telephone operators, 99.9% female, had "virtually intolerable" working conditions including "authoritarian" work rules, and pay ceilings of $5,000–$6,000 a year, with almost no advancement possibilities, the EEOC report charged.

AT&T and the General Services Administration (GSA) Sept. 20, 1972 announced an agreement for AT&T to increase and upgrade the employment of women and minority-group members.

The Labor Department's Office of Federal Contract Compliance (OFCC) told the GSA and AT&T Sept. 29 that it was "assuming jurisdiction" over their agreement. An OFCC spokesman said the office would probably require the parties to negotiate a more extensive agreement. Women's and minority organizations had criticized the accord as inadequate.

The GSA accord would have required AT&T to promote 50,000 women and 6,600 minority group members into better jobs within 15 months, and to try to hire 6,600 women for jobs usually filled by men and 4,000 men to traditionally female jobs, for a goal of 10% women among new employes in outside craft jobs and 5% men among newly hired operators. All qualified persons who applied for the opposite-sex jobs would be hired, as long as positions were open.

AT&T pledged that minorities and women would constitute a percentage of all new employes in each affiliated company equivalent to one and one half times the percentage of that minority group in the local area. AT&T would conduct semiannual progress reviews, subject to GSA inspection.

The plan was immediately criticized by some civil rights groups. The National Organization for Women (NOW), the National Association for the Advancement of Colored People (NAACP) and the Mexican-American Legal Defense Fund filed formal objections Sept. 29. They said the plan violated federal law in failing to provide for back pay to victims of past discrimination, ignoring job test procedures that were unfair to women or minorities, and ignoring unfair transfer policies. The groups asked that any local AT&T affiliate with a poor record of minority hiring be required to make a greater effort than the plan required nationally, and they asked for maternity leave standards in accordance with Equal Employment Opportunity Commission (EEOC) rules.

In a 10,000-page brief released Aug. 1, AT&T had disputed the EEOC's charges of massive discrimination, in preparation for Federal Communication Commission (FCC) hearings on whether the company's employment policies ought to influence FCC rate decisions. The company claimed that over the past three years minorities had accounted for one quarter of all new employes, so that blacks constituted 10% of the total work force, and the number of Spanish-speaking employes had nearly doubled.

One third of AT&T managers were women, the company said, more than half of whom earned over $10,000 annually, and the number of women at middle management and higher levels had increased seven times as fast as all management jobs in the three-year period. About 40% of all managers and officials were women, compared with a 15% figure for the nation as a whole.

Although most of the 53.5% of its employes who were women were operators or clerks, the company criticized the EEOC's "disparagement" of the operator job, which it called "a good one." AT&T said the commission had ignored the "realities of the labor market" and the company's responsibility to provide good services.

AT&T, the Labor Department and the EEOC Jan. 18, 1973 reached an agreement under which the company would pay $15 million to 15,000 women and minority male employes as compensation for past discriminatory hiring and promotion practices. The company also agreed to pay $23 million a year in pay increases to 36,000 women and minority workers who had moved to higher paying jobs without being credited with seniority gained in lower category jobs. In return, the EEOC agreed to drop its opposition to rate increases for AT&T.

AT&T also agreed to a set of percentage goals for women in craft jobs and for men in traditionally female operator and clerical jobs that were about twice as high as those provided in the 1972 AT&T accord with the General Services Administration, which had been rejected by the Labor Department's Office of Contract Compliance.

In a departure from previous cases, women would receive back pay, upon moving into craft jobs, even if they had failed to apply for the jobs under the impression that the company would deny the request. The settlement was the largest job bias compensation ever awarded, although the EEOC said the total payments would be far less than what the employes would have earned if they had been promoted earlier. The settlement did not remove the company's liability in about 1,-000 pending job bias cases by individual employes, which the EEOC would continue to process.

AT&T agreed to develop programs at all its facilities toward a goal of 38%–40% women in inside craft jobs and 19% women in outside craft jobs, and set a hiring goal of 10% men in operator jobs and 25% men in clerical jobs. About 1,500 women college graduates would be moved into a rapid-advance management training program allegedly closed to women in the past.

EEOC Chairman William H. Brown 3rd said he hoped the agreement "would be used as a model for government's negotiations with companies." Labor Department assistant solicitor William J. Kilberg said the settlement showed that the Nixon Administration backed numerical goals and timetables as methods of ending job bias. But the National Organization for Women criticized the plan for failing to set specific timetables for the numerical goals.

A federal district court judge in Philadelphia Oct. 13, 1973 denied a petition by the Communications Workers of America (CWA) to block implementation of the AT&T-government settlement.

The CWA contended that the settlement had infringed upon the union's rights as bargainer for AT&T employes. Judge A. Leon Higgenbotham Jr. ruled, however, that the union had remained "persistently aloof" from the negotiations leading to the agreement, refusing numerous invitations to join. The union had therefore lost any right to delay "even for one hour" implementation of the agreement.

The court noted that the CWA had consistently failed to attempt action against discriminatory practices by the company, having filed only one minor complaint with the EEOC.

AT&T was reported May 14, 1975 to have agreed to step up its efforts to implement the 1973 agreement. A supplemental accord, reached by AT&T and four federal agencies, called for "priority" hiring and promotion of workers where the 1973 goals had not been met.

Expected to cost up to $2.5 million during 1975 and 1976, the new agreement called for back pay ranging from $125 to $1,500 to "an undetermined number of employes whose promotions may have been delayed." Under the new agreement, an AT&T spokesman said, an estimated 5,000 workers who should have been hired or promoted under the original decree would be given special attention.

The supplemental agreement remedied "the failure of a number of Bell System [AT&T] companies to fully implement the 1973 consent decree in a timely mannet," said Labor Department solicitor Kilberg.

Government agencies participating in the new agreement were the Labor Department, the Justice Department, the General Services Administration and the Equal Employment Opportunity Commission.

NLRB reversal in Lubbock. The National Labor Relations Board (NLRB) Nov. 11, 1971 ruled, 3–1, that a Lubbock, Tex. employer had not discriminated against black and Chicano employes. The ruling reversed a 1968 decision of the board and was seen as an indication of the leanings of Republican members appointed in 1970.

The board majority in the latest decision said that "in a plant where 85%–90% of the employes belong to minority groups," any actions by the employer "are likely to be subject to claims of discrimination." The lone dissenter, Howard Jenkins Jr., noting that whites held 85% of the higher-paid jobs, said "such statistics, in themselves, sufficiently demonstrate the existence of racial discrimination."

The 1968 decision found the Farmers' Cooperative Compress guilty of unfair labor practices in opposing organization by the United Packinghouse Workers, since merged into the Amalgamated

Meatcutters. The board at that time ruled that discrimination against workers could be considered an unfair practice under NLRB jurisdiction, and ordered the firm to bargain with the union on the issue.

The U.S. Court of Appeals for the District of Columbia upheld the 1968 ruling, but ordered the NLRB to make a specific finding on whether discrimination had occurred. An NLRB trial examiner then found that the firm was in fact discriminating, but the Nov. 11 decision overturned that finding.

Sam A. Zagoria, former NLRB member who participated in the 1968 ruling, said Nov. 11 that the board members at that time had "no doubt" that "rampant discrimination" existed.

Federal efforts criticized. U.S. government programs to assure equal job rights for employes and prospective employes of federal contractors were criticized by the outgoing head of the Office of Federal Contract Compliance in June 1972 as ineffectual.

George Holland, director of the OFCC since February, submitted his resignation June 1, effective July 1, charging that a recent reorganization of the agency had diminished its effectiveness in enforcing equal job opportunities in firms doing business with the federal government.

In his letter of resignation Holland charged that the reorganization, which decentralized the agency and merged its field offices with other Labor Department units, "diminishes program impact, diffuses program authority and denies program uniformity."

Steel Industry

U.S. Steel charges federal 'threat.' The chairman of the United States Steel Corp. accused the Justice Department Dec. 14, 1970 of threatening a law suit to force the company to hire more black office and clerical personnel at its plant in Fairfield, Ala.

According to E. H. Gott, the chairman, when the corporation refused to accept the government's racial job quota, the Justice Department filed suit against U.S. Steel, charging it with discrimination.

(The Justice Department had filed a suit in federal district court in Birmingham Dec. 11, charging the steel firm with discriminating against blacks at its Fairfield plant. The suit also charged the United Steelworkers of America and the AFL-CIO and 12 Alabama steelworker locals with violating the 1964 Civil Rights Act and being parties to the alleged discriminating practices.)

Gott said Justice Department officials demanded Dec. 10 that U.S. Steel, the nation's largest steel company, allocate 50% of all office and clerical jobs at its Fairfield division to blacks within five years. Another Justice Department demand, Gott said, was that blacks constitute 40% of all personnel promoted to management levels through 1975 at the Fairfield steelworks.

Gott said the hiring figures "were the price U.S. Steel was asked to pay to forestall immediate filing of a pattern and practice suit against Fairfield Works by the Justice Department." He termed the government's proposals "grossly outrageous demands." U.S. Steel rejected the figures the same day they were received.

The Justice Department confirmed Dec. 14 that it had used the figures cited by Gott in negotiations with the company. The spokesmen said, however, that it was erroneous to characterize the proposed hiring figures as demands. He added that "resolution of these issues would not have stopped the filing of the suit."

When the suit was filed Dec. 11 in Birmingham, U.S. Steel issued a statement denying "any pattern or practice of discrimination at its Fairfield operations. The company included in the statement a listing of the programs it had initiated to help black workers.

Gott said the government's proposed racial job quotas were "in direct opposition to the premise of Title VII of the Civil Rights Act, which provides there be no discrimination in employment and upgrading because of race, color, creed, national origin or sex." He said the quotas' provisions exceeded the ratio of blacks to whites in Jefferson County, where the Fairfield plant was located.

Company & union lose suit—A federal judge in Birmingham May 2, 1973 ordered U.S. Steel and the United Steelworkers to end discriminatory hiring and seniority systems at the Fairfield Works.

The ruling by Judge Sam C. Pointer Jr. created a uniform seniority system to replace 10 separate systems and established the right of workers to transfer from one line of promotion to another without losing seniority rights, opening previously closed jobs to blacks. Back pay was ordered for employes who had been held in menial jobs.

Timetables were set under which one black apprentice would be chosen for each white apprentice until 25% of all journeymen positions were held by blacks, and one black supervisor would be hired for every two white supervisors until 20% of all management positions were held by blacks. Blacks who had been laid off were given special rehiring rights.

The ruling was to take effect Aug. 1 after an "intense education program" at the Fairfield Works and other company plants in Alabama, all of which were affected.

Judge Pointer said his order marked the first time a federal judge had attempted to restructure a seniority system rather than deal with individual cases.

A federal appeals court Oct. 11, 1975 overturned a ruling by Pointer that 2,700 black workers at the Fairfield Works should not get back pay sought on the grounds of racial discrimination by the company and union. Pointer had awarded back pay to 61 employes but denied it to workers on the production and maintenance force because he lacked the resources to determine individual awards.

In reversing the decision, the Fifth Circuit Court of Appeals in New Orleans stated that the fact that so many persons had been discriminated against neither lessened the liability of the company nor

made the individual workers any less entitled to back pay.

Bethlehem Steel ruling. The U.S. 2nd Circuit Court of Appeals June 21, 1971 ordered the United Steelworkers of America and Bethlehem Steel Co. to permit black workers to transfer from "hotter and dirtier" jobs at Bethlehem's plant in Lackawanna, N.Y. to higher paying and cleaner jobs with no loss in seniority or pay.

The decision was believed to be the first time a federal court had outlawed transfer and seniority provisions that violated Title VII of the Civil Rights Act of 1964. Such violations were interpreted as penalizing black employes who sought to shift their jobs within a plant.

In a unanimous ruling, the court held that "in hiring, jobs were made available to whites rather than to blacks in a number of ways. There were no fixed or reasonably objective standards and procedures for hiring." The court also said that over 80% of the black workers at the Lackawanna plant were placed in departments "which contained the hotter and dirtier jobs in the plant." Blacks, the court held, were excluded from "higher-paying and cleaner jobs."

The case was brought to the appeals court by the federal government. The government had succeeded in getting a lower court to rule that the company and union did discriminate, but could not obtain a lower court order that "would have made the exercise [of transfer rights] more attractive."

A federal panel had accused Bethlehem Steel Jan. 5 of discriminating against blacks through its seniority system. A report by the panel was forwarded Jan. 5 to Labor Secretary James D. Hodgson.

In a statement accompanying the report, Bethlehem denied the charge but agreed to set new hiring, promotion and training quotas for Negro employes.

The three-member federal panel delivered a unanimous decision against Bethlehem but disagreed on what corrective measures should be taken. Two of the panelists accepted the company's new job quotas, but the third termed the quota proposal "seriously deficient" and asked for adoption of a plan presented by the federal government.

The plan, which was drawn up by the Office of Federal Contract Compliance, was rejected by the majority as unworkable and inappropriate in the steel industry.

Seniority change ordered—The Department of Labor Jan. 16, 1973 ordered into effect a new series of changes in seniority practices at Bethlehem Steel's Sparrows Point, Md. plant, to wipe out the continuing effects of past discrimination in job placement of blacks.

The order, which a department spokesman called "the most far-reaching" affirmative action program so far ordered, was issued under the Executive Order enforcing job rights in federal contracts, but Labor Secretary James D. Hodgson rejected a request by the Office of Contract Compliance that sanctions be imposed, "in light," he said, "of the company's spirit of cooperation." The order was the first to concern seniority rights.

The three-member federal panel had reported at the beginning of 1971 that as of November 1967, 81% of the 7,864 black workers at the plant had been employed in all-black or predominantly black departments with lower pay and less sought-after jobs, including refuse disposal and coke oven maintenance, while most of the 12,602 white employes worked as timekeepers and sheet metal workers. Changes in hiring practices since March 31, 1968 eliminated discrimination against new workers, the government ruled, but limited transfer rights perpetuated the effects of previous policy.

The order provided that all employes hired before March 31, 1968 who had never transferred out of a black department be given written transfer offers, provided they could perform the new job "with minimal training." Bethlehem was ordered to see that "reasonable requirements" be set for jobs, and training be provided.

Employes asking for transfer to a predominantly white department would be hired for the first "available permanent vacancy" on the basis of total years of "plant service" in any department. Blacks transferring to a white department would retain their accrued seniority and their pay, if higher than the new job would otherwise provide.

TV, Radio & Films

Negroes win radio-TV accord. A black citizens' group in Atlanta announced March 30, 1970 that it had just negotiated agreements with 22 of the city's 28 TV and radio stations calling for increased black involvement in programming and employment. Details of the agreements varied with the size of the 22 stations.

The accord was reached after the Federal Communications Commission (FCC) had granted the bargainers for both sides an additional 30 days to settle their disputes over minority hiring and increased programming aimed at Atlanta's black community. The citizens' group, the Community Coalition on Broadcasting, had asked the FCC to grant the 30-day extension in February after protracted negotiations had been stalemated.

The coalition announced March 30 that it would actively oppose the relicensing of the four stations that failed to ratify the accord.

The agreements included more coverage of black community news, more black employes in both the technical and broadcasting fields and the placement of blacks in decision-making posts at the stations.

Film-makers set job plan. Seventy-two movie studios and television companies said March 31, 1970 that they had agreed to implement immediately an equal employment plan for their industries that included hiring, training and upgrading of minorities and setting racial quotas. The agreement was worked out with the aid of lawyers from the Justice Department who entered the negotiations after the movie and television industry had been criticized during hearings in 1969 for practices of racial discrimination in hiring.

Among the major companies signing the agreement were Columbia Pictures Industries, the Columbia Broadcasting System, Warner Brothers, Metro-Goldwyn Mayer, Bing Crosby Productions, Paramount Pictures Corp., Lucille Ball Productions, Walt Disney Productions and 20th Century Fox Film Corp.

The agreement would ban all job discrimination within the movie-making industry and the affiliated unions that served it. The jobs were nonacting employment, such as hair stylists, make-up artists, set designers, film editors and electrical technicians. The firms also agreed to prohibit discriminatory job testing and to set up a minority pool in some jobs in which two of every five new employes would be members of a minority group. The firms also agreed to establish a job-training program with participation consisting of two-fifths Negroes and two-fifths Mexican-Americans, with all of them guaranteed jobs within the industry.

Radio station gift. The Washington Post Co. said Dec. 10, 1970 that it was turning over its FM radio station valued at $750,000 to Howard University. The gift of WTOP-FM was aimed at improving employment opportunities of minority groups in all phases of broadcasting.

Minority cable channels set. Two major cable television franchisers and a coalition of 16 minority group organizations announced an agreement in San Francisco Nov. 29, 1972 that would give the groups control of several cable channels and train minority workers in broadcast skills.

The companies, Cox Communications, Inc. and American Television Communication, Inc., said the plan would be effective upon completion of pending merger plans. The new company would provide, over a five-year period, up to three full-time channels in each of their eight California franchise areas at a token fee of $1 a year to nonprofit minority organizations, provide all necessary video equipment in four of the areas, and begin training minority individuals in technical and program skills.

The 16 minority groups in the agreement included the Black Panther Party, the western office of the National Association for the Advancement of Colored People and the Mexican-American Political Alliance.

Report on broadcast jobs. The Federal Communications Commission reported June 26, 1973 that in 1972 about 10% of broadcast employes were members of four key minority groups—black, 6.6%; Spanish-surnamed, 3%; Oriental, .5%; and American Indian, .4%. The study was compiled from mandatory reports filed by stations with five or more full-time employes.

The study also showed women making up 23% of the 130,656 employes covered.

Black network starts—The National Black Network, the nation's first black-owned and operated radio news network, began operations July 2, 1973 with news feeds to 40 affiliated stations. The network, based in New York City, was scheduled to provide news reports of interest to black listeners daily.

Private Industry Efforts

Businessmen praised. President Nixon lauded the National Alliance of Businessmen March 15, 1969 for producing jobs for the hard-core unemployed. In a brief talk at the second annual meeting of the alliance, a non-partisan group organized during the Johnson Administration, Mr. Nixon told the group that its program had "the complete, unqualified support of this Administration." He suggested that the alliance focus especially on the problem of finding jobs for youths and, if possible, that it extend its program to smaller towns and cities.

The alliance's outgoing chairman, Henry Ford 2d, chairman of the Ford Motor Co., reported that 145,000 persons had been hired under the alliance program and that 87,850 of them were still on the job. Of the latter, 73% were black,

17% white, 8% "Spanish-surnamed," 1% Indian and 1% Oriental.

GM reports gains. James M. Roche, chairman of the board of the General Motors Corp. (GM), reported Feb. 6, 1970 that the company had made significant gains in its minority group hiring, although the number of salaried blacks at GM remained relatively low. He said that at the end of 1969 97,150 of its U.S. employes, or 15.3%, were Negroes, Orientals, Indians or Spanish Americans. Roche said that in 1965 the figure was 66,469 or 11.5%.

Roche said that "since 1965, 60% of the employes we have added, both hourly and salaried, have been minority Americans." Roche said that in the last year the number of GM's salaried employes who were minority group members had increased 30%, to 5,086 from 3,894. General Motors had about 143,000 salaried employes, meaning that minority group members made up about 3.5% of the salaried worker total.

PUSH in action. A new black organization active in fighting job discrimination was PUSH (People United to Save Humanity), an offshoot of the Southern Christian Leadership Conference. In 1972 PUSH took over from the conference the sponsorship, in Chicago Sept. 27–31, of the fourth annual Black Expo.

The exposition of black business and cultural efforts drew over 700,000 visitors and grossed about $500,000 to help PUSH's economic programs.

PUSH leader Rev. Jesse L. Jackson, according to a Sept. 27 report, said the group's boycott and picketing tactics had obtained over $100 million in concessions from major corporations and banks in the form of hiring and promotion, deposits in black banks and contracts with black suppliers.

Government Employment

Although government was charged with enforcing equal-opportunity laws and regulations in private industry, there was growing complaint that it was *not keeping its own house in order. Charges of racial and sex discrimination in employment were made against all levels of government—federal, state and local.*

State & local regimes accused. The U.S. Civil Rights Commission charged in a 1969 report that "state and local governments consciously and overtly discriminate in hiring and promoting minority group members." Excerpts from the report:

FINDINGS
Background of the problem

1. In recent years State and local government employment has grown rapidly in total numbers, in the range of services provided, and in the occupational categories required to perform these services. Because they are relatively large institutions, have broad potential, and need a variety of talent, State and local governments can provide an important source of jobs for members of minority groups.

2. State and local governments are the largest single group of employers in the United States for which no comprehensive information is available on the racial and ethnic composition of their work force. These governments also are the only large group of employers in the Nation whose racial employment practices are almost entirely exempt from any Federal nondiscrimination requirements.

Extent of equal opportunity

3. Minority group members are denied equal access to State and local government jobs.

(*a*) Negroes, in general, have better success in obtaining jobs with central city governments than they do in State, county, or suburban jurisdictions and are more successful in obtaining jobs in the North than in the South.

(*b*) Negroes are noticeably absent from managerial and professional jobs even in those jurisdictions where they are substantially employed in the aggregate. In only two central cities, out of a total of eight surveyed, did the overall number of black employees in white-collar jobs reflect the population patterns of the cities.

(*c*) Access to white-collar jobs in some departments is more readily available to minority group members than in others. Negroes are most likely to hold professional, managerial, and clerical jobs in financial administration and general control.

(*d*) Negroes hold the large majority of laborer and general service worker jobs—jobs which are characterized by few entry skills, relatively low pay, and limited opportunity for advancement.

(e) Spanish Americans hold a substantial number of State and local jobs in the Houston area governments but hold proportionately fewer State and local jobs in the San Francisco-Oakland area governments. They have been more successful in obtaining higher level jobs than Negroes but less successful than majority group members.

(f) Oriental Americans are more successful in obtaining State and county jobs than central city jobs. Although the distribution of Oriental Americans in professional and clerical occupations is equal to or better than that of the majority group. Oriental Americans have not obtained full access to managerial positions.

Barriers to equal opportunity

4. State and local government employment opportunities for minorities are restricted by overt discrimination in personnel actions and hiring decisions, a lack of positive action by governments to redress the consequences of past discrimination, and discriminatory and biased treatment on the job.

(a) A merit system of public personnel administration does not eliminate discrimination against members of minorities. It proclaims objectively, but does not assure it. Discrimination occurs both in recruiting and in selection among final applicants.

(b) Governments have undertaken few efforts to eliminate recruitment and selection devices which are arbitrary, unrelated to job performance, and result in unequal treatment of minorities. Further, governments have failed to undertake programs of positive action to recruit minority applicants and to help them overcome barriers created by current selection procedures.

(c) Promotional opportunities are not made available to minorities on an equal basis by governments that rely on criteria unrelated to job performance and on discriminatory supervisory ratings.

Barriers in police and fire departments

5. Barriers to equal employment are greater in police and fire departments than in any other area of State and local government.

(a) Negroes are not employed in significant numbers in police and fire departments.

(1) Although 27 percent of all central city jobs surveyed are in police and fire departments, only 7 percent of the black employees in central cities are policemen and firemen.

(2) Fire departments in most of the cities surveyed employ even fewer uniformed personnel than do the police departments.

(3) Negro policemen and firemen hold almost no positions in the officer ranks.

(4) State police forces employ very few Negro policemen. Four of the States employed no Negro policemen in the metropolitan areas surveyed.

(b) Spanish Americans are employed as policemen and firemen on the average less than half as frequently as Anglos.

(c) Police and fire departments have discouraged minority persons from joining their ranks by failure to recruit effectively and by permitting unequal treatment on the job including unequal promotional opportunities, discriminatory job assignments, and harassment by fellow workers. Minority group hostility to police and fire departments also deters recruitment, and this has not been overcome by the departments.

Impact of the Federal Government

6. The Federal Government has established no effective Federal requirements for equal opportunity in State and local employment, and no effective standards and guidelines for affirmative action to correct past discriminatory practices and increase opportunities for minority groups. The limited efforts to do so have not been successful.

(a) The nondiscrimination clause, included in the Federal merit standards since 1963, applies only to a small fraction of State and local government employment and has had no discernible effect in increasing employment opportunities for minority groups in State and local government. Present enforcement of the clause provides neither effective protection, nor effective avenues of redress to members of minority groups who encounter discrimination. The Office of State Merit Systems has provided no guidelines for State action either to eliminate discrimination or to increase opportunities.

(b) Federal housing agencies have made virtually no efforts to enforce the nondiscrimination clause included since the 1950's in their contracts with local public housing and urban renewal agencies. Neither have they assured that affirmative action has been taken to increase opportunities for minorities.

U.S. exam challenged. Eight black federal employes charged in a suit filed Feb. 4, 1971 that the Federal Service Entrance Examination, the principal test that qualified college graduates for civil service posts, was "culturally and racially discriminatory."

The eight plaintiffs, employes of the Department of Housing and Urban Development's (HUD) Chicago Regional Office, alleged that the exam violated the equal opportunity guarantees of the Fifth Amendment. They also said it violated the 1964 Civil Rights Act, several executive orders and the regulations of HUD and the Civil Service Commission.

Named defendants in the suit were George Romney, HUD secretary, and three Civil Service commissioners. The

Black Employment As a Percentage of Total Employment, 1960 & 1969

Numbers in thousands

	Total employment (number)	Total	White collar	Managers and officials	Technicians	Office and clerical	Blue collar	Craftsmen	Operatives	Laborers	Service workers
1960: All industries	64,647	10.2	3.8	2.3		4.6	10.5	4.9	10.7	25.8	28.1
1969: All industries (EEO-1)	28,739	10.4	5.1	2.1	6.9	7.0	13.3	5.6	14.1	22.9	28.2
Nonwhite		9.5					12.6	5.0	13.4	21.8	26.9
Negro		12.4					2.7	1.2	2.9	27.1	27.1
Food processing	1,094	12.8	4.1	1.5	5.6	6.1	14.3	6.1	13.8	27.7	33.4
Textile mills	784	10.3	2.9	1.7	2.0	3.6	11.1	8.9	11.2	15.8	19.5
Apparel and other textiles	604	8.8	1.7	.6	2.9	2.9	11.1	4.6	11.1	17.2	21.1
Paper products	564	6.3	3.5	1.8	3.4	5.6	7.6	2.1	10.4	19.0	32.7
Printing and publishing	541	7.8	1.6	.7	2.0	2.8	12.2	4.7	13.0	22.7	23.5
Chemicals	930	13.6	3.7	1.0	4.1	5.7	17.0	6.7	19.1	25.3	19.0
Primary metals	1,079	9.1	2.1	1.7	2.6	4.0	11.6	3.4	13.0	17.5	17.8
Fabricated metals	881	5.6	1.4	.8	1.9	3.1	7.8	6.2	9.0	14.9	13.5
Machinery (Excluding electrical)	1,394	7.3	1.5	.5	1.6	2.3	10.2	4.2	11.5	12.7	19.2
Electrical machinery	1,748	10.4	2.3	.9	1.9	2.6	14.4	6.2	18.4	20.6	24.8
Transportation equipment	1,670	7.8	2.0	1.4	3.1	3.9	8.8	3.0	5.7	30.0	47.8
Railroad transportation	616	7.4	2.2	1.4	.6	3.8	8.8	3.0	13.6	15.7	31.9
Communications	853	5.2	8.8	.8	2.4	2.6	6.4	1.9	8.6	25.3	32.8
Electric, gas, sanitation services	569	6.9	3.4	2.4	1.6	11.6	13.9	6.3	13.6	22.7	23.2
Wholesale trade	1,345	7.8	3.1	2.0	3.2	5.3	14.6	4.3	14.9	21.0	24.1
Retail and general merchandise	1,554	6.5	5.8	2.9	6.1	4.1	10.7	6.2	13.4	13.8	13.4
Food stores	731	7.5	5.6	1.8	7.6	7.4	13.6	6.8	15.9	20.9	28.6
Banking	651	6.2	6.4	3.5	5.9	5.2	20.1	5.1	17.5	45.4	29.4
Insurance carriers	837	9.7	6.6		4.6	7.6	14.2	5.5	18.2	19.8	32.9
Educational services	863		4.9		10.2	8.0					

From a report by Andrew F. Brimmer, Federal Reserve Board member, at the NAACP convention in Minneapolis July 6, 1971.

class action suit was filed in U.S. district court in Washington.

The plaintiffs charged that the exam "has served systematically to exclude qualified blacks and members of other minority groups from obtaining managerial and professional level positions in the federal service, and has by other means denied plaintiffs and their class equal employment opportunities."

The suit asked the court to bar the use of the examination until its allegedly biased aspects were eliminated, and it requested that other testing procedures be stopped until a determination could be made of their relation to specific job requirements.

According to the plaintiffs, about 49% of the 100,000 persons who took the test in 1969 finished with scores above 70, with "a disproportionately low percentage" of blacks and other minority group members passing.

Bias in GPO. The U.S. Civil Service Commission, releasing the findings of an inquiry it had begun in November 1968, said June 19, 1969 that there was evidence of racial discrimination in the Government Printing Office (GPO). The report cited a lack of minority group members in higher level supervisory and administrative positions. The report said however that the GPO had a favorable minority employment record compared with the private printing industry and other federal agencies.

GSA bias found. Black employes of the General Services Administration (GSA) charged in a report July 21, 1969 that the agency practiced racial discrimination in its staffing and promotion procedures. Russell Gaskins, chairman of a task force formed by 100 Negro employes, said they were submitting a petition demanding changes to GSA Administrator Robert L. Kunzig.

(Kunzig had acknowledged July 8 that patterns of racial discrimination in employment existed in the GSA. He had pledged to support a biracial committee to correct the inequities in the agency's promotion procedures.)

Though the report said the employe group was encouraged by the GSA management's commitment to equal employment opportunities, individual members expressed dissatisfaction with the agency's new promotion procedures. One member said the new practice under which employes rated each other was "the same old soup warmed over."

Postal Service accused of job bias. The Rev. Jesse Jackson, leader of the Operation Breadbasket arm of the Southern Christian Leadership Conference, charged Aug. 2, 1971 that the Postal Service was discriminating against blacks as it reorganized.

Jackson made the charge in Washington, the second stop on his eight-city tour to pick up support for a national coalition of postal workers.

As it was proceeding, Jackson said, the reorganization of the Postal Service had placed thousands of black employes a step closer to welfare rolls. He explained that since the majority of black postal workers were in lower job categories, they were the first to be let go in any reorganization plans that included layoffs. Jackson also criticized the Postal Service decision to place some new district offices in the suburbs. He said that in Chicago, the new district office was being placed in Cicero, "where it is not even safe for blacks to pass through—let alone live."

He added that when the new offices were opened in suburban areas, "local residents get priority" for the new postal jobs.

Jackson said the alleged discrimination was attributable to a newfound interest in Postal Service jobs by whites.

Bias charged in HUD. A federal hearing examiner ruled that the Housing and Urban Development Department (HUD) and its predecessor agencies had been guilty of systematic discrimination against blacks in hiring and promotion, at least until late 1970, it was disclosed Oct. 21, 1971.

Minority Employment in Federal Government 1963 & 1970

Pay category	Total full time employees	Minority groups Number	Minority groups Percent of total	Negro Number	Negro Percent of total	Spanish surnamed Number	Spanish surnamed Percent of total	American Indian[1] Number	American Indian[1] Percent of total	Oriental[2] Number	Oriental[2] Percent of total	All other Number	All other Percent of total
1963													
Total, all pay systems	2,298,808	374,321	16.3	301,889	13.1	51,682	2.2	10,592	0.5	10,158	0.4	1,924,487	83.7
Total, general (or similar) schedule	1,103,051	125,596	11.4	101,589	9.2	15,292	1.4	5,315	.5	3,400	.3	977,455	88.6
GS-1 through GS-4	355,329	78,170	22.0	66,169	18.6	7,520	2.1	3,373	1.0	1,108	.3	277,159	78.0
GS-5 through GS-8	315,203	33,851	10.7	26,452	8.4	4,809	1.5	1,311	.4	1,279	.4	281,352	89.3
GS-9 through GS-11	243,325	10,433	4.3	7,016	2.9	2,178	.9	481	.2	758	.3	232,892	95.7
GS-12 through GS-18	189,194	3,142	1.7	1,952	1.0	785	.4	150	.1	255	.1	186,052	98.3
1970													
Total, all pay systems	2,592,956	501,871	19.4	389,355	15.0	73,968	2.9	17,446	.7	21,102	.8	2,091,085	80.6
Total, general (or similar) schedule	1,272,310	186,170	14.4	140,919	10.9	24,302	1.9	10,480	.8	10,469	.8	1,106,140	85.6
GS-1 through GS 4	308,315	84,078	27.3	67,253	21.8	9,258	3.0	5,655	1.8	1,912	.6	224,237	72.7
GS-5 through GS 8	372,939	64,278	17.2	50,392	13.5	8,186	2.2	2,724	.7	2,976	.8	308,661	82.8
GS-9 through GS 11	318,077	25,572	8.0	16,272	5.1	4,663	1.5	1,472	.5	3,165	1.0	292,505	92.0
GS-12 through GS 18	292,979	12,242	4.2	7,002	2.4	2,195	.8	629	.2	2,416	.8	280,737	95.8
GS-12 through GS 13	215,720	9,736	4.5	5,723	2.7	1,700	.8	477	.2	1,836	.9	205,984	95.5
GS-14 through GS 15	71,788	2,395	3.3	1,204	1.7	478	.7	146	.2	567	.8	69,393	96.7
GS-16 through GS 18	5,471	111	2.0	75	1.4	17	.3	6	.1	13	.2	5,360	98.0

[1] Surveyed only in Arizona, California, Montana, New Mexico, North Carolina, Oklahoma, and South Dakota in 1963.

[2] Surveyed only in California, Oregon, and Washington in 1963.

Source: U.S. Civil Service Commission, "Study of Minority Group Employment in the Federal Government," 1963 and 1970.

Julia P. Cooper, an Equal Employment Opportunity Commission lawyer appointed examiner by the Civil Service Commission, recommended that HUD repay 106 employes who had lost a day's pay after an October 13, 1970 protest during work hours against alleged discrimination. Miss Cooper found that, at least until the time of the protest, HUD supervisory personnel had frequently kept blacks in low grade levels while whites advanced, hired blacks at grade levels beneath their qualifications, limited or denied training opportunities to blacks, and penalized those who complained of these practices.

HUD officials, who had asked the Civil Service Commission to investigate the charges, admitted that discrimination had existed in the past. But Secretary George Romney denied, after the examiner's report was disclosed, that the problem remained. He cited a rise in minority employment at the agency to 40.5%, including 19.6% of those in grades 7 and above.

Samuel J. Simmons, HUD assistant secretary for equal employment opportunity, accepted Cooper's proposal Nov. 23 and agreed to the payments to the 106 employes. He conceded that there had been in the past "an accumulation of incidents of disparate treatment suffered by minorities," but he said that steps had been taken since 1970 "in an attempt to correct the problems."

Administration claims rights gains. A White House staff report on civil rights gains was released by Communications Director Herbert G. Klein Feb. 15, 1972 at a news conference at which Klein's assistant Stanley Scott and other black appointees were present.

Scott said that while "some insist there is no commitment," the Administration had "nothing to be ashamed of." The reports included the assertion that federal civilian minority employment had risen to 19.5% by May 1971, including seven black ambassadors and nearly 100 blacks in "super-grade" jobs, as opposed to 63 in 1969.

A color brochure by the National Republican Congressional Committee entitled "Meet Some of the Blacks in the Nixon Administration" was also distributed at the press conference.

U.S. job efforts scored. Federal programs to assure equal job rights at government agencies were criticized in 1972 by the Public Interest Research Group, a Ralph Nader unit.

The Public Interest Research Group report, issued June 24, charged the Civil Service Commission with inadequate and unsympathetic supervision of job rights complaint procedures in government agencies, and with failing to require agencies to provide training and promotion programs to compensate for past discrimination against blacks and women.

The report charged that half of all complaints closed in the 1970 fiscal year and reviewed by the commission had taken over six months to process, despite regulations requiring action within two months. Of those cases reviewed by the commission, a finding of discrimination was made in only 7.4% of the cases in fiscal 1970 and 4.8% in the first half of fiscal 1971. In 1970, supervisors were disciplined in only 1.8% of the cases, and only through reprimands or training classes. The Civil Service Board of Appeals and Review had rejected complaints in over 98% of the cases it reviewed.

Commission chairman Robert Hampton said June 24 "the data the conclusions are based on is quite dated."

Black named to FCC. President Nixon announced April 11, 1972 that he was nominating Benjamin L. Hooks, 47, a black Memphis lawyer and Baptist minister, to a seven-year term on the Federal Communications Commission (FCC).

The Congressional Black Caucus had asked Nixon March 8 to name a black to the FCC, charging that the commission had ignored the needs of blacks in license renewal cases.

Minority gains. The U.S. Civil Service Commission reported July 1, 1972 that the number of blacks, Spanish-Americans and other minority group members had increased in all grade levels of federal service above the lowest in the year ending November 1971. Overall federal minority employment excluding the Postal Service rose by 2.1% in the period, although the proportion of minorities in federal service dropped from 19.6% to 19.5% in the year, taking into account extensive postal job cutbacks.

The gains in high-paying jobs resulted from a one-third minority share of the 31,485 increase in U.S. white collar jobs.

The commission said Dec. 18 that a survey of government workers taken in May showed that the number of blacks and other minority group members in general schedule grades 12–18, earning $15,000–$36,000 a year, had increased 12.5% over a year earlier, and that minority group members had accounted for about 25% of the increase in personnel in those grades. But the nearly 16,000 high-level minority workers still accounted for only 5% of the work force in those grades.

Overall, blacks, Spanish-surnamed people, Orientals and Indians held 505,-568 federal jobs as of May 31, 19.6% of the total.

EEOC aide charges bias. A white senior investigator in the Equal Employment Opportunity Commission's New York district resigned June 5, 1972 after filing a formal complaint that the EEOC "discriminates in favor of Negroes and Spanish-surnamed Americans in hiring, promotion and terms and conditions of employment."

Carl Shiffman, who had worked for two years at the EEOC, said he had been denied a promotion because he was white and Jewish, and because he had opposed the firing of another white employe who had made similar charges in 1971.

U.S. granted bias suit immunity. U.S. District Court Judge Frank M. Johnson Jr. ruled in Montgomery, Ala. that the federal government could not be sued in a job discrimination case because of the doctrine of sovereign immunity, it was reported Oct. 14, 1972.

But, in a suit by two blacks who charged they had been denied promotions despite years of service in Air Force jobs, Johnson refused to apply the doctrine to government officials, and left as defendants all Cabinet officers except the secretary of state. Johnson criticized the government for invoking the doctrine, after "having so vigorously brought and prosecuted actions against various Alabama agencies to insure equal education and employment for blacks."

The suit asked for promotions and back pay for the men, and for a general injunction against racial discrimination by federal employers, charging that only 2.6% of general schedule federal civil servants in Alabama were blacks, although blacks constituted 36% of the state's population.

Alabama government bias barred. U.S. District Court Judge Frank M. Johnson Jr. in Montgomery, Ala. July 29, 1970 had ordered seven Alabama state agencies to stop discriminating against Negroes in their hiring practices and to give immediate job consideration to 62 Negro applicants turned away earlier.

He directed state authorities to take steps to eliminate all future racial discrimination in hiring practices.

In reviewing the case, which was brought into court by the Justice Department in 1968, Johnson noted that Alabama was the only state that had refused to adopt a regulation formally banning racial discrimination and providing for a system of redress in such cases. In his decision the judge said that the state "engaged in, and continues to engage in, a systematic practice of discrimination against qualified Negro applicants by preferring lower-ranking white applicants." He ordered the departments to offer to the 62 Negro applicants the first available positions in a classification and at a pay rate commensurate with what they would have been earning but for the discrimination. Johnson also directed the seven. agencies to hire Negroes and appoint them to positions other than custodial, domestic or laborer, when such applicants were listed as qualified and eligible.

Judge Johnson ordered Alabama's Department of Public Safety Feb. 7, 1972 to hire an equal number of whites and blacks until the proporation of black personnel rose to 25%, or roughly the proportion of blacks in the state population.

None of the 644 state policemen were black. Johnson charged that discrimination had been practiced, but left it up to the state to find the qualified blacks.

The suit had been brought by the National Association for the Advancement of Colored People.

An Associated Press survey reported Feb. 1 found only 27 blacks among 5,000 state police personnel in eight Southeastern states. Alabama and Mississippi had none, Georgia and Florida two each, South Carolina and Louisiana four each, Tennessee six and North Carolina nine.

Police job developments—District Court Judge John P. Fullam July 8, 1972 issued a preliminary injunction continuing his order that the Philadelphia Police Department hire one black for each two whites hired. He extended the order to include promotions.

Three blacks were graduated Sept. 2 from the Mississippi highway patrol training academy, becoming the first patrolmen of their race in the state.

A U.S. district court judge ruled that Cleveland could hire 188 new policemen to replace transferred personnel, but must reserve 18% of the places for blacks or individuals with Spanish surnames, it was reported Dec. 23.

U.S. sues 2 cities. The Justice Department, citing provisions of the 1972 Equal Employment Opportunity Act, filed suits Aug. 7, 1972 against local government agencies in Montgomery, Ala. and Los Angeles charging them with racial discrimination in hiring for public jobs.

The suits marked the first time the department had initiated action against state or local government agencies under the 1972 employment act.

In the Montgomery suit, filed in U.S. district court in Montgomery, the Justice Department accused the city, its water department, sanitary sewer board and the city-county personnel board of giving some black workers lower-paying job classifications even though they performed the same work as higher-paid whites.

(The Justice Department reported Jan. 24, 1973 that the Montgomery suit had been resolved by a consent decree filed Oct. 3. The department said that the decree "substantially expanded employment opportunities for blacks in the city government.")

The Los Angeles Fire Department was accused of pursuing "policies and practices that discriminate against black, Mexican-American and Oriental applicants for employment."

In its suit. the department asked the U.S. district court in Los Angeles for a permanent injunction to end the alleged job bias.

Imperial Valley order. A federal judge in San Diego Sept. 8, 1972 ordered the Imperial Irrigation District to hire blacks or Mexican-Americans to fill two-thirds of all new vacancies until the minority proportion of the district work force, then 15.2%, rose to the minority percentage of the Imperial County population, 49.5. According to California Rural Legal Assistance, which had filed the suit, the two-thirds hiring ratio was the highest ever ordered by a federal judge.

Anti-Bias Powers Enlarged

EEOC authority expanded. A bill to give the Equal Employment Opportunity Commission (EEOC) power to seek court enforcement of its findings of job

discrimination and to expand its jurisdiction was approved by 62–10 Senate
vote March 6, 1972 and by 303–110 House
vote March 8.

The bill as approved by a Senate-
House conference Feb. 29 followed the
more liberal Senate version in extending
EEOC coverage to 10.1 million state and
local government workers, all employes
of public and private educational institutions and all companies and unions
with at least 15 workers, instead of the
previous minimum of 25.

Two House provisions were dropped
that would have curbed class action suits
and made the EEOC the only federal
agency with job bias authority.

The conferees gave the EEOC, rather
than the Justice Department, power to
bring suits against a "pattern and practice" of union or employer bias. An
independent EEOC general counsel
was provided for, appointed by the
President and subject to Senate confirmation, but acting only under orders of
the commission.

The measure was a substitute for a
stronger proposal, favored by civil
rights and women's rights groups, that
would have given the EEOC the power to
issue cease-and-desist orders.

In earlier action in the Senate, conservative Republicans and Southern Democrats had succeeded Jan. 26 in delet-
ing by a 49–36 vote a provision transferring the Office of Federal Contract
Compliance from the Labor Department to the EEOC. The Office enforces
executive orders requiring racial balance
among employes of federal contractors.

EEOC files first suit—In its first use
of its newly enacted powers, the EEOC
filed suit in federal district court
in Jacksonville, Fla. May 11 against the
Container Corp. of America, four international unions and six union locals,
charging job discrimination against
women and blacks.

The suit alleged that women were
confined to low-paying clerical positions,
while blacks were denied training for
better jobs, victimized by "unvalidated
tests" for advancement, and confined
to "more arduous and lower-paying
jobs" than whites.

The court was asked to order a revision of seniority practices, special
training programs, elimination of the
tests, payment of back wages, hiring of
blacks and women in specified ratios
and revision of union by-laws.

The unions involved were the Inter-
national Association of Machinists, the
International Brotherhood of Electrical
Workers, the Brotherhood of Painters
and the Pulp, Sulphite and Paper Mil'
Workers Union.

Quota Controversy

Nixon bans job quotas. President
Nixon banned minority employment hir-
ing quotas in the federal government
Aug. 24, 1972.

The order, transmitted by Civil Ser-
vice Commission (CSC) chairman
Robert Hampton, was in response to a
letter sent Aug. 4 by the American Jewish
Committee (AJC) to President Nixon and
Democratic presidential nominee George
McGovern expressing concern over the
use of job quotas.

Hyman Bookbinder of the AJC said
Aug. 25 that quotas had become "particularly serious in our government education programs." Bookbinder said the
AJC's position was not intended to
"mean we should reduce efforts to increase the number of blacks, women and
Chicanos [in jobs]. But we mustn't do
it on a quota basis."

The CSC had asserted that no quota
practices existed, but according to the
Washington Post Aug. 25, the government's "affirmative action" hiring programs were, in effect, de facto quota systems.

In his reply to the AJC, McGovern
also opposed the use of quotas; however,
he had also often promised jobs to
blacks in his administration in proportion to their number in the population,
the Post said.

Nixon had included criticism of quota
systems in his acceptance speech Aug.
23 at the Republican presidential nominating convention.

Nixon referred to the controversy again in a Labor Day statement Sept. 3. "Quotas are intended to be a short cut to equal opportunity," he said, "but in reality they are a dangerous detour away from the traditional value of measuring a person on the basis of ability."

Philadelphia Plan in question. Administration leaders denied Sept. 3–7, 1972 that they were planning to drop the Philadelphia Plan. But the Labor Department said the programs were undergoing reviews in light of President Nixon's statements opposing job quotas for minority groups.

The New York Times reported Sept. 3 that Arthur A. Fletcher, former assistant secretary of labor, and current Labor Department sources, had said that the Philadelphia Plan would be dropped, in part to attract support from labor union members who opposed it.

In all, about 56 cities had adopted similar programs, often called "home town" plans, geared to the minority proportion of the general population, although all but four had been voluntarily adopted. Contractor associations and labor unions had frequently opposed the plans, while civil rights groups charged lax federal enforcement.

Labor Secretary James D. Hodgson said in a Sept. 3 statement that no decision had been made to drop the program, although all programs that might involve quotas "were being reviewed." He denied that the Philadelphia Plan was "a quota system," but rather a system of "goals and timetables," which contractors must make a "good-faith effort" to achieve. White House Press Secretary Ronald Ziegler made the same distinction Sept. 4, and said the Times story was "without substance."

Secretary of Health, Education and Welfare (HEW) Elliot L. Richardson reinforced the denial Sept. 7. He said a team of Labor and HEW experts would be sent to Philadelphia to review recent progress. But the Sept. 5 Wall Street Journal cited one Labor Department official as saying that since "it's possible to apply" goals and timetables "in a quota form," all programs of the Office of Federal Contract Compliance, which administers the plan, would be reviewed.

Hodgson memo disputed. In the continuing debate over Administration enforcement of equal employment objectives, civil rights groups charged that a memorandum dated Sept. 15 from Labor Secretary James D. Hodgson to "all heads of agencies" in the federal government had nullified minority hiring plans.

The memo stated that the Office of Federal Contract Compliance did not require "quotas or proportional representation" of minorities, although "the goals required of government contractors" may have been "misinterpreted or misapplied." Hodgson said the goals were merely "targets," and failure to reach them "is not to be regarded as, per se, a violation."

In a Sept. 25 NAACP-NOW conference, Herbert Hill, NAACP labor director, said the memo implied abandonment of the Philadelphia Plan and similar programs, since it removes the "major standard for measuring good-faith efforts in all previous minority hiring plans." He charged that the Administration "retreat" on the issue was "in large part, part of a political payoff to the AFL-CIO" for its neutrality in the presidential election.

Hill criticized the Administration, contractors and building trades unions for hindering enforcement of the Philadelphia Plan, the first federal minority hiring agreement, but admitted that more blacks were employed in the Philadelphia building trades than when the plan was begun in 1969, and said it should be retained.

Secretary of Housing and Urban Development George Romney Sept. 28 ordered a Philadelphia construction contractor barred from further federal building work after determining that the firm, Russell Associates, had not complied with provisions of the plan. The firm had held a $225,000 plumbing contract on a 1970–71 housing project, and was the third company to be debarred under the plan.

Public Policy

Federal Failures Charged

By 1973 the Nixon Administration was under continuing fire from civil rights and women's groups and even from government advisory panels for alleged failures to support the employment rights of minorities and women.

Rights unit criticizes Administration. The U.S. Commission on Civil Rights charged in a report to Congress Feb. 9, 1973 that most federal agencies were failing to enforce civil rights laws adequately.

The commission laid much of the responsibility for the government's poor record on a lack of "Presidential leadership." It predicted that without such leadership "a steady erosion of the progress toward equal rights" would take place, because of the historically crucial role of the President as a moral and political leader. The Administration had "no government-wide plan for civil rights enforcement," the report charged, and even agencies with related civil rights responsibilities, such as the Civil Service Commission, the Equal Employment Opportunity Commission (EEOC) and the Office of Federal Contract Compliance (OFCC), did not work together effectively.

The 425-page report by the independent, Congressionally created agency was the last prepared under the direction of the Rev. Theodore M. Hesburgh, who had resigned in November.

Even when civil rights agencies recognized their duties and initiated action, the report said, "enforcement proceeds at a snail's pace." The commission warned that "the long-term stability of this nation demands an end to discrimination."

In the job rights area, the report charged the OFCC had been downgraded. It said the agency had "no adequate procedures to resolve compliance problems" on hiring agreements with contractors. The EEOC, while it had made "potentially effective" procedural changes, had an ever-growing backlog of complaints, expected to reach 70,000 by June, 1973, and assigned low priority to enforcing agreements. The Civil Service Commission, while it had "improved" its complaint handling mechanisms and now required federal agencies to adopt hiring goals and timetables, had failed to change the "pronounced disparate treatment" of minority employes in federal departments. Though minorities constituted 15.2% of federal employes in 1972, up from 14.7% in 1970, they still made up

Employment Status of Selected Labor Force Groups

[Numbers in millions]

Selected groups	Annual averages			Seasonally adjusted quarterly averages							
				1974				1975			
	1973	1974	1975	I	II	III	IV	I	II	III	IV
Civilian labor force	88.7	91.0	92.6	90.5	90.7	91.3	91.7	91.8	92.5	93.1	93.2
Total employment	84.4	85.9	84.8	85.9	86.1	86.2	85.5	84.3	84.4	85.1	85.2
Men, 20 years and over	47.9	48.4	47.4	48.6	48.5	48.5	48.2	47.3	47.3	47.6	47.5
Women, 20 years and over	29.2	30.1	30.3	29.8	30.1	30.4	30.0	29.9	30.1	30.5	30.7
Both sexes, 16 to 19 years	7.2	7.4	7.0	7.5	7.4	7.4	7.3	7.1	7.0	7.1	7.0
Part-time for economic reasons	2.3	2.7	3.5	2.6	2.5	2.7	3.2	3.7	3.7	3.3	3.3
Unemployed	4.3	5.1	7.8	4.6	4.6	5.1	6.1	7.5	8.1	8.0	7.9
Unemployment rates (percent):											
All workers	4.9	5.6	8.5	5.0	5.1	5.6	6.7	8.1	8.7	8.6	8.5
Men, 20 years and over	3.2	3.8	6.7	3.4	3.4	3.8	4.9	6.2	7.0	7.0	7.0
Women, 20 years and over	4.8	5.5	8.0	5.0	5.0	5.5	6.5	8.0	8.4	7.9	7.9
Both sexes, 16 to 19 years	14.5	16.0	19.9	14.8	15.2	16.3	17.6	19.8	20.2	20.2	19.5
White	4.3	5.0	7.8	4.5	4.6	5.1	6.0	7.5	8.0	7.9	7.8
Negro and other races	8.9	9.9	13.9	9.1	9.0	9.7	11.7	13.4	14.1	14.1	14.0

NOTE: Detail may not add to totals because of rounding.

From "Employment and Training Report of the President," submitted by President Ford to Congress, June 1976

less than 3% of those in policy-making positions, the report said.

Most regulatory agencies, the report charged, continued "to deny the full scope of their civil rights responsibilities." Despite an opinion by the Justice Department that the Federal Power Commission had authority to enforce fair hiring practices in the power industry, the commission said, the agency refused to take action, as had the Interstate Commerce Commission. The Federal Communications Commission had failed to enforce fully the hiring plans submitted by broadcasters, while the agencies responsible for the financial community had not even begun "to collect racial and ethnic data," including the Federal Reserve Board, the Comptroller of the Currency, the Federal Deposit Insurance Corporation and the Federal Home Loan Bank Board." The Civil Aeronautics Board and the Securities and Exchange Commission were also criticized, as were the Interior Department, the Law Enforcement Assistance Administration and the Civil Rights Offices of the Departments of Justice and of Health, Education & Welfare.

5 U.S. agencies criticized—Another report by the Commission on Civil Rights, made public Nov. 12, 1974, charged five federal regulatory agencies with failure to combat job discrimination in the industries they regulated. The study cited four agencies—the Interstate Commerce Commission (ICC), the Civil Aeronautics Board (CAB), the Federal Power Commission (FPC) and the Securities and Exchange Commission (SEC)—for not having issued rules forbidding job discrimination. The report called anti-discrimination rules issued by the Federal Communications Commission (FCC) "highly inadequate."

The agencies "appear to assume that their independent regulatory status allows them to stand above the national commitment to equal employment opportunity," the commission said in a cover letter to Congress and the President. "This commission finds," the letter said, "their position neither legally nor morally justifiable."

The study found heavy underutilization of minorities and women in the industries regulated by the ICC, CAB and FPC, except in lowest job classifications. Although petitions on equal opportunity employment regulations had been before the ICC and CAB since 1972, neither agency had yet acted, the report said. Moreover, the FPC had not accepted a Justice Department opinion affirming its authority to combat industry discrimination, the report added. The SEC had a poor record of employment of minorities in general and of women above the clerical level, the study commented, "but the SEC has refused to adopt mandatory equal employment guidelines for its regulatees."

U.S. contract rule ignored. The General Accounting Office May 4, 1975 reported substantial noncompliance with the 1965 executive order prohibiting federal contractors from discriminating on the basis of race, sex, creed or national origin. The GAO said it found a pattern of "almost non-existence of enforcement actions."

The report had been requested by the Congressional Joint Economic Committee panel studying the economic status of women. But Rep. Richard Bolling (D, Mo.), in releasing the report, said the GAO had "found so many problems in the over-all [antidiscrimination] program that it was meaningless to assess the program against sex discrimination alone."

New job board urged. The U.S. Commission on Civil Rights July 15, 1975 recommended the creation of a national employment rights board because of what it called "fundamentally inadequate" efforts by the federal government to end job discrimination.

The commission said in a 673-page report: "Not only does the federal government suffer from unmistakable underutilization of minorities and women in its middle and higher ranks, but it also has a record of overt discrimination against these groups in the past, which has resulted historically in preference being given to nonminority [white] males." It

Employed Persons: Annual Averages by Occupation Group & Color

NUMBER EMPLOYED (thousands)

Year	Total employed	White-collar workers Total	Professional and technical	Managers and administrators ex. farm	Sales workers	Clerical workers	Blue-collar workers Total	Craft and kindred workers	Operatives Total	Operatives Except transport	Operatives Transport equipment	Nonfarm laborers	Service workers Total	Private household workers	Other service workers	Farmworkers Total	Farmers and farm managers	Farm laborers and supervisors
White																		
1961	58,912	27,771	7,380	6,946	4,135	9,310	20,989	8,191	10,326	(2)	(2)	2,472	6,020	1,046	4,974	4,133	2,504	1,629
1962	59,698	28,459	7,658	7,219	4,012	9,570	21,269	8,240	10,586	(2)	(2)	2,443	6,088	1,001	5,087	3,879	2,392	1,487
1963	60,622	28,681	7,821	7,101	4,029	9,730	21,922	8,446	10,996	(2)	(2)	2,480	6,327	1,011	5,316	3,689	2,221	1,468
1964	61,922	29,477	8,043	7,257	4,111	10,066	22,344	8,456	11,365	(2)	(2)	2,523	6,512	1,043	5,469	3,591	2,168	1,423
1965	63,445	30,359	8,348	7,136	4,364	10,511	23,114	8,695	11,699	(2)	(2)	2,720	6,517	993	5,524	3,454	2,100	1,354
1966	65,019	31,424	8,759	7,198	4,403	11,064	23,650	8,989	11,989	(2)	(2)	2,614	6,740	976	5,764	3,206	1,963	1,243
1967	66,361	32,395	9,287	7,287	4,387	11,435	23,863	9,259	12,002	(2)	(2)	2,635	6,971	934	6,037	3,130	1,862	1,268
1968	67,751	33,561	9,685	7,551	4,489	11,836	24,063	9,359	12,023	(2)	(2)	2,681	7,065	947	6,118	3,062	1,828	1,234
1969	69,518	34,647	10,074	7,733	4,527	12,314	24,647	9,484	12,368	(2)	(2)	2,795	7,289	917	6,372	2,935	1,759	1,176
1970	70,182	35,641	10,374	7,992	4,674	12,601	24,230	9,466	11,905	(2)	(2)	2,859	7,514	906	6,608	2,797	1,665	1,132
1971	70,716	35,808	10,314	8,333	4,875	12,286	23,831	9,515	11,162	(2)	(2)	3,154	8,355	872	7,483	2,723	1,603	1,120
1972	73,074	36,517	10,638	7,711	5,161	13,007	25,136	10,061	11,708	8,974	2,734	3,367	8,616	853	7,763	2,806	1,634	1,172
1973	75,278	37,545	10,876	8,270	5,207	13,192	26,147	10,479	12,239	9,425	2,814	3,429	8,814	833	7,981	2,772	1,602	1,170
1974	76,620	38,761	11,368	8,562	5,203	13,629	26,029	10,603	11,880	9,075	2,805	3,547	9,037	755	8,282	2,793	1,579	1,214
1975	75,713	39,126	11,711	8,493	5,218	13,705	24,568	10,177	11,042	8,274	2,768	3,349	9,319	728	8,590	2,700	1,538	1,162
Negro and other races																		
1961	6,832	1,117	318	174	97	528	2,694	426	1,393	(2)	(2)	875	2,241	989	1,252	780	202	578
1962	7,004	1,175	372	189	105	509	2,783	428	1,408	(2)	(2)	947	2,295	1,022	1,273	753	195	558
1963	7,140	1,268	434	192	122	520	2,853	469	1,468	(2)	(2)	916	2,344	1,018	1,326	675	167	508
1964	7,383	1,385	499	192	125	568	2,998	525	1,515	(2)	(2)	957	2,381	998	1,383	621	145	476
1965	7,643	1,493	524	204	135	630	3,133	521	1,646	(2)	(2)	966	2,419	963	1,456	599	138	461
1966	7,875	1,644	551	207	138	748	3,300	600	1,782	(2)	(2)	918	2,472	928	1,544	460	128	332
1967	8,011	1,837	592	209	138	899	3,398	617	1,882	(2)	(2)	899	2,353	835	1,519	423	107	317
1968	8,169	1,991	641	225	158	967	3,462	656	1,932	(2)	(2)	874	2,315	777	1,538	403	98	305
1969	8,384	2,197	695	254	166	1,083	3,591	709	2,004	(2)	(2)	877	2,239	714	1,525	356	84	272
1970	8,445	2,356	766	297	180	1,113	3,561	692	2,004	(2)	(2)	866	2,199	652	1,546	328	87	241
1971	8,403	2,444	756	342	191	1,154	3,353	663	1,821	(2)	(2)	868	2,321	615	1,706	285	63	222
1972	8,628	2,575	821	320	193	1,240	3,440	749	1,841	1,366	475	850	2,350	584	1,766	263	55	208
1973	9,131	2,840	901	374	209	1,356	3,721	809	2,030	1,547	483	883	2,314	520	1,794	255	62	193
1974	9,315	2,977	970	379	214	1,414	3,747	874	2,041	1,553	488	833	2,337	474	1,863	254	64	190
1975	9,070	3,101	1,037	398	242	1,423	3,394	795	1,814	1,363	451	785	2,339	443	1,896	237	56	181

² Not available

From "Employment and Training Report of the President," submitted by President Ford to Congress, June 1976 also charged that there was "no one person, agency or institution which could speak for the federal government" on this matter and that, as a result, "employers, employes and aggrieved citizens are left to their own devices in trying to understand and react to a complex administrative structure."

The proposed board would have "cease and desist" authority and would be able to initiate procedures against any employer, private or government, if it believed Title 7 of the Civil Rights Act had been abridged. It could bar federal contractors from doing business with government agencies it found in violation of antidiscrimination laws.

Although the report also criticized the Labor Department's Office of Federal Contract Compliance and the Equal Employment Opportunity Coordinating Council, it had especially strong words for the Civil Service Commission and the Equal Employment Opportunity Commission.

It recommended that the civil service agency adopt procedures making employers set goals and timetables for increasing female and minority employment. The civil service should abolish the "rule of three," requiring a government employer to hire from a list of three top candidates, because "current ranking and testing procedures are unreliable and unjustifiably screen qualified minorities and women." Until minority persons in a ratio equal "to the numbers in the available work force" were hired, the service should allow agencies to make sex and ethnic background criteria for employment.

The report advised the Equal Employment Opportunity Commission to focus on systematic discrimination by moving against large employers. Each of its commissioners except the chairman should be given a specific area of responsibility. Persons whose grievances had been on record more than 180 days should be told they could bring private suit.

Lax enforcement on aid funds. The U.S. Commission on Civil Rights charged Nov. 11, 1975 that the federal government had not properly enforced the 1964 Civil Rights Act prohibition against discriminatory use of federal aid funds.

The commission said that while some of the staffs of a number of U.S. agencies that administered $50 billion in expenditures in about 400 federal aid programs had tried to comply with Title 6 of the act, their efforts were largely futile due to inadequate government-wide leadership.

The commission concluded that federal agencies did not adequately monitor their aid programs for discrimination. It further charged that no strong and prompt corrective action was taken when evidence of bias was found.

The commission, an advisory body only, urged President Gerald R. Ford to transfer responsibility for Title 6 enforcement from the Justice Department to the White House Office of Management and Budget (OMB) with orders that it develop standards within 90 days. OMB, the commission said, would be better able to monitor the agencies during the course of its budgetary hearings and could apply sanctions in the form of budget cutbacks. The move would also "serve notice of a Presidential decision" to actively enforce the law, the commission said.

The commission also recommended that Ford issue an executive order barring sex discrimination—not mentioned in the 1964 law—in federal aid programs.

26% of blacks unemployed. The National Urban League asserted Jan. 28, 1976, in a statement entitled "The State of Black America," that 26% of black workers were unemployed during 1975. According to the league's statement:

The most realistic manner of reporting what took place with the black worker during 1975 is to describe the general situation for blacks as worse than at any time since the Great Depression of the 1930s.

During the third quarter of 1975 black unemployment rose by 14,000 to a record high of 3,075,000, taking into account those workers who had become discouraged and dropped out of the labor market and those workers holding parttime jobs because they could not find full-time jobs. Over the year, this unofficial but more accurate black jobless rate remained at an almost constant 26 percent. Thus, from the beginning of the year, one out of every four black

Employment by Occupation Group & Race (Annual Averages)

PERCENT DISTRIBUTION

White

Year	Total employed	White-collar workers					Blue-collar workers						Service workers			Farmworkers		
		Total	Professional and technical	Managers and administrators ex. farm	Sales workers	Clerical workers	Total	Craft and kindred workers	Operatives Total	Except transport	Transport equipment	Nonfarm laborers	Total	Private household workers	Other service workers	Total	Farmers and farm managers	Farm laborers and supervisors
1960	100.0	46.6	12.1	11.7	7.0	15.7	36.2	13.9	17.9	(2)	(2)	4.4	9.9	1.7	8.2	7.4	4.3	3.0
1961	100.0	47.1	12.5	11.8	7.0	15.8	35.6	13.8	17.5	(2)	(2)	4.2	10.2	1.8	8.4	7.0	4.3	2.8
1962	100.0	47.7	12.8	12.1	6.7	16.0	35.6	13.8	17.7	(2)	(2)	4.1	10.2	1.7	8.5	6.5	4.0	2.5
1963	100.0	47.3	12.9	11.7	6.6	16.1	35.9	13.9	18.1	(2)	(2)	4.1	10.4	1.7	8.8	5.8	3.5	2.4
1964	100.0	47.6	13.0	11.7	6.6	16.3	36.1	13.7	18.1	(2)	(2)	4.1	10.5	1.7	8.8	5.4	3.3	2.3
1965	100.0	47.9	13.2	11.2	6.9	16.6	36.4	13.8	18.4	(2)	(2)	4.3	10.3	1.6	8.7	5.4	3.3	2.1
1966	100.0	48.3	13.5	11.1	6.6	17.0	36.4	13.9	18.5	(2)	(2)	4.0	10.4	1.5	8.9	4.9	3.0	1.9
1967	100.0	48.8	14.0	11.0	6.6	17.2	36.0	13.8	18.1	(2)	(2)	4.0	10.5	1.4	9.1	4.7	2.7	1.9
1968	100.0	49.5	14.3	11.1	6.5	17.5	35.5	13.6	17.7	(2)	(2)	4.0	10.4	1.4	9.0	4.5	2.7	1.8
1969	100.0	49.8	14.5	11.1	6.7	17.7	35.5	13.6	17.8	(2)	(2)	4.0	10.5	1.3	9.2	4.2	2.5	1.7
1970	100.0	50.8	14.5	11.4	6.7	18.0	34.5	13.5	17.0	(2)	(2)	4.1	10.7	1.3	9.4	4.0	2.4	1.6
1971	100.0	50.6	14.6	11.8	6.9	17.4	33.7	13.5	15.8	(2)	(2)	4.5	11.8	1.2	10.6	3.9	2.3	1.6
1972	100.0	50.0	14.6	10.6	7.1	17.8	34.4	13.8	16.0	12.3	3.7	4.6	11.8	1.2	10.6	3.8	2.2	1.6
1973	100.0	49.9	14.4	11.2	6.9	17.5	34.7	13.9	16.3	12.5	3.7	4.6	11.7	1.1	10.6	3.7	2.1	1.6
1974	100.0	50.6	14.8	11.2	6.8	17.8	34.0	13.8	15.5	11.8	3.7	4.6	11.8	1.0	10.8	3.6	2.1	1.6
1975	100.0	51.7	15.5	11.2	6.9	18.1	32.4	13.4	14.6	10.9	3.7	4.4	12.3	1.0	11.3	3.6	2.0	1.5

Negro and other races

Year	Total employed	White-collar workers					Blue-collar workers						Service workers			Farmworkers		
		Total	Professional and technical	Managers and administrators ex. farm	Sales workers	Clerical workers	Total	Craft and kindred workers	Operatives Total	Except transport	Transport equipment	Nonfarm laborers	Total	Private household workers	Other service workers	Total	Farmers and farm managers	Farm laborers and supervisors
1960	100.0	16.1	4.8	2.6	1.5	7.3	40.1	6.0	20.4	(2)	(2)	13.7	31.7	14.2	17.5	12.1	3.2	9.0
1961	100.0	16.3	4.7	2.5	1.4	7.7	39.4	6.2	20.4	(2)	(2)	12.8	32.8	14.5	18.3	11.4	3.0	8.5
1962	100.0	16.8	5.3	2.7	1.5	7.3	39.7	6.1	20.1	(2)	(2)	13.5	32.8	14.6	18.2	10.8	2.8	8.0
1963	100.0	17.8	6.1	2.7	1.7	7.3	40.6	6.6	20.6	(2)	(2)	12.8	32.8	14.3	18.6	9.5	2.3	7.1
1964	100.0	18.8	6.8	2.7	1.7	7.7	40.6	7.1	20.5	(2)	(2)	13.0	32.2	13.5	18.7	8.4	2.0	6.4
1965	100.0	19.5	6.9	2.6	1.8	8.2	41.0	6.8	21.5	(2)	(2)	12.6	31.6	12.6	19.0	7.8	1.8	6.0
1966	100.0	20.9	7.0	2.6	1.8	9.5	41.9	6.9	22.6	(2)	(2)	11.7	31.4	11.8	19.6	5.8	1.6	4.2
1967	100.0	22.9	7.4	2.6	1.7	11.2	42.4	7.7	23.5	(2)	(2)	11.2	29.4	10.4	19.0	5.3	1.3	4.0
1968	100.0	24.4	7.8	3.0	1.9	11.8	42.4	7.7	23.6	(2)	(2)	11.0	28.3	9.5	18.8	4.9	1.2	3.7
1969	100.0	26.2	8.3	2.8	2.0	12.9	42.8	8.5	23.9	(2)	(2)	10.5	26.7	8.5	18.3	4.2	1.0	3.2
1970	100.0	27.1	9.1	3.5	2.1	12.8	42.8	8.2	23.7	(2)	(2)	10.3	26.0	7.7	18.3	3.9	1.0	2.9
1971	100.0	29.1	9.0	4.1	2.3	13.7	39.9	7.9	21.7	(2)	(2)	10.3	27.6	7.3	20.3	3.4	.7	2.6
1972	100.0	29.8	9.5	3.7	2.2	14.4	39.9	8.7	21.3	15.8	5.5	9.9	27.2	6.8	20.5	3.0	.6	2.4
1973	100.0	31.1	9.9	4.1	2.3	14.9	40.8	9.4	22.2	16.7	5.2	8.9	25.1	5.7	19.6	3.0	.6	2.4
1974	100.0	32.0	10.4	4.1	2.3	15.2	40.2	9.4	21.9	16.7	5.2	8.9	25.1	5.1	20.0	2.7	.7	2.1
1975	100.0	34.2	11.4	4.4	2.7	15.7	37.4	8.8	20.0	15.0	5.0	8.7	25.8	4.9	20.9	2.7	.7	2.0

From "Employment and Training Report of the President," submitted by President Ford to Congress June 1976

[2] Not available

workers in the nation was unemployed.

Even when the "official" measurement of the Department of Labor is used (this excludes the two categories used in the unofficial tabulation) black unemployment remained virtually unchanged at 14.1 percent for the first three quarters of 1975, while white unemployment dropped from 8.0 percent to 7.6 percent.

Using the unofficial rates, over half of all black workers in many poverty areas were unemployed during the past year, while over two-thirds of the teenagers could not find jobs.

Further aggravating the employment situation was the ineligibility of over half of all the black unemployed for unemployment compensation.

Complicating the employment picture for blacks is the factor of long-term unemployment. Among unemployed black males, 26 percent of them were out of work half-a-year or more, followed by 16 percent of the adult women, 10 percent of the male teenagers, and 5 percent of the female teenagers.

These figures mean that those who have been out of work the longest are remaining out of work.

A major issue that emerged full blown during the year was that of seniority as opposed to affirmative action. With lay-offs occurring in industry because of the economic downturn, the question arose as to how these lay-offs would affect the minority worker since in many instances he was the last hired and under the strict observance of seniority would be the first to go. This meant that in some instances blacks who had been victims of past discrimination were unfairly penalized.

Blacks also found themselves losing ground in other employment areas. The National Urban League completed a survey of prime sponsor hiring practices under Title II and Title VI of the Comprehensive Employment and Training Act (CETA) that showed there has been a shifting of emphasis from helping people most in need of jobs to helping those recently unemployed and with higher educational levels.

Additionally, a Department of Labor report indicates there has been a substantial drop in manpower training funds available to the nation's inner-cities where unemployment is highest, with more of these funds going to suburban and rural areas. Here again is an example of the minority poor being made even poorer as funds are diverted to other areas. . . .

Private Industry & Government Action

Construction job plans. Representatives of construction unions and employers and of minority groups April 6, 1973

signed a three-year agreement to make a "good faith effort" to achieve 6% black membership in each local construction union in New York's Nassau and Suffolk Counties.

It was the first "hometown plan" to be approved by the Office of Federal Contract Compliance of the U.S. Department of Labor since President Nixon emphatically rejected the "quota" concept of minority job advancement in 1972.

The plan had been delayed for nine months because of Administration insistence that the phrase "good faith effort" be inserted before mention of the 6% goal. The agreement could be canceled after each year, 60–90 days after written notification by any of the participant groups.

Barely 15 months later the Labor Department July 2, 1974 imposed mandatory minority hiring goals on the contractors and 101 construction union locals in 21 areas. The department said the unions had failed to meet employment obligations under their voluntary plans.

Under the new orders, contractors bidding on projects receiving federal funds would be required to see that unions met percentage goals, which were based on population composition of individual cities and regions. Failure to make "good-faith" efforts could result in loss of contracts or suspension.

(The Equal Employment Opportunity Commission had reported June 29 that in the 1969–72 period, minority membership in construction unions had increased from 13.2% to 15.6% [an increase of 52,000 workers], but mostly in lower-paying job categories. The report said that in 1972, only 6.9% of the members of higher-paying construction industry unions [such as iron workers, plumbers and sheetmetal workers] were from minorities, while minorities represented 37.6% of the laborers' union.)

Airline pact approved. An anti-discrimination agreement between the federal government and Delta Air Lines was approved by Federal District Court Judge Charles A. Moye in Atlanta, it was reported May 3, 1973. The consent order followed a suit filed April 16 by the Departments of Justice and Labor.

Unemployment Rates by Race, Sex & Age (Annual Averages)

Item	Total, 16 years and over	16 and 17 years	18 and 19 years	20 to 24 years	25 to 34 years	35 to 44 years	45 to 54 years	55 to 64 years	65 years and over	14 and 15 years
WHITE										
Male										
1968	2.6	12.3	8.2	4.6	1.7	1.4	1.5	1.7	2.8	8.3
1969	2.5	12.5	7.9	4.6	1.7	1.4	1.4	1.7	2.1	8.5
1970	4.0	15.7	12.0	7.8	3.1	2.3	2.3	2.7	3.1	10.1
1971	4.9	17.1	13.5	9.4	4.0	2.9	2.8	3.2	3.4	10.8
1972	4.5	16.4	12.4	8.5	4.0	2.5	2.5	3.0	3.3	10.7
1973	3.7	15.1	10.0	6.5	3.5	1.8	2.0	2.4	2.9	10.7
1974	4.3	16.2	11.5	7.8	3.5	2.4	2.2	2.5	2.0	11.9
1975	7.2	19.7	17.2	13.2	6.3	4.5	4.4	4.1	5.0	13.0
Female										
1968	4.3	13.9	11.0	5.9	3.9	3.1	2.3	2.1	2.7	5.4
1969	4.2	13.8	10.0	5.5	4.2	3.2	2.4	2.1	2.4	6.4
1970	5.4	15.3	11.9	6.9	5.3	4.3	3.4	2.6	3.3	7.4
1971	6.3	16.7	14.1	8.5	6.3	4.9	3.9	3.3	3.6	8.3
1972	5.9	17.0	12.3	8.2	5.5	4.5	3.5	3.3	3.7	8.1
1973	5.3	15.7	10.9	7.0	5.1	3.7	3.1	2.8	2.8	7.8
1974	6.1	16.4	13.0	8.2	5.7	4.3	3.6	3.3	3.9	9.9
1975	8.6	19.2	16.1	11.2	8.5	6.6	5.8	5.1	5.3	10.7
NEGRO AND OTHER RACES										
Male										
1968	5.6	26.6	19.0	8.3	3.8	2.9	2.5	3.6	4.0	26.0
1969	5.3	24.7	19.0	8.4	3.4	2.4	2.4	3.2	3.8	22.1
1970	7.3	27.8	23.1	12.6	6.1	3.9	3.3	3.4	3.4	29.0
1971	9.1	33.4	26.0	16.2	7.4	4.9	4.5	4.7	6.9	32.2
1972	8.9	35.1	26.2	14.7	6.8	4.8	3.8	4.6	3.6	31.8
1973	7.6	34.4	22.1	12.6	5.8	4.0	3.2	3.6	5.6	34.1
1974	9.1	39.0	26.6	15.4	7.2	4.1	4.0	3.6		37.9
1975	13.7	39.4	32.9	22.9	11.9	8.3	9.0	6.1	9.5	38.6
Female										
1968	8.3	33.7	26.2	12.3	8.4	5.0	3.2	2.8	2.4	28.9
1969	7.8	31.2	25.7	12.0	6.6	4.5	3.7	2.9	1.1	23.1
1970	9.3	36.9	32.9	15.0	7.9	4.8	4.0	3.2	3.9	30.9
1971	10.8	38.5	33.7	17.3	10.7	6.9	4.2	3.5	3.9	33.3
1972	11.3	38.3	38.7	17.4	10.2	7.2	4.7	4.0	2.0	39.3
1973	10.5	36.5	33.3	17.6	9.7	5.3	3.7	3.0	2.9	35.6
1974	10.7	36.2	33.7	18.0	8.6	6.7	4.3	3.3	1.5	37.9
1975	14.0	38.9	38.3	22.5	12.9	8.6	6.7	5.3	3.1	41.8

From "Employment and Training Report of the President," submitted by President Ford to Congress June 1976

The agreement, effective for five years, would allow women and minority employes the opportunity to transfer to higher level jobs, held predominantly by white males. Delta said such applicants would be allowed to transfer only if qualified and when positions were actually open.

Under terms of the pact, the first 1,000 persons transferred would be eligible for $200–$1,000 in back pay based on job classification and $100 for each year of employment.

■ The 10th U.S. Circuit Court of Appeals had ruled Oct. 11, 1972 that United Airlines had not been guilty of unfairly discriminating against a black employe when it had refused to give him a pilot's job when more qualified whites had applied. The plaintiff had said United's requirement of a college education and 500 hours flight time discriminated against blacks; he himself had spent two years in college and had clocked 204 hours flight time.

EEOC suits charge bias. The Equal Employment Opportunity Commission (EEOC) announced April 5, 1973 that it had filed 20 suits alleging employment bias on the basis of race, color, national origin, religion and sex, most of them against major corporations and unions.

EEOC had filed only 28 previous suits in the year since it was granted authority to initiate suits.

Among the defendants cited in the suits were General Motors Corp. and United Auto Workers locals in Euclid and Cleveland, Ohio, National Steel Corp. and the Independent Steelworkers Union at Weirton, W. Va., General Electric Co. in Lynchburg, Va., Sunshine Biscuits Inc. and the American Bakery Union in Oakland, Calif., Chesapeake & Ohio Railway and the Seafarers International Union in Newport News, Va., General Insurance Co., in Seattle, Metropolitan Life Insurance Co., in New York, Philip Morris Inc. in Richmond, Va., the Missouri Pacific Railroad in St. Louis, and locals of the United Steelworkers Union and the International Longshoreman's Association.

The commission July 19 announced its first suit against a television station. WREC-TV in Memphis, owned by the New York Times, was accused of discriminating against women and blacks in hiring, recruiting and job classification. Another suit announced the same day accused the Seattle Post-Intelligencer—a Hearst Corp. newspaper—and locals of the Newspaper Guild and the International Typographical Union of discrimination against blacks in hiring and apprenticeship programs, against women by hours restrictions and pregnancy-leave policies, and against men by denying them lounges and rest periods, which were provided for female employes.

The EEOC Aug. 28 announced a suit charging the Xerox Corp. with engaging in "policies which exclude Spanish-surnamed persons from employment" in California. The suit asked for a permanent injunction against the company to prevent discrimination based on national origin.

Two other suits announced Aug. 29 accused Avondale Shipyards Inc. of New Orleans and the Red Arrow Corp., a St. Louis trucking company, of job discrimination against blacks.

The EEOC was reported Sept. 18 to have notified four large corporations and several unions that it had filed employment bias charges against them.

Reports (later confirmed by the companies and unions) identified the firms as General Motors Corp., Ford Motor Co., General Electric Co. and Sears, Roebuck & Co. The unions identified included the United Auto Workers, the United Electrical Workers and the International Union of Electrical, Radio and Machine Workers. (The National Electrical Contractors Association and the International Brotherhood of Electrical Workers confirmed Sept. 20 that they had been notified by the EEOC of similar charges.)

The action was the first taken by the EEOC's new National Programs Division, which was created to deal with discrimination cases involving large numbers of workers on a company-wide basis. The charges involved wages, benefits, terms and conditions of employment, promotion, training and testing programs, layoff and seniority procedures.

The companies and unions reacted to the charges with surprise, and a spokesman for the United Electrical Workers noted that his union had been trying to get the EEOC to "end its lethargy and enforce the anti-discrimination laws."

Herbert Hill, labor director for the National Association for the Advancement of Colored People, said his organization had previously filed complaints with the EEOC against the four companies. Hill called the commission's action significant because it recognized that discrimination was not merely "random acts of bigotry" but part of "broad patterns that are codified in collective bargaining agreements."

Accords with utilities—The EEOC announced Oct. 16, 1973 that the Pacific Gas & Electric Co. of San Francisco had given its voluntary pledge to increase employment opportunities for women and minorities in its managerial, craft and technical categories.

The agreement called for the company to review all its 3,000 women and 5,000 minority employes for possible advancement or transfer. Recruitment programs were to be instituted with special emphasis on placing Asian-Americans in high-paying craft jobs. The accord also provided for special management training programs for all minority groups and women.

The EEOC and the El Paso Natural Gas Co. agreed Jan. 8, 1974 on a plan for increased job opportunities for minorities and women.

The agreement provided back pay and salary increases for women and minority employes whose current pay was below the norm for white males "of similar background and training." In addition, the company would seek during the next seven years to hire specific percentages of women, blacks, Spanish-surnamed and American Indians, with the percentages varying according to population makeup in the company's geographically-defined operating areas.

Other utility bias cases. U.S. District Court Judge Damon J. Keith Oct. 2,

1973 ordered the Detroit Edison Company to pay $4 million in punitive damages to blacks who, he said, had been subjected to "deliberate" and "invidious" racial discrimination. Judge Keith also assessed a local of the Utility Workers of America for damages of $250,000 for abetting the company's discriminatory practices.

A class-action suit had originally been filed in 1971 by three black employes, who were joined as plaintiffs by the Justice Department in 1972.

Judge Keith ordered that the damages be paid to the court for later determination of distribution among plaintiffs. The court also directed the company to make restitution in the form of back pay to blacks who had been denied promotion or jobs for racial reasons.

The decision established a quota system for hiring and promotion designed to achieve an overall work force 30% black, with 25% of skilled jobs to be filled by blacks.

The U.S. 6th Circuit Court of Appeals March 11, 1975, however, reversed a lower court ruling that blacks who had not applied for jobs with Detroit Edison during 1965-73 because of its reputation for racism in hiring were entitled to compensation. In a unanimous decision, the appellate court held that restitution should be ordered only for Detroit Edison employes and those rejected for jobs during the period 1969-72.

The Justice Department Jan. 31, 1974 got a final court decree ordering the Georgia Power Co. to pay retroactive wages and pension benefits of almost $2.1 million to black employes who had been denied equal job rights. The order settled a suit, originally filed in 1969, which an appeals court had remanded to federal district court Feb. 14, 1973 for determination of back benefits.

The order also required the company to increase black employment to 17% of the work force within five years. Currently, 9.3% of the company's 8,278 employes were black.

Benefits to Chrysler killer. A Michigan state hearing referee ruled that Chrysler Corp. had to pay workmen's compensation benefits, including psychiatric care expenses, to a black employee whose nondisabling psychotic tendencies had been aggravated by plant racism and unfair work conditions, causing him to kill three supervisors after he was fired in 1970, it was reported March 7, 1973.

James Johnson had been found legally insane at his trial and placed in a state mental hospital. In the latest ruling, a state examiner said Johnson had developed paranoic feelings toward whites during his childhood on a Mississippi plantation. He had then been unfairly assigned to undesirable jobs at the plant, denied advancement opportunities, called "nigger" and "boy" by a foreman, denied medical benefits, suspended unfairly and fired after refusing what he considered a dangerous job.

Eastex decree. The Justice Department Feb. 8, 1974 obtained a court decree in a job discrimination suit involving black and female employes of Eastex Inc., a paper manufacturing subsidiary of Time Inc. The company was ordered to pay $325,000 in back wages and transfer bonuses, adopt percentage goals for hiring and job assignments, and modify its seniority system to allow black and women employes to transfer to previously-closed jobs without losing seniority rights.

Supreme Court decisions. Among Supreme Court rulings in job bias cases:

The court Nov. 19, 1973, over Justice William O. Douglas' dissent, upheld the right of the Farah Manufacturing Co. of El Paso, Tex. to refuse to hire resident aliens to work in its San Antonio clothing plant. In his majority ruling, Justice Thurgood Marshall said the legislative history of the Civil Rights Act of 1964 made it clear that U.S. citizenship was not included in the ban on discrimination based on national origin.

The court ruled June 25, 1975 that victims of hiring or promotion bias did not have to prove bad faith on the part of their employer to qualify for compensatory awards of back pay. In so ruling, the court concluded that back pay was a remedy that federal courts could apply at their

discretion in such cases. It rejected arguments that employers who had not acted in bad faith should not be required to give back pay and instead asserted that the court's concern was not with an employer's motives but with the consequences of his employment practices.

The court Dec. 1, 1975 let stand an appellate court ruling ordering the integration of racially segregated longshoremen's union locals in Texas Gulf Coast ports.

Retroactive seniority ordered—The Supreme Court ruled, 5–3, March 24, 1976 that applicants denied jobs because of race, and then later hired by the same organization, should be awarded the seniority and benefits they would have accumulated if hired in the first instance.

The ruling, based on the Civil Rights Act of 1964, would apparently extend to cases involving discrimination based on sex, national origin, or religion, as well as race. It applied to cases where individuals had been refused jobs after the Civil Rights Act went into effect. The ruling did not consider the issue of retroactive seniority for persons who claimed they had not originally applied for a job because they knew that a discriminatory hiring policy had existed.

The ruling was greeted as a major victory by civil rights groups, who had maintained that recent advances in minority employment were being destroyed by recession layoffs made under the "last-hired, first-fired" policy.

Recognizing that the ruling could result in the relative loss of seniority standing by some whites, Justice William J. Brennan Jr. in the opinion wrote that "the burden of the past discrimination" must be shared by whites with blacks. Joining Brennan in the majority were Justices Potter Stewart, Byron R. White, Thurgood Marshall and Harry A. Blackmun.

Chief Justice Warren E. Burger, dissenting, said: "I cannot join in judicial approval of 'robbing Peter to pay Paul'." Justices Lewis F. Powell Jr. and William H. Rehnquist also dissented; Justice John Paul Stevens did not participate in the decision.

The ruling came on a suit brought by two black former employes against

Bowman Transportation Co., a trucking firm located in Atlanta.

Steel industry in job pact.

Nine major steel companies, the United Steelworkers of America and the federal government signed agreements April 15, 1974 to provide back pay and expanded job opportunities for minorities and women The accord, similar to earlier broad settlements in the trucking and communications industries, was contained in consent decrees filed in U.S. district court in Birmingham, Ala., resolving a Justice Department discrimination suit filed at the same time.

The companies were: Allegheny-Ludlum Industries, Inc., Armco Steel Corp., Bethlehem Steel Corp., Jones & Laughlin Steel Corp., National Steel Corp., Republic Steel Corp., U.S. Steel Corp., Wheeling-Pittsburgh Steel Corp. and Youngstown Sheet & Tube Co. According to the Justice Department, the companies produced about 73% of the nation's raw steel and employed 347,679 workers, of whom 52,545 were black, 7,646 Spanish-surnamed and 10,175 women.

The accord also set timetables under which half of the openings in trade and craft positions would be filled by minorities and women, and additional first-year goals calling for women in 20% of production and maintenance vacancies, minorities in 15% of technical and clerical openings, and selection of minorities and women for 25% of vacancies in supervisory positions and for management training.

Employes would also be allowed to transfer to departments or seniority categories offering better advancement opportunities previously reserved for white males, without suffering pay cuts even if the new job had a lower wage scale.

The National Association for the Advancement of Colored people, which had opposed the settlement as inadequate and an obstruction to other litigation under the Civil Rights Act, filed suit in the Birmingham court April 23 to have the consent decrees set aside.

The nine companies agreed Aug. 18, 1975 to sign consent orders to end job bias, comply with the federal antidiscrimination laws and create a $31-million back-pay fund. The consent orders, which covered 245 steel plants in 25 states and affected some 61,000 women, blacks and Spanish-surnamed Americans, were approved by the U.S. 5th Circuit Court of Appeals. The court ordered the companies to pay the employes back pay from the fund.

Rail clerks get minorities pact.

The leadership of the AFL-CIO Brotherhood of Railway Clerks announced an accord with U.S. railroads Nov. 5, 1975 on a special agreement to provide new job opportunities for women and minorities.

The agreement, the first in the industry on equal employment practices, would permit transfer in certain areas without loss of seniority to a better job if the applicant were qualified or could be trained for the opening. Applications would be allowed only for vacant jobs that were not claimed by other employes with seniority rights to that position.

The clerks' union had about 175,000 railroad members. Application of the agreement, if extended throughout the industry, would affect an estimated 20,000 employes.

Merrill Lynch to make amends.

Merrill Lynch, Pierce, Fenner & Smith, Inc., the U.S.' largest brokerage firm, agreed in consent decrees June 4, 1976 to pay about $1.9 million to victims of past discrimination and to set up targets for minority and female job recruitment. The settlements, filed in U.S. District Court in Pittsburgh, involved two anti-discrimination suits. One had been filed by the Equal Employment Opportunity Commission, the other by Helen O'Bannon, a woman whose application for a job as an account executive had been rejected by Merrill Lynch. (O'Bannon's suit was joined by the EEOC.)

Merrill Lynch promised to spend $1.3 million on advertising over a five-year period in an effort to attract minority and female applicants. The agreement specified the following hiring quotas for female and minority account executives: For women, 10% in 1976, increasing by 2% each year to 18% in 1980; for blacks, 3.5% each year during the five-years and for persons with Spanish surnames, 2.6% annually during the same period. Merrill Lynch agreed to pay O'Bannon $10,000 plus $182,000 in legal fees.

Blacks win $1 million job bias award. A federal district judge in Birmingham, Ala. June 12, 1975 ordered the American Cast Iron Pipe Co. to pay 833 current and former black employes $1 million previously denied them because of the company's discriminatory promotion policies. Judge Seybourne Lynne's order to distribute the back pay ended nine years of court action by the black employes of the Alabama company, who had charged in their original suit in 1966 that the firm had promoted whites over blacks with more seniority. The company had also been accused of cutting wage rates for blacks hired to fill jobs formerly held by whites.

Judge Lynne in 1972 had ruled that the employes had not been discriminated against, but the U.S. 5th Circuit Court of Appeals reversed his ruling and remanded the case to the district court with an order that Lynne grant back pay and develop a plan for eliminating future discrimination.

Government protection sought against job bias. The NAACP, at its 1975 convention, held in Washington June 30–July 4, called on government agencies to protect job rights of women and minority members during the current economic slump.

The main resolution passed at the five-day gathering, which attracted over 3,500 delegates to the Shoreham and Sheraton-Park hotels, called on the government "to assure that blacks and other minorities and women who have secured employment or promotion as the result of affirmative action or other equal employment programs not be deprived of the benefits of that employment under the last-hired, first-fired theory." Those named in the controversial resolution included "the Equal Employment Opportunity Commission, the Civil Service Commission, the [Department of Labor's] Office of Federal Contract Compliance and other administrative agencies, federal and state." Although the statement in its final form passed quickly, it had gone through several changes of wording in order to avoid antagonizing NAACP members whose connections with organized labor made them reluctant to tamper with the principle of job seniority. William F. Pollard, director of civil rights for the American Federation of Labor and Congress of Industrial Organizations (AFL-CIO), remarked June 30: "Seniority did not create this recession, and the abolition of it won't cure it." He pointed out the following day that seniority "is color-blind. We have over two million blacks in the AFL-CIO, and seniority protects them too."

Layoffs by seniority ruled valid. A judge of the U.S. Court of Appeals for the 5th Circuit ruled July 16, 1975 that the last-hired, first-fired provisions of the seniority system were constitutional. Black workers laid off by the Continental Can Co., Inc. had tried to show that hiring discrimination in effect before the passage of civil rights laws had put them at the bottom of the seniority system. The judge called the argument "historical, not personal" and declared that plaintiffs who "have never suffered discrimination at the hands of the company are in no better position to complain of the recall system than are the white workers who were hired contemporaneously with them." The verdict overturned a decision by Federal District Court Judge Fred J. Cassibry of New Orleans, who had ordered Continental Can to recall enough black workers to restore the ratio of black/white employes that had obtained in 1971.

Broadcasting bias. The Wall Street Journal reported July 21, 1975 that the FCC had published revisions of its equal opportunity guidelines that would compel radio and television stations to set up "employment goals and timetables" where "an extremely low rate of minority or female employment persists in a station's work force." Stations with 50 or more fulltime employes would be obliged to report periodically how women and minorities were doing in terms of job titles.

Rep. Augustus F. Hawkins (D, Calif.) introduced in the Congressional Record May 25, 1976 an FCC summary of the 1975 employment patterns of the broadcasting industry involving women and minorities. According to the summary:

More women were employed in 1975 (38,-347) than in 1974 (35,765) and accounted for 26.2 percent of the total, compared to 25.2 percent in 1974 and 24.0 percent in 1973.

Minority groups employment (male and female), including Negro, Oriental, American Indians and Spanish-surnamed Americans, accounted for 12.9 percent of the total, compared to 12.3 percent for 1974 and 11.7 percent for 1973. Blacks, the largest minority group, increased from 11,188 in 1974 to 11,818 in 1975, or 8.0 percent of the total in 1975 compared to 7.8 percent in 1974 and 7.5 percent in 1973. Spanish-surnamed Americans comprised 3.6 percent of the total in 1975 as against 3.3 percent in 1974 and 3.1 percent in 1973.

Walter E. Fauntroy, delegate of the District of Columbia, had introduced in the Congressional Record April 26, 1976 a letter in which FCC aide Clarence V. McKee provided this data from an FCC report on broadcasting employment as of December 1975:

"*Officials and Managers Categories:* The total number of females employed in the officials and managers categories in the industry in 1971 was 9%. In 1975, that figure had increased to 16.2%, or a 7.2% increase over the five year period. However, for Black females, the same figures were .4% and 1%, for an increase of .6% over the same period. Black males went from 1.8% to 2.3% for a total increase of .5%.

"*Professional Categories:* In 1971, the total percentages of females in professional positions was 10.2% and in 1975 was 16.8% for an overall increase of 6.6%. For Black females, the corresponding figures were .9% and 1.9% for an increase of 1%. The increase of Black males in this category was only .7% going from 4.5% in 1971 to 5.2% in 1975.

"*Technicians:* Total female percentages in 1971 were 1.5% and in 1975, 3.8% for an increase of 2.3%. Black female percentages only increased .5% going from .1% in 1971 to .6% in 1975. Black males went from 4% to 6.1% for an increase of 2.1%.

"*Sales Workers:* In the sales worker categories, total female increases have been the greatest in the top categories going from 8.5% in 1971 to 16% in 1975 for a net increase of 7.5%. However, Black females only increased .5% from .2% to .7% and Black males had an even smaller increase going from 2.5% to 2.9% for a .4% increase."

Turning away from the national industry totals, and to the broadcast *headquarters* totals, the statistics also indicate that females, overall, have far outpaced Black females and Black males. The best examples in the *Professional Categories* where female percentages went from 18.6% in 1971 to 25.3% in 1975 for an increase of 6.7%. Black female percentages only increased 1% and Black males actually *decreased* .2%. In the *Sales Workers* categories Black male percentages *decreased* .9%, and Black female percentages showed *no gain* being at .6% in 1971 and .6% in 1975.

Waterway project scored. According to a study by staff members of the House Subcommittee on Equal Opportunities, the U.S. Corps of Engineers had failed to assure equal employment opportunities on its Tennessee-Tombigbee waterway project in Alabama and Mississippi. Excerpts from the study, as inserted in the Congressional Record by Rep. Augustus F. Hawkins (D, Calif.) June 15, 1976:

The Corps of Engineers' Tennessee-Tombigbee Waterway Project is a $1.8 million project involving construction of 5 dams and 10 locks and a 27-mile cut to provide a 253-mile inland waterway from Demopolis, Alabama to the Tennessee River. The construction is in an economically depressed rural area of Alabama and Mississippi in which Blacks comprise approximately 40 percent of the population. The project was justified partly on the basis of economic benefits to the region and alleviation of problems of low income and unemployment. However, Blacks have not been included in most of the planning groups involved in the waterway; no comprehensive affirmative action program has been adopted or imposed on the contractors of the waterway; it has been estimated that Blacks comprise less than 20 percent of the present work force on construction projects underway and that one-third to one-half of the labor is being brought in from outside the area. In response to concerns that minority people receive a fair and proportionate share of the benefits, a local organization known as the Minority People's Council has been formed to attempt to secure the equal opportunities that have been claimed by proponents of the project.

A local office at RTP, Inc. (Recruitment and Training Program) under contract with the Department of Labor, has been established to assist in recruitment and placement of minorities and women on the Tennessee-Tombigbee Waterway construction projects. However, neither the Minority People's Council nor RTP have been included in planning and decision-making for the development of the Waterway and their assistance in regard to employment of minorities has not been sought. A hometown affirmative action program was developed by the local organization with participation of the unions, contractors, Corps of Engineers, and Federal compliance agencies but was not adopted because of lack of action and cooperation from the Corps of Engineers.

It is recommended that the hometown plan be adopted and with monitoring and enforcement by the contract compliance offices of the Departments of Defense and Labor. This plan includes goals and timetables to assure 40 percent minority participation, provisions for recruitment, training and placement, and a mechanism for review. In addition, it is recommended that the Department of Defense adopt special bid conditions with goals and timetables and provisions for sanctions. It is also recommended that representatives from minority organizations be included in all decision-making groups for Waterway development. . . .

One affirmative action program, the "Gainesville Plan" was developed and used as a bid condition for the Gainesville project. While this plan represents a positive step toward affirmative action, it establishes a goal of only 20 percent minority participation and applies only to the Gainesville project. For the more recent contracts, no affirmative action program is being required. In absence of a program, the Corps of Engineers has sent letters to the contractors simply directing compliance with the non-specific requirements of the equal opportunity clause of the contract required by Executive Order 11246 and instructing contractors to display equal opportunity posters as required by Executive Order 11246. The company is urged to develop an equal opportunity policy if it does not have one. No program for affirmative action or requirements related to establishing of goals and timetables is mentioned. . . .

Federal Employment

NASA ex-aide rehired. Ruth Bates Harris, a black woman who had been dismissed in 1973 by the National Aeronautics and Space Administration (NASA) during a dispute over the agency's hiring policies, was rehired to a different position at a higher salary, it was

reported Aug. 18, 1974.

Mrs. Harris' new post was deputy assistant administrator for community and human relations; the position from which she had been dismissed carried the same rank in NASA's equal employment programs. A complaint she had filed with the Civil Service Commission had not been ruled upon.

Sen. William Proxmire (D, Wis.), chairman of the Senate Appropriations subcommittee overseeing funds for the NASA, had ordered the space agency Jan. 11 to double the fiscal 1975 budget of its equal employment office and to report to the subcommittee every three months on progress in hiring minorities and women.

Proxmire acted after a hearing during which NASA did not dispute figures showing that as of mid-1973 it had the lowest percentage (5.1%) of minority and female employes of any federal agency, with two-thirds of them in low-level jobs.

NASA documents revealed that the agency had also failed to act against project contractors which had not met minority hiring goals.

Congress job bias found. The Congressional agency responsible for referring and placing applicants for staff jobs, admitted Aug. 19, 1974 that the offices of some congressmen had filed job requests specifying discriminatory criteria, including race ("white only"), religion ("no Catholics") and astrology ("no water signs"). The agency said the requests were usually honored.

The accusations of discrimination had been published Aug. 18 by the Fort Worth (Tex.) Star-Telegram, which said it had obtained documents showing that at least 20 Congressional offices (19 representatives and one senator) had placed such requests.

The Office of Placement and Office Management, a unit of the Joint Committee on Congressional Operations, said it had found no evidence that the congressmen had personally made the requests. By Aug. 19, 15 of the 20 cited by the Star-Telegram had issued either outright denials of discriminatory practices or statements that the requests had been made without their knowledge.

Sen. Lee Metcalf (D, Mont.), chairman of the joint committee, said Aug. 19 that he had ordered the placement unit to cease accepting discriminatory requests. (The Justice Department, Equal Employment Opportunity Commission and Civil Service Commission said Aug. 20 that because of language in job discrimination laws, they were powerless to act against alleged bias in Congressional hiring.)

EEOC guilty of bias. U.S. District Court Judge Gerhard Gesell ruled Sept. 23, 1975 in Washington that the Equal Employment Opportunity Commission had discriminated against George Rogers, a black who was deputy director fof the EEOC's district office in Philadelphia.

Rogers had charged that he had been passed over for promotion to director because of race. The commission countered that even if race had been considered in the selection, Rogers had not been the best qualified candidate for the job.

Gesell ruled that since "race played a part" in the hiring decision, it was enough to "taint" the selection.

Black employes accuse Labor Department. Twenty-six black employes in the Atlanta office of the Labor Department filed a class action complaint charging the department with racial discrimination in its employment practices, it was reported Sept. 9, 1975.

The complaint, filed on behalf of all black employes in the department's eight-state southeast region, alleged that fewer blacks were employed in high-paying jobs in 1975 than in 1971. During the same 1971–75 period, the complaint said, the concentration of blacks in low-paying positions became more pronounced.

According to the complaint, blacks made up 8.2% of the regional work force in 1971, including 7.2% of the employes in the highest civil service grades and 22% of the employes in the lowest four grades. By January 1975, blacks constituted 15.7% of

the work force, but only 5.4% were in high grades, while 32.7% were in the lowest grades, the complaint said.

This disparity between high-level black and white employes arose largely because of discrimination, the complaint said. Most of those hired in the region, the complaint claimed, had come from other agencies that had traditionally excluded blacks. It said whites were hired into high grades despite the availability of blacks with equivalent or better educational and job experience qualifications. In addition, the department tended not to advertise to blacks the availability of promotional opportunities, the complaint said.

U.S. agencies accused. Rep. John E. Moss (D, Calif.) May 6, 1975 made public seven hitherto secret Civil Service Commission studies showing that certain federal agencies hired and promoted employes without adequate regard for civil service and equal employment rules designed to protect women and minorities from discriminatory job practices.

Moss, who suggested that the commission had not been "vigorous" in pressing for internal change in these agencies," said that the reluctance of the commission to make the studies public raised questions about its commitment to enforcement of anti-discrimination rules. However, a commission spokesman called the reports "problem oriented and negative, and . . . done for internal use. They contain names of people and could be an invasion of privacy and so we do not make them public."

The agencies cited in the studies were: the Equal Employment Opportunity Commission, the National Science Foundation, the Small Business Administration, the Merchant Marine Academy, the Smithsonian Institution, the Department of Transportation, the Social Security Administration and the Atomic Energy Commission.

White wins reverse bias complaint. Robert J. Neyhart, a white employe of the Labor Department's Office of Equal Employment Opportunity, was awarded a delayed promotion and back pay after a Civil Service Commission examiner upheld his complaint that he had been discriminated against because he was not Spanish-surnamed, it was reported March 11, 1975. In his complaint, Neyhart said that Velma M. Strode, the office's director, told him he would be named to the $28,000-a-year deputy directorship. Subsequently, Neyhart asserted, Strode changed her mind because of instructions from the White House to place more Spanish-surnamed persons in top positions.

Bias charged in ACTION. The federal volunteer agency ACTION was charged June 2, 1976 with employment discrimination against "women and blacks, especially black women." The charge was made in a suit filed in U.S. District Court Washington, D.C. by Local 2027 of the American Federation of State, County and Municipal Employes, which represented ACTION workers. The suit alleged discrimination in recruiting, job classification, promotion and firing.

Other Government Jobs

Revenue-sharing anti-bias effort hit. Charging that federal enforcement of regulations prohibiting discrimination in the spending of revenue-sharing funds had been "fundamentally inadequate," the U.S. Commission on Civil Rights urged Congress Feb. 14, 1975 to appropriate $7.5 million to ensure proper monitoring of the program.

The panel reported "abundant evidence . . . that discrimination in the employment practices and delivery of benefits of state and local governments is far-reaching, often extending to programs funded by general revenue sharing." (The report noted that it was sometimes difficult to trace the uses of revenue sharing funds, as some recipients used the funds to free money that was in turn used for discrimi-

natory purposes.)

To bring about effective enforcement of antidiscrimination regulations, the commission report said, the revenue-sharing office of the Treasury Department should delegate compliance work to other, presumably more experienced federal agencies working under standards developed by the Justice Department. The report also urged that statistical data on public employment by states and localities be reviewed regularly for evidence of discrimination and that Office of Revenue Sharing cut off or defer quarterly payments to recipients failing to correct discriminatory practices.

Six months later, four important national organizations made public a report Aug. 19 charging the $30.2-billion federal revenue sharing program with "financing widespread discrimination in public employment and local services."

The report, entitled "Equal Opportunity under Revenue Sharing," cited what it said were the most recent figures available on public employes as evidence of the existence of "a nationwide pattern of underrepresentation of minorities and women." State and local government spent federal funds on contracts to discriminatory private employers and on inadequate municipal services for the poor and minority neighborhoods, the report said.

The report was also critical of the Treasury Department's Office of Revenue Sharing, which distributed revenue-sharing funds and was responsible for seeing they were not spent in a discriminatory way. The office "delays unconscionably in dealing with complaints" and "has done almost nothing" to remedy such inadequacies in the communities it funded, the report said.

The organizations involved in the study were the Center for National Policy Review, the National Urban Coalition, the League of Women Voters and the Center for Community Change.

In a separate development, Elmer Staats, U.S. controller general and chief administrator of the General Accounting Office, told a Senate subcommittee July 23 that a GAO study of federal revenue sharing had determined that state and local recipients were able to evade federal antidiscrimination regulations by using their own money in areas where civil rights compliance problems might be encountered. Summarizing the GAO study before the Government Operations Subcommittee on Intergovernmental Relations July 23, Staats urged that the revenue sharing act be broadened to provide that "a government receiving revenue sharing could not discriminate in any of its programs or activities regardless of the source of funding, and revenue-sharing funds would be withheld, after due process, pending acceptable actions to correct discriminatory practices."

U.S. sues Boston on fire hirings. The Justice Department filed a civil suit in federal court in Boston Jan. 24, 1973, charging that the city of Boston, Boston Fire Commissioner James H. Kelly and the members of the Massachusetts Civil Service Commission had discriminated against blacks and Spanish-surnamed people in hiring new firemen.

Out of 2,100 firemen, only 16 were black and three had Spanish surnames, though these groups constituted 16% and 4% of the city's population, respectively. The department said the city had failed or refused to hire minority people on an equal basis with whites, and had used tests and qualifications that discriminated against minorities although they had "not been shown to be required by the needs of the fire department or predictive of successful job performance."

The Justice Department asked the court to order the defendants to begin an active recruiting program, hire enough minority group members to compensate for past discrimination and compensate individuals who had taken fire department examinations but had been unfairly denied jobs.

Bridgeport police order. U.S. District Judge Jon O. Newman ordered Bridgeport, Conn. Jan. 29, 1973 to hire blacks and Puerto Ricans to fill half the vacancies in the police force until they constituted 15% of the force.

Newman said the city's Civil Service Examination denied equal protection of the law to minority groups. Only 14 blacks and three Peurto Ricans were on the 485-member force, though the groups constituted 25% of the city's population. All future job tests would be submitted to the court for approval.

Newman also set minority hiring quotas for detective, sergeant, lieutenant and captain positions over the next two years.

Cairo, Ill. found polarized. The U.S. Commission on Civil Rights released a report Feb. 6, 1973 charging that racially divided Cairo, Ill. suffered from a "breakdown in law and justice."

Since 1969 Cairo had been the scene of recurrent racial violence—riots, fire bombings, shootings.

Cairo's population of 6,300 was 38% black.

The report was based on two years of "monitoring" and three days of public hearings in March 1972. Some of its conclusions:

"Blacks have been underrepresented or excluded from city and county boards and commissions responsible for establishing policy and hiring of personnel." By March, however, blacks were being appointed to a few positions.

Of Cairo's police force the report said, "The rights of certain citizens have not been adequately safeguarded, and existing remedies appear to be insufficient. The police force has been biased and unprofessional in the performance of its public trust."

Among the report's recommendations were proposals to professionalize Cairo police and hire black police officers.

LEAA & police bias. The Law Enforcement Assistance Administration (LEAA) March 9, 1973 issued a guideline requiring all police departments, correctional and court facilities which receive LEAA funds to eliminate minimum height requirements for employment, unless an agency could "convincingly demonstrate that such requirements are necessary for certain job categories."

LEAA said the height requirements had sometimes tended "to disproportionately disqualify persons of certain national origins and races and women." According to the Leadership Conference on Civil Rights, which had advised LEAA on minority employment, Puerto Ricans, Mexican-Americans and Japanese-Americans had been among the affected groups.

LEAA also issued a proposed guideline requiring all law enforcement agencies receiving funds, and operating in an area whose work force was more than 3% composed of minority groups, to implement affirmative action programs to obtain "full and equal opportunity for women and minorities." Correctional facilities would have to increase recruitment among minority groups even if located in suburban or rural areas with few minority individuals.

The American Civil Liberties Union Sept. 3, 1975 filed a class-action suit in federal court in Washington asking that the LEAA be enjoined from giving funds to police departments that discriminate against blacks and women. The suit, brought by the ACLU on behalf of a national black police officers association, a national woman police officers organization and several individual plaintiffs, charged that the LEAA had illegally given millions of dollars in federal money to departments that regularly violated federal laws against discrimination in hiring and promotion practices.

An LEAA spokesman responded that the agency had already cut off funds to 20 departments, pending their compliance with LEAA equal employment guidelines. In 17 additional cases, the LEAA threatened funding cutoffs, the spokesman said.

California cities accused. Four civil rights groups filed a complaint March 13, 1973 with California's Fair Employment Practices Commission against the state's 28 largest cities, charging job bias against blacks and Spanish-surnamed people in police and fire departments.

The organizations said the two groups constituted 27% of the cities' population, but only 9% of the police and 5% of the firemen. They asked the commission to order population parity in the positions by 1977, to open up about 8,000 jobs.

Complainants were the National Association for the Advancement of Colored People, the League of United Latin-American Citizens, the American GI Forum and the Mexican-American Political Association.

U.S. acts against Chicago. The Department of Justice filed a civil suit in federal court in Chicago March 15, 1973 charging that the city had discriminated against blacks and Spanish surnamed persons in hiring and promoting firemen.

The department noted that only 4% of Chicago's 5,000 firemen were black and only .5% Puerto Rican or Mexican-American, although 32% of the city's people were black and 11% had Spanish surnames. The suit sought a change in hiring practices, including elimination of allegedly unnecessary and discriminatory hiring and promotion tests, a recruitment program and compensation for past discrimination.

The department, in a suit filed Aug. 14, accused the Chicago police of job discrimination against blacks, women and Spanish-surnamed people.

The police suit was the first brought by the Justice Department under the antibias regulations of the department's Law Enforcement Assistance Administration, which had granted funds to the police.

Federal Judge John Lewis Smith Jr. Dec. 18, 1974 ordered the Treasury Department's office of Revenue Sharing to stop making revenue-sharing payments to Chicago until the city took affirmative action to end racial discrimination in its police department. The action followed a finding Nov. 7 by Federal Judge Preston Marshall that the Chicago police department's hiring, promotion and personnel practices discriminated against blacks and women.

Judge Smith, who issued his decision in Washington, was acting on a suit by two civil rights groups, the Chicago branch of the National Association for the Advancement of Colored People (NAACP) and the Afro-American Patrolmen's League of Chicago. The plaintiffs charged the police department with discriminatory hiring practices and asserted that the city violated the law by using revenue-sharing funds for the department.

A spokesman for the Revenue Sharing Office said the $19.3 million quarterly check due to be mailed to the city Jan. 3, 1975, would be held because of Smith's order. While attorneys for the Treasury Department said they would not appeal the order, Chicago officials asserted that Chicago was "in total and complete compliance" with all court orders and directives concerning police department employment.

Meanwhile, Judge Marshall Dec. 16 accepted an interim hiring plan for the police department calling for 600 new employes. Of the 600 hired, 400 were to be from minority groups or women.

Marshall Dec. 26 refused to vacate Judge Smith's ruling that the federal funds be withheld. He reaffirmed the ruling April 21, 1975.

Mayor Richard J. Daley said April 22, 1975 that Chicago would hire 200 more police officers, most of them black and women, in an effort to regain the federal funds. ($38 million had been withheld by then.)

Marshall Jan. 5, 1976 ordered the Chicago police to set racial quotas for the hiring of police officers. He simultaneously enjoined the Treasury Department from sending revenue-sharing funds (then amounting to $76 million) to the city until his orders had been obeyed.

The quotas specified by the judge were: 42% black and hispanic males, 16% women, and 42% white males. At the time of the ruling, blacks and hispanics made up 17% of the police force (in contrast to a 40% share of the general city population).

Buffalo police accused. In a civil suit filed Aug. 14, 1973, the Justice Department accused the Buffalo, N.Y. police department of practicing discrimination against blacks, women and Spanish-surnamed persons in employment opportunities and conditions of employment.

The suit charged that the proportion of minority-group members employed by the police was far below the minority percentage of the city's population.

San Francisco police & fire quotas. In decisions reported Dec. 2, 1973, U.S. district judges in San Francisco ordered quota systems for the employment of minorities in the city's police and fire departments.

Concerning the police department, Judge Robert F. Peckham ordered that three minority persons (defined by Peckham as "blacks, Latinos and Asians) be hired for every two whites at the level of patrolman until minority representation reached 30%. A one-to-one ratio in appointments to the rank of sergeant was to be in effect until 30% of that rank were from minorities.

Peckham also enjoined the city's Civil Service Commission from using a hiring and promotion test which he said was discriminatory. He ordered future tests submitted to him for approval.

The city's fire department was ordered by Judge William T. Sweigert to fill half of more than 200 vacancies with members of racial minorities.

Maryland decree. The Justice Department Jan. 7, 1974 obtained a consent decree requiring the Maryland State Police to hire women and more blacks and to assign them on a nondiscriminatory basis. The department had filed a civil suit against the state Jan. 4.

The agreement set a goal of a force 16% black within five years and banned the use of pre-employment tests that had been found discriminatory against blacks and women.

Jackson, Miss. job quotas set. The city of Jackson, Miss. and the U.S. Justice Department reached an agreement providing quotas for the increased placement of blacks on the municipal payroll and back pay up to $1,000 for currently-employed blacks who had been denied promotion opportunities, it was reported March 31, 1974.

Quotas in the plan set a five-year goal of a 40% black work force, approximately the same percentage as in the city's population. Currently, about 800 of the 3,000 workers were black, most in low-paying job classifications. The 40% figure would apply to both police and fire departments.

The accord also provided that at least one-third of city jobs would be filled by women.

Black state troopers ordered. The U.S. 5th Circuit Court of Appeals April 19, 1974 upheld a lower court decision that the Alabama Department of Public Safety must revise its hiring policies so that the state's highway patrol force could become 25% black.

Department Director C. E. Dothard said that within the next month 25 blacks would enroll in the 625-man force, bringing black representation to 4%. Blacks already made up 23% of the department's support personnel, Dothard said.

In a related decision reported March 31, the court had found that the Mississippi highway patrol discriminated against blacks, but stopped short of ordering quota hiring. The court said, however, that a lower court could, "within the bounds of discretion," set temporary hiring quotas, a freeze on hiring of whites "or any other affirmative hiring relief until the patrol is effectively integrated." According to the court, five of Mississippi's 548 patrolmen were black.

Minorities in police number 6%. A study by the Police Foundation, a unit of the Ford Foundation, showed that about 6% of the nation's police officers were from racial minorities and less than 2% were women, it was reported April 21, 1974.

The survey found that hiring standards varied widely between men and women, with stricter educational requirements but more relaxed physical and back-

ground-check requirements for women.

The study also noted that the 6% figure was inflated by the high minority representation on the forces in Washington, D.C. (37% black) and Hawaii (more than 95% minority).

Nationally, the center said, blacks constituted 1.5% of the state police forces. American Indians and Hispanics made up about an equal percentage. The figures contrasted with employment data for the nation's 50 largest urban police forces. Of the 86,065 persons employed on these forces, 9% were black, the center said.

Figures on minorities in police forces were amplified by the Race Relations Information Center in Nashville, Tenn., which announced in the last issue of its bimonthly Race Relations Reporter that it had been forced to close because of lack of funding (reported Dec. 10, 1974).

Firemen's job plan set. The Justice Department obtained a consent decree June hiring in the Los Angeles fire department and requiring a recruiting program which would emphasize that women would be eligible for employment. The city also agreed to replace the term "fireman" with "firefighter."

The agreement provided a long-range goal of hiring racial minorities in proportion to their representation in the city's civilian labor force. To meet the goal, city agreed that, beginning July 1, 50% of appointments as firefighters would be from black, Mexican-American and Asian-American applicants. The agreement also included a court injunction forbidding discrimination against employees already hired.

The department noted that when a suit was filed against the city in 1972, 1.5% of 3,150 firefighters were black, 3% were Mexican-American, and none were Asian-American.

Milwaukee police, fire bias charged. The Justice Department filed a civil suit Oct. 17, 1974 charging Milwaukee's police and fire departments with bias in the hiring of women and minority-group members. At the same time, a consent order was filed resolving the suit against the fire department and setting hiring goals for minorities.

Under the consent order, the fire department—which had six black men and no women among its 1,120 firefighters—agreed to recruit and hire blacks, persons with Spanish surnames and American Indians until the three groups made up 14% of the department's uniformed personnel. The department agreed to adopt a goal of making at least 40% of its appointments from among qualified applicants from the three minority groups.

The fire department also had to recruit and hire women in numbers reflecting their interest and ability to qualify.

The suit against the police department said that of Milwaukee's 2,200 police officers, only 58 were black and 16 were women.

Tallahassee decree. After filing a suit, the Justice Department April 11, 1975 obtained a consent decree under which Tallahassee, Fla. agreed to hire qualified black persons for every type of city job in proportion to the number of blacks in the city's civilian labor force. The city was ordered to establish a biracial selection committee to identify blacks rejected because of race and notify them of their right to apply for listing on a priority register.

The government suit, filed Dec. 13, 1974, had charged Tallahassee with bias against black job applicants and current black employes. Filed in U.S. District Court in Tallahassee, the suit was the first brought under the Revenue Sharing Act of 1972 as the result of a routine compliance review by the Justice Department.

The suit accused the city of discriminating against blacks in recruiting, job assignments, hiring and promotion. The department's compliance review and subsequent suit focused on 11 city departments, which had received some of the $1,054,264 in revenue-sharing funds given Tallahassee since 1972.

Alabama cities accused of bias. The Justice Department May 27, 1975 filed a civil suit in U.S. District Court in Birmingham, Ala. charging that city and 11 others in Jefferson County with discrimination against blacks and women in

government jobs, thereby violating provisions of the Revenue Sharing Act of 1972.

Supreme Court rulings. The Supreme Court April 14, 1975 upheld a ruling that ordered towns and cities in Massachusetts to give preference in hiring to blacks and Spanish-surnamed individuals to alleviate past racial discrimination in fire departments.

The court June 16 upheld a ruling a Georgia official was liable for damages for refusing to accept a job application from a white man because he was married to a black woman.

D.C. test upheld—The Supreme Court June 7, 1976 upheld, 7–2, the validity of a test given to Washington, D.C. police force applicants. The action reversed a federal appellate court ruling that threw out the test because of a "racially disproportionate impact." (The failure rate for blacks taking the test was four times that of whites.)

The high court, in ruling on a claim that the test violated the Constitution's ban on racial discrimination, maintained that "discriminatory purpose" must be proved as well as "disproportionate impact" for a "law or other official act" to be held unconstitutionally biased. The court acknowledged that some tests had been invalidated as biased without evidence of a discriminatory purpose, but it said that those decisions had been based on the 1964 Civil Rights Act, not on the Constitution.

The decision, written by Justice Byron R. White, noted that the ruling might have implications for discrimination suits filed in a number of areas besides job tests, including urban renewal and zoning. White, in a footnote, cited a number of cases in which lower courts had ruled in favor of discrimination suits, and said, "The cases impressively demonstrate that there is another side to the issue; but, with all due respect, to the extent that those cases rested on or expressed the view that proof of discriminatory racial purpose is unnecessary in making out an equal protection violation [of the 14th Amendment], we are in disagreement."

Philadelphia police order sought. Continuing a six-year effort to increase the percentage of black policemen in Philadelphia, the Pennsylvania Justice Department Jan. 8, 1976 asked a federal judge to order the city's police department to hire one black candidate for every white person hired. Nineteen per cent of the members of the force and 33.6% of the city population were black.

State attorneys asked that the blacks be chosen from among 286 who passed a new entrance examination, which had been designed to be bias-free at a cost of over $200,000 to the city. The city had agreed to give those blacks some kind of preference in hiring because they previously had failed examinations ruled to be discriminatory by a federal judge.

More than half of the 286 blacks scored below the top 3,000 applicants on the new test. All new policemen hired during the next two to three years were expected to be chosen from among the top 3,000 tested. Attorneys for the state and the blacks requested the one for one hiring order on grounds that the new test was still discriminatory.

The state also asked the judge to draw up an interim procedure for investigating applicants' backgrounds until a nondiscriminatory procedure could be designed by the city.

Police quotas upheld. U.S. District Court Judge Clifford S. Green Feb. 19, 1976 dismissed two suits challenging the constitutionality of a 1974 consent decree that established minority hiring and promotion quotas for the Pennsylvania State Police. Green ruled the "reverse discrimination" suits brought by three white applicants to the force and three white troopers were "an improper collateral attack" on the consent decree.

Under the so-called "Bolden" decree approved by Green in June 1974, the State Police agreed to hire one qualified minority applicant for every two whites hired and to promote one minority trooper for every three whites promoted. The quota system was to remain in effect until black and Hispanic troopers composed 9.2% of the force, matching minority representation in the overall Pennsylvania

labor force. When the decree was signed, members of minorities made up 1.5% of the 4,100-member State Police force.

Monessen loses federal funds. The U.S. Economic Development Administration had revoked a $309,000 federal grant to Monessen, Pa. on the ground that the city was continuing to operate an all-white volunteer fire department, it was reported Feb. 25, 1976. The funds had been earmarked for remodeling the city's fire station but were withheld when city officials would not agree to permit blacks to serve on the force.

Affirmative Action, Quotas & Reverse Discrimination

Controversy continued during the mid-1970s over whether "affirmative action" in redressing the evils of racial and sex discrimination required the imposition of probably illegal quotas and resulted in instances of "reverse discrimination."

Social Democrats vs. quotas. At a meeting held May 11–12, 1974, the national committee of Social Democrats, U.S.A. adopted a resolution opposing quotas and analyzing the situation leading to the controversy over their use. The resolution said:

Lying at the heart of the controversy over quotas and preferential treatment for racial minorities are two phenomena. The first is the persistence of racial inequality in American life, despite the significant progress made during the past decade toward breaking down patterns of discrimination and segregation.

The second is the disastrous consequences of the economic policies of the Nixon Administration. There would obviously be no seriously considered demands for affirmative action formulas which extend preference to blacks and Spanish-speaking workers had the Administration committed itself to a policy of full employment....

Prejudice and the shortcomings of Nixonian economics do not fully resolve the question of why the quota principle is rapidly becoming embedded in American society. Another consideration is the attitude of some liberals, much of the news media, and a large segment of the business com-

Elements of an Affirmative Action Program

The U.S. Civil Service Commission listed the following nine points as "elements" of "a comprehensive program of equal employment opportunity" (EEO). These "elements of an affirmative action program," the commission said, "are based on the specific requirements of Executive Order 11478 and the Equal Opportunity Act of 1972...."

1. Adequate and competent staff and dollar resources throughout the organization to assure administration and implementation of a results-oriented program of equal employment opportunity which is involved in every aspect of personnel management policy and practice.

2. Recruitment activities designed to reach and attract job candidates from all segments of the population. Where appropriate, these activities are tailored to improve their effectiveness among members of specific groups.

3. Full identification and utilization of the present skills of employees on the rolls, facilitating movement through job restructuring techniques, establishment of trainee positions, and assuring that qualifications of requirements are realistic in terms of the jobs to be done.

4. Opportunities for employees to enhance their skills, perform at their highest potential, and advance in accordance with their abilities and the availability of opportunities. These efforts include programs of career counseling and planning, training and education, job analysis and redesign, and elimination of any unnecessary barriers to upward mobility.

5. Encouragement of EEO program understanding and support by supervisors and managers through practical training and advice, effective use of incentive systems, and evaluating supervisory and managerial performance in the EEO area.

6. Managerial support for and participation in community efforts to improve conditions—such as housing, transportation, and education—which affect employability.

7. Systematic evaluation of EEO program progress, identification of problem areas, and assessment of the effectiveness of program activities.

8. Systems providing for the informal resolution of EEO-related employment problems wherever possible, and for prompt, fair, and impartial consideration of formal complaints of discrimination in any aspect of employment.

9. Special programs to provide employment and training opportunities for the economically and educationally disadvantaged.

munity towards white working people. The outright snobbery prevalent during the 1960's has been replaced by a more subtle elitism which rejects the validity of the jobs of working people, the aspirations of their children, and the legitimacy of their labor leadership and political representatives. Although 70 per cent of the poor are white, public attitudes and government policy implies that only some groups—minorities and women—merit the help of government.

The dangers of these attitudes and the policies they generate are obvious: an exacerbation of the divisions between blacks and white working people, the perpetuation of an unhealthy, tribalistic form of ethnic consciousness, and a tendency to define social injustices as a function of racial, rather than class differences. A society which apportions jobs and college admissions on the basis of race and sex will inevitably confront demand for even further compartmentalization. We are already told that only black policemen should patrol the ghetto, that only Puerto Rican teachers can relate to Puerto Rican children, that only women can effectively serve as the political representatives of women.

Quotas also have a profoundly destructive psychological impact on those who benefit from them. Quotas infer that minority groups must be given something in order to have something. We reject such a condescendingly racist notion as demonstrably absurd. Society, however, may reach a different conclusion if the quota doctrine becomes institutionalized. The majority will never accept the minority as having achieved something through their own worth; the minority will be plagued by self-doubts as to whether they have really made it on their own.

We also reject quotas as both undemocratic and anti-democratic. The demand for ratio political representation implies that the natural democratic process is inherently and unalterably biased, a suggestion effectively refuted by the substantial political progress blacks have made, including the election of congressional and mayoral candidates in communities with white majorities, and to suggest, as some have, that quotas do not represent reverse discrimination, that quotas are simply "preferential inclusion" is simply semantic evasion. To include members of one group in order to fill a numerical goal is to exclude others. Quotas are quotas, whether they are called goals, preferential inclusion, affirmative action, or whatever. . . .

. . . Vigorous affirmative action programs must be continued. However we oppose the use of goals and timetables since as part of these programs, as now interpreted, they are simply a euphemism for quota systems.

Finally, we reject the proposition that quotas are the legacy of the civil rights movement. The leaders of the struggle for racial equality sought to expand opportunity for all who were oppressed by an unjust

social and economic order. They were opposed to reverse discrimination for both practical and principled reasons. The quota principle does not reflect the civil rights movement's values, but rather signifies their abandonment.

Tower sees affirmative action as invalid. Sen. John Tower (R, Tex.) told the Senate May 13, 1975 that he considered affirmative action programs "unconstitutional" as well as in violation of the Civil Rights Act of 1964. He quoted from Title VII of the 1964 act:

(a) It shall be an unlawful employment practice for an employer—

(1) to fail or refuse to hire or discharge any individual, or otherwise to discriminate against any individual . . . because of such individual's race, color, religion, sex, or national origin; or

(2) to limit, segregate, or classify his employees in anyway which would deprive or tend to deprive any individual of employment opportunities or otherwise adversely effect his status as an employee because of such individual's race, color, religion, sex or national origin. . . .

(j) Nothing contained in this title shall be interpreted to require any employer . . . to grant preferential treatment to any group because of the race, color, religion, sex or national origin of such individual or group on account of an *imbalance* which may exist with respect to the total number or percentage of persons of any race, color, religion, sex, or national origin employed by any employer . . . (emphasis added.)

"To prevent any misunderstanding of the language of this section," Tower said, the Senate floor managers for the act provided the following interpretation:

There is no requirement in Title VII that any employer maintain a racial balance in his work force. On the contrary, any deliberate attempt to maintain a racial balance whatever such a balance may be, *would involve a violation of Title VII* because maintaining such a balance would require an employer to hire or refuse to hire on the basis of race. (Emphasis added.)

Jackson proposes quotas. The Rev. Jesse L. Jackson, president of PUSH (the People United to Save Humanity), proposed Sept. 25, 1975 that employees be hired and laid off on the basis of a "quota principle" in order to minimize the impact of the recession on members of groups which in the past had been discriminated against by employers.

Hill defends affirmative action. Herbert Hill, national labor director of the NAACP, defended the affirmative action principle in a statement inserted in the Congressional Record by Rep. Charles B. Rangel (D, N.Y.) March 1–2, 1976. Excerpts from Hill's statement:

A major manifestation of the sharp turning away from the goal of racial equality is to be found in the shrill and paranoid attacks against affirmative action programs. The effort to eliminate the present effects of past discrimination, to right the wrongs of many generations was barely underway when it was aborted. And now, even the very modest gains made by black men and women through affirmative action are being erased, as powerful institutions turn the clock of history back to the dark and dismal days of "separate but equal."

Judging by the vast outcry, it might be assumed that the use of numerical goals and timetables to eliminate racist job patterns has become as widespread and destructive as discrimination itself. As with the much distorted subject of busing, the defenders of the racial status quo have once again succeeded in confusing the remedy with the original evil. The term "quota" like "busing" has become another code word for resistance to demands for the elimination of prevailing patterns of discrimination.

This issue is now a major national controversy and because it has become the focus of conflicting forces in current civil rights struggles it is necessary to identify, within the limits of this paper, the leading opponents of affirmative action. The attack comes from many places, among these are the academic community and the educational bureaucracy, big business and organized labor, white ethnic organizations and, of course, the federal government itself. Although

The clarion call in the ideological war against affirmative action was sounded by Professor Sidney Hook in a widely quoted article that appeared on November 5, 1971 in the New York Times, followed by his article in *Freedom At Issue* and other publications. Hook denounced affirmative action programs in institutions of higher learning and called upon his colleagues to resist all such demands from civil rights groups. He was soon joined by many distinguished academicians and the Committee for a Rational Alternative emerged (later known as the University Center for Rational Alternatives) followed by the Committee on Academic Non-discrimination and Integrity. These groups, using the names of some of the most prestigious figures in academia and with virtually unlimited access to the media have conducted a steady drumbeat of attack against affirmative action programs in colleges and universities. Since January 1972 the pages of *Commentary* magazine, which described the EEOC as the "quota commission," have been repeatedly

filled with self-righteous denunciations of affirmative action by the ideologues of the new atack upon racial equality. . . .

The Anti-Defamation League of B'nai B'rith and the American Jewish Congress both condemned affirmative action requirements imposed by the federal government. . . . On August 4, 1972, the American Jewish Committee in an open letter to President Nixon urged him to "reject categorically the use of quotas and proportional representation" in civil rights programs, and on January 12, 1973 six national Jewish organizations charging "reverse discrimination" against white males sent a protest to the Department of Health, Education and Welfare urging it to "prevent or eliminate preferential treatment."

Typical of the position of most labor unions is the resolution adopted by the AFL–CIO Building and Construction Trades Department which stated:

"Racial quotas, under any guise are repugnant to all Americans. When a proposal is made to establish racial quotas as public policy, honest men must protest . . . We prefer the free choice of free men and we are certain that the vast majority of Americans, white and nonwhite alike prefer such freedom."

Spokesmen for corporate enterprise issued equally sanctimonious expressions of outrage and in March of 1973 Fortune magazine further distorted the issue by warning against the dangers of job quotas. Its executive editor, Daniel Seligman, wrote, "For a democratic society to systematically discriminate against 'the majority' seems quite without precedent."

Another major source of organized opposition to the mandate of affirmative action developed in litigation under Title VII, comes from the newly emerging network of groups based on the white ethnic working class population. . . .

The diverse forces united in their intense opposition to affirmative action programs deliberately distort the issue by equating affirmative action based upon numerical goals with a fiction called the "quota system" and "reverse discrimination." But there is a fundamental distinction between quotas and numerical goals. Quotas are used to exclude, while numerical goals are a means to include those workers who have been systematically excluded in the past. Quotas establish a ceiling—that is a maximum. Numerical goals used in affirmative action establish only a minimum which can, and often should, be exceeded. In short, quotas have been used as a limitation, while numerical goals represent the exact opposite.

Those who attack the use of numerical goals often argue that affirmative action programs will penalize innocent whites who are not responsible for past discriminatory practices. This argument turns on the notion of individual rights and sounds very moral and high-minded, indeed. But it ignores basic social reality. For example, black workers have not been denied jobs as individuals but as a class—no matter what their personal merits and qualifications. Women have not been denied training and jobs as individuals, but as a class regardless of their individual talent or lack of it. Correspondingly, while males as a class have benefitted from this systematic discrimination. Wherever discriminatory employment patterns exist, hiring and promotion without affirmative action perpetuates injustice.

The federal courts have recognized in Title VII ligitation that employment discrimination is by its nature class discrimination. This was established in *Parham* v. *Southwestern Bell Telephone Company, Oatis* v. *Crown Zellerbach Corporation* and *Bowe* v. *Colgate-Palmolive Company,* among many other cases. It was also established that relief must go to the entire injured class and the use of specified numerical goals can be most effective in achieving compliance with the law.

Common to most attacks upon affirmative action programs is the assumption that such approaches constitute "reverse discrimination" and that the quality of performance and work standards will be severely diminished as a result of the employment of nonwhites and women. The *a priori* assumption that no "qualified" blacks or women exist is implicit in this argument. Also implicit in the assumption that if blacks and women were to be employed, the allegedly high standards now in force would be diminished. But in reality, the so-called merit system operates to give preference to mediocre or incompetent whites at the expense of highly talented blacks, as well as at the expense of mediocre and incompent blacks. . . .

Under the guise of defending "merit systems" that in reality do not exist, the opponents of affirmative action are, in fact, attempting to maintain unstated but traditional discriminatory practices that result in the exclusion of blacks, women and others from desirable, high-paying, skilled jobs. A major factor in the resistance to new legal remedies is that white male expectations, based on the systematic denial of the rights of minorities, have become the norm. Thus any alteration of this norm is considered "reverse discrimination."

It should be evident that what is really involved in the debate over affirmative action programs is not that blacks and women will be given preference over white males, but that a substantial body of law now requires that discriminatory systems which operate to favor white males at the expense of women and blacks must be eliminated. . . .

During the past quarter of a century, the federal courts have increasingly recognized the validity of numerical goals in eliminating traditional forms of discrimination. The courts have used this approach as a remedy to end systematic discrimination in the selec-

tion of juries and it has also been utilized in legislative reapportionment litigation, and in school segregation cases.

In *Swann* v. *Charlotte-Mecklenburg Board of Education,* the Supreme Court held that:

"Absent a constitutional violation there would be no basis for judicially ordering assignment of students on a racial basis. All things being equal, with no history of discrimination, it might well be desirable to assign pupils to schools nearest their homes. But all things are not equal in a system that has been deliberately constructed and maintained to enforce racial segregation. The remedy for such segregation may be administratively awkward, inconvenient and even bizarre in some situations and may impose burdens on some; but all awkwardness and inconvenience cannot be avoided in the interim period when remedial adjustments are being made to eliminate the dual school systems."

Significantly, the Court ruled that mathematical racial ratios could be used as "a starting point in the process of shaping a remedy."

Although the courts have repeatedly spoken on this issue the extensive public discussion of affirmative action programs has ignored the major legal interpretations of the validity of numerical goals and timetables in civil rights enforcement efforts. In the last half of the 1960s, as a result of an emerging body of law relating to employment discrimination, new forms of implementation were developed to obtain compliance with legal requirements. Among the most important of these was the concept of numerical goals to be achieved within stated time frames . . .

In *Carter* v. *Gallagher,* a case involving the Minneapolis Fire Department brought under Sections 1981 and 1983 of the Civil Rights Act of 1866 the district court decreed:

"That the defendants . . . give absolute preference in certification of fire fighters with the Minneapolis Fire Department to twenty/(20) Black American Indians or Spanish Sur-named American applicants who qualify for such a position . . ."

The municipality appealed this decision and, in response, the circuit court held that "The anti-preference treatment section of the new Civil Rights Act of 1964 does not limit the power of a court to order affirmative relief to correct the effects of past unlawful practices."

In *Associated General Contractors of Massachusetts, Inc.* v. *Altshuler,* a federal court validated a statewide affirmative action plan requiring building contractors to employ a specified minimum percentage of minority workers. In rather eloquent language the court explained the necessity for such approaches.

"It is by now well understood, however, that our society cannot be completely color-blind in the short term if we are to have a color-blind society in the long term. After centuries of viewing through colored lenses, eyes do not quickly adjust when the lenses are removed. Discrimination has a way of perpetuating itself, albeit unintentionally, because the resulting inequalities make new opportunities less accessible. Preferential treatment is one partial prescription to remedy our society's most intransigent and deeply rooted inequalities."

On November 30, 1973 the First Circuit Court of Appeals sustained the use of "numerical objectives" in all state financed construction projects in Massachusetts and on April 22, 1974 the Supreme Court refused to review.

On the basis of these and other federal court decisions, it is evident that a substantial body of case law has established not only the permissibility, but indeed the necessity, of numerical goals and affirmative action programs to eliminate discriminatory employment patterns. But the opponents of affirmative action persist in their campaign of distortion, deliberately confusing goals with the pejoratively labeled "quotas" and denouncing affirmative action as "reverse discrimination."

A well orchestrated nationwide propaganda operation, based upon systematic misrepresentation and the manipulation of racial fears among whites has succeeded in causing the federal government to retreat on this crucial issue. Administrative enforcement of affirmative action requirements contained in the comprehensive body of civil rights laws and executive orders has, for all practical purposes, ceased and the process of administrative mullification begun under President Nixon continues under President Ford.

The Office of Federal Contract Compliance, for example, has become functionally useless, and the less said about the Office for Civil Rights in H.E.W. the better. The Report of the United States Commission on Civil Rights issued July 1975 sums up the matter: "Instead of imposing sanctions on contractors who do not follow the affirmative action requirements, the compliance agencies and OFCC devote substantial resources to extend conciliation, which can often stretch out over several years." . . .

There is every reason to believe that the current unemployment crisis will last for a decade or more. A most important aspect of the long-term economic forecast is that at the same time that the nation is expected to experience a continuing high rate of unem-

ployment many millions of workers will remain on the job. Not everyone will be unemployed. In fact, 85 million are now working. It is clear that the pattern of unemployment is unevenly distributed with black people, as usual, hurt the most. Therefore, the fundamental question now and for the next ten years and perhaps longer will be WHO WORKS? Industry-wide patterns of discrimination based on race and sex are a decisive factor in determining who does or who does not work.

The EEOC, if it is to survive as a viable agency, must reject the pressures to retreat that are exerted upon it by other organs of the federal government, such as the Civil Service Commission, the Department of Labor, and the Department of Health, Education and Welfare, among others. These agencies have crippled civil rights enforcement in their respective jurisdictions and they have done this by rejecting the concept of affirmative action and substituting instead an abstraction called voluntary compliance. But programs based upon voluntarism, with their expressed or implied promise not to enforce the law, have failed to eliminate discriminatory employment practices.

Voluntary compliance programs avoid the concept that racial discrimination is illegal, that black workers and other minorities have fundamental rights which cannot be bargained away, and that the institutions which discriminate against them are required by law to change their conduct. . . .

In the final analysis affirmative action is an attempt at redistribution, an attempt to achieve a limited but necessary reallocation of jobs and income within the existing legal structure. It is part of a long-term civil rights strategy to make the law operate as an instrument of social change. When the law is permitted to function at its best, it fulfills its historic role of preserving public order while, at the same time, redressing collective grievances and thereby giving the institutions of society an opportunity to change without fatal trauma.

The history of the twentieth century teaches us that if those victimized by injustice are denied relief under law, then the alternative is violence and violence. whatever its motivation, is certain to result in disaster. But the opponents of affirmative action are succeeding in nullifying the law, are confirming the belief that black people are indeed powerless in American society. . . .

Women

Equal Rights Amendment

Champions of women's rights have been struggling for more than half of this century to win the adoption of a constitutional amendment stating explicitly or in effect that "equality of rights under the law shall not be denied or abridged by the United States or by any state on account of sex." This Equal Rights Amendment (or ERA), introduced in Congress every year since 1923 without previously coming to a vote, was finally approved by the House in 1970 and by the Senate in 1972, but it could not become part of the Constitution unless ratified by at least 38 states within seven years. Supporters of ERA held that the amendment would be invaluable in protecting women against job bias. Opponents of the measure argued that it would rob women of protections they had already won.

House passes ERA. The proposed Equal Rights Amendment was passed by 350–15 vote of the House of Representatives Aug. 10, 1970 after an unusual maneuver was used to dislodge the measure from committee.

The rarely used device of a discharge petition—to discharge the Judiciary Committee from further consideration of the bill—was employed to gain House consideration of the measure, which had never been granted hearings or any other consideration by the committee during the 21 years that Rep. Emanuel Celler (D, N.Y.) had been its chairman. In arguing against the maneuver and the measure, Celler said "there is no equality except in a cemetery" and "more difference between a male and a female than between a horse chestnut and a chestnut horse." Celler also said the amendment might invalidate some laws designed to protect women.

Senate hearings. Opening hearings of the Senate Judiciary Committee's Constitutional Amendments Subcommittee on the Equal Rights Amendment May 5, 1970, Subcommittee Chairman Birch Bayh (D, Ind.) asserted that "women have often been left behind in the struggle to make American society a fair and just one. Despite the passage of Title VII of the 1964 Civil Rights Act and the Equal Pay Act of 1963, widespread employment discrimination continues throughout the United States. In a recent management survey, for example, 59% of the companies admitted that they continue to disqualify women from jobs solely on the basis of sex; 63% recruit at men's schools while only 30% recruit at women's schools; and 47% continue to use separate 'male' and 'female' classified advertisements despite Equal Employment Opportunity Commission regulations against such placement."

Mrs. Myra Ruth Harmon, president of the National Federation of Business & Professional Women's Clubs, told the subcommittee that by blocking laws "discriminating between men and women on the basis of sex alone," ERA would nullify legislation that could no longer be described as "protective." "Women do not need protection" against sweatshops and other "oppressive conditions which have ceased to exist," she said. "Special labor legislation for women restricts as fully as it was originally intended to protect. These laws operate to prevent millions of women from competing on equal terms with men. . . ." Through such legislation, she declared, "employers have been able to deny . . . women jobs, promotions, seniority benefits, wage increases and overtime; to prevent these women from being hired, promoted, transferred. . . ."

Prof. Norman Dorsen of New York University School of Law told the Senate Judiciary Committee Sept. 15 that "the crazy quilt of state protective laws reveal graphically that there is no consensus on what is needed protection for either men or women and that much of the legislation . . . actually 'protect' them out of jobs that they are perfectly capable of fulfilling." He added that "laws that confer genuine benefits can and .should be extended to men under the Equal Rights Amendment."

Senate passage. The Equal Rights Amendment was passed by 84–8 Senate vote March 22, 1972. It then went to the states for ratification.

Provisions offered by Sen. Sam J. Ervin (D, N.C.) to exempt women from the draft, bar them from assignment to combat units, and preserve laws that "extend protections or exemptions to women" were defeated by large margins March 21.

The amendment had been endorsed by President Nixon March 18.

ERA was ratified in 1972 by 22 states: Alaska, California, Colorado, Delaware, Hawaii, Idaho, Iowa, Kansas, Kentucky, Maryland, Michigan, Massachusetts, Nebraska, New Hampshire, New Jersey,

New York, Pennsylvania, Rhode Island, Tennessee, Texas, West Virginia and Wisconsin.

Opposition to ERA. Ratification of ERA was rejected by the Utah legislature Jan. 24, 1973. Ann Scott, director of legislative work for the National Organization for Women, said "about two weeks ago we began to realize we were hitting well-organized, well-financed opposition." Phyllis Schlafly, leader of a group called Stop ERA, said her group had coordinators in 26 states, and several thousand members working to defeat the measure.

Nebraska, one of the 30 ratifying states, voted March 15 to reject the amendment, although the counsel to the U.S. Senate Judiciary Committee had informed the state in December 1972 that an attempt by a state to rescind ratification would be "null and void." The Supreme Court had ruled in 1939 that the legality of a state's ratification was entirely under Congressional control, noting that the 14th and 15th Amendments had been declared adopted even though some of the necessary number of states had tried to rescind their approval.

The Tennessee legislature April 23, 1974 also voted to rescind its ratification of the amendment.

'75 ERA drive planned. Representatives of 26 national organizations supporting ERA said Dec. 10, 1974 that they would concentrate their campaign in 10 states in an effort to achieve final ratification in 1975. The states, cited in a plan devised by a political consultant firm, were Illinois, Missouri, North Carolina and North Dakota—all listed as almost certain of prompt favorable action; Arizona and Oklahoma—regarded as good but not certain of favorable action; Florida—deemed good for later ratification; and Indiana, Nevada and South Carolina.

The number of legislatures having approved the ERA rose to 34, when the North Dakota legislature endorsed the amendment Feb. 4, 1975. The ERA had been submitted to the North Dakota legislature in 1973, but had been rejected.

The proposal failed to gain ratification in seven other states, however. State legislatures rejecting the ERA in the first month and a half of 1975 were in Louisiana, Oklahoma, Virginia, Arizona, Georgia, Utah and Nevada.

In March and April, ratification efforts were defeated in Indiana, Missouri, Florida, Illinois, South Carolina and North Carolina.

ERA advocates attributed the stalling of the ratification drive to several factors: fundamentalist religious views on the woman's role in society, especially among legislators in the Deep South; opposition among some segments of the Catholic Church who were fearful of the ERA's effect on institutions maintaining separate educational facilities for boys and girls; and fears in the nation's insurance industry that passage of the ERA would require a major rewriting of policies with special clauses governing women. Moreover, ERA proponents admitted that of the 16 states that had not ratified the amendment, only eight or 10 were realistic possibilities.

Phyllis Schlafly, a prominent opponent of the ERA, said rejection of the ERA had happened "where full debate and discussion occurred." Just because the ERA had not been approved in 1975, it was not a dead issue, said Schlafly, who indicated she would continue her battle against ratification, if need be, until March 1979, the deadline for passage.

Her most effective arguments against the proposed amendment, Schlafly said, were that the woman's "special role" in the family would be endangered and that ERA ratification would mean women would have to be sent into military combat.

58% favor ERA, Gallup Poll indicates. The results of a Gallup Poll made public April 10 indicate that 58% of 1,542 persons sampled March 7–10 supported ratification of the ERA. According to a Gallup spokesman, 58% backed the ERA, 24% opposed it and 18% had no opinion. Broken down by sex, the poll showed 63% of the males surveyed favoring passage, compared to 54% of the women. Geographically, backing for the amendment was higher in the East (67%) and the West (62%) than in the South (52%) and the Middle West (53%);

ERA rejected in N.Y. & N.J. Equal rights amendments—proposed as amendments to the state constitutions to declare that equality of rights under the law should not be denied or abridged on account of sex—were defeated by more than 400,000 votes in New York State and 60,000 votes in New Jersey Nov. 4, 1975. The ERA won by a vote of 449,214 to 310,900 in New York City but was opposed statewide by a vote of 1,463,985 to 914,617.

Abzug assesses situation—Rep. Bella Abzug (D, N.Y.) evaluated the ERA situation in a Dec. 22, 1975 article in the Village Voice. She wrote:

To put ERA in perspective, the federal amendment has been ratified by 34 states and has until 1979 to get the necessary ratification by four other states. Fifteen states have enacted state equal rights provisions or amendments to their own constitutions. In none of these states have any of the horrors conjured up by the anti-ERA forces materialized.

Instead, the amendment is providing the framework and impetus for review and reform of hundreds of existing laws to eliminate unequal treatment that primarily victimizes women but also in some instances victimizes men. ERA also stands as a barrier against enactment of discriminatory legislation.

Under the attorney general opinions interpreting state ERAs, most states have been extending benefits to the excluded group rather than doing away with the benefits. These include such benefits as the right to support or alimony, the right to receive pension benefits based on the employment record or occupation of one's spouse. . . .

Even after the New York defeat, a national Harris Poll showed a 70 to 15 per cent majority of Americans in favor of ERA, with 73 per cent of women favoring it, compared with a 68 per cent majority of men. Similarly, a Gallup Poll in September reported that 71 per cent of Americans feel the country would be governed as well or better with more women in public office, and 73 per cent said they would vote for a qualified woman for president. New York voters, while defeating ERA, elected 60 per cent of the women who ran for various offices around the state, continuing a national trend that has seen the election of thousands of women to local and state office in the past few years. The trend didn't just happen. It was in response to the "Win With Women" campaign developed by the multipartisan National Women's Political Caucus, which has been on the scene only since 1971. . . .

Effort continues in '76. ERAmerica, an organization created to win ratification of the amendment, opened offices in Washington, D.C. Feb. 25, 1976. Heading the organization were Liz Carpenter, a Democrat, and Elly Peterson, a Republican. Peterson accused opponents of ERA of "lies and misrepresentations," citing in particular claims by opponents that ERA was connected with abortion, and that it would deny women the choice to be supported by their husbands.

Phyllis Schlafly, chairman of the Stop ERA organization, said at a news conference Feb. 13 that the supporters of the amendment wanted to turn child care over to the government. She claimed as evidence a report issued by a study group set up by Ohio governor James A. Rhodes, which had said that ratification of ERA would create a "need for universally available child-care centers," in order to free mothers to take jobs.

Schlafly castigated the proposal as downgrading the institution of marriage.

An ERAmerica spokesman said Feb. 13 · that the daycare center proposal was not in the section of the report concerned with actions that would be legally required by the amendment, and that Schlafly had misrepresented the report.

In Kentucky, the state house of representatives Feb. 18 voted 57 to 40 to rescind its 1972 approval of the amendment.

The Arizona state senate March 1 failed to approve the measure on a 15–15 vote. The Arizona house had killed the amendment in committee earlier, so the Senate action closed off any possibility of approval by the state legislature for the current year.

Women's Groups Active

Nationwide protests. Thousands of women demonstrated Aug. 26, 1970 in response to a "Women's Strike for Equality" call and to celebrate the 50th anniversary of women's right to vote in the U.S. Organized by a loose coalition of groups including the National Organization for Women (NOW) and Women's Liberation, women protesters, joined by

male supporters of the movement, demonstrated in large rallies and marches in East Coast cities, San Francisco and Los Angeles and in dozens of smaller observances throughout the nation. Organizers called for a women's "strike."

President Nixon marked the day with a proclamation noting the 50th anniversary of the 19th Amendment and honoring the "brave and courageous women" who had "fought long and hard for woman suffrage." He urged that the nation "recognize that women surely have a still wider role to play in the political, economic and social life of our country."

Demonstrations in New York City drew the largest crowds. At least 10,000 joined an evening rush-hour march down 5th Avenue, and up to 40,000 attended the rally that followed. The main speaker was Mrs. Betty Friedan, a founder of NOW who had originated the "strike" notion and was credited with revitalizing the women's rights movement with her 1963 best-seller, "The Feminine Mystique."

Mrs. Friedan, who said the success of the "strike" was "beyond our wildest dreams," said at the rally "this is a political movement. . . . Man is not the enemy, man is a fellow victim." (According to reports from companies with large numbers of women employes, the call to strike, even in New York, was largely ignored.)

Demonstrators in Washington centered their efforts on urging passage of the Equal Rights Amendment.

Political caucus under way. More than 200 women met in Washington, D. C. July 10–11, 1971 to mobilize the women's rights movement to achieve political power. The National Women's Political Caucus (NWPC) set as its goal the equal representation of women with men at all levels of the nation's political system. The group declared it would support candidates, men and women, who would fight against "sexism, racism, violence and poverty."

The NWPC elected a 21-member steering committee to coordinate the efforts of the new women's group. The caucus settled on a program, to be carried out by NWPC state and local units, to rally support for women candidates, force political parties to accept women in decision-making roles and register new women voters.

Rep. Bella Abzug (D, N.Y.), in a speech to the opening meeting July 10, said the caucus should seek to double the number of women in Congress by 1972. She said: "We should campaign for women—and men candidates—who are good on women's issues. We should work to defeat those who are not."

Betty Friedan, a founder of NOW, pointed out that when men comprised "98 or 99 per cent of the House, Senate, the State Assembly, City Hall, women are outside the body politic." Writer Gloria Steinem said: "No one gives political power. It must be taken. And we will take it."

Another speaker, Fannie Lou Hamer, a black civil rights leader in Mississippi, said she would fight "for the liberation of all people, because nobody's free until everybody's free. . . . I've passed equal rights; I'm fighting for human rights."

The four speakers were all elected to the policy council, whose members were announced at a press conference July 12. Also chosen for the 21-member council were Rep. Shirley Chisholm (D, N.Y.), Indian rights leader La Donna Harris and Beulah Sanders, vice president of the National Welfare Rights Organization (NWRO). The only woman under 30 elected to the council was Paula Page, representing the National Student Association. However, following pressure by a radical caucus four additional seats were reserved for younger women and Spanish speaking women.

The other members of the council were Shana Alexander, Virginia Allen, Nikki Beare, Joan Cashin, Mary Clarke, Myrlie Evers, JoAnne Evans Gardner, Elinor Guggenheimer, Wilma Scott Heide, Dorothy Height, Olga Madar, Vivian Carter Mason, Midge Miller.

The NWPC made public a set of issues adopted as "guidelines" for support of political candidates. The statement said priority issues were: passage of ERA; repeal of "all laws that affect a woman's right to decide her own reproductive and sexual life"; amendment of the 1964 Civil Rights Act and extension of the 1963 Equal Pay Act to provide more protection for women; enforcement of existing anti-discrimination legislation and strengthening of the enforcement powers of the Equal Employment Opportunity Commission; and elimination of tax inequities involving women and children.

The NWPC's first convention was held in Houston Feb. 9–11, 1973. The delegates passed a series of resolutions supporting pending bills on child care, minimum wage, welfare reform, full health services including abortion and family planning aid, consumer credit discrimination and sex discrimination in government-aided programs. Another resolution opposed the Administration's impoundment of social welfare funds.

"Top priority" was given to ratification of ERA.

By a razor-thin margin, the convention voted Feb. 9 to admit men as nonvoting members at large, and to allow local caucuses to decide their membership policies. Some state caucuses had already enrolled men, and spokeswomen from the Texas delegation said they feared discrimination lawsuits if a sex bar were allowed.

The 1975 meeting was held in Boston June 25–29, and delegates agreed to work in the 1976 election campaigns for the election of state legislators who would help ratify ERA.

The caucus gave its highest priority to the 1976 campaign for ERA passage and allocated $213,000 for this goal.

NOW's program. The 1973 convention of the National Organization for Women was held in Washington Feb. 18–20. It approved a resolution Feb. 19 asking each chapter to set up a committee to work for a $2.50 an hour federal minimum wage which would cover domestics for the first time, a federalized welfare system which would not require any single parent or guardian of a young child to work, federally aided day care and child development programs, and federally guaranteed full employment.

Other resolutions approved Feb. 19 called for repeal of all laws against prostitution and an end to discrimination based on sexual preference in employment.

Black feminist group formed. Citing the need to "demolish myths" about the role of black women in society, a group announced in New York Aug. 15, 1973 the formation of the National Black Feminist Organization.

New York City Human Rights Commissioner Eleanor Holmes Norton, a founder of the group, said that in recent years of increasing black awareness, women had been expected to suppress their aspirations in deference to black men. Margaret Sloan, another founder, said the new organization should "remind the black liberation movement that there can't be liberation for half a race."

The sponsors said chapters had already been formed in several cities, including Chicago, Cleveland and San Francisco.

Federal Action

Guidelines vs. sex bias. The Labor Department June 9, 1970 issued guidelines prohibiting sex discrimination in employment by government contractors and subcontractors. Elizabeth Duncan Koontz, director of the department's Women's Bureau, announced the guidelines, which applied to companies with government contracts of $50,000 or more or those that employed more than 50 people.

At the same time the White House released a 33-page report by the President's Task Force on Women's Rights and Responsibilities. The guidelines were one of the recommendations in the report, which was completed nearly six months before its release.

The guidelines, to take effect immediately, prohibited sex discrimination in employment opportunities, wages, hours or other job conditions. Advertisements for employes could not express a sex preference, unless sex was "a bona fide occupational qualification." Distinctions between married and unmarried employes were to be applied equally to men and women, and an employer could not discriminate against a woman with young children "unless the same exclusionary policy exists for men." Women could not

be penalized for taking time off to bear children.

The guidelines prohibited seniority based solely on sex and banned "discriminatorily restricting one sex to certain job classifications and departments." In addition, an employer could not discriminate against a woman on the basis of state laws requiring the protection of female employes.

The regulations were to be enforced by the Labor Department's Office of Federal Contract Compliance. Contracts could be withheld from employers who failed to comply.

The task force report was prepared by a 13-member panel headed by Virginia R. Allan, executive vice president of Cahalan Drug Stores Inc. (Wyandotte, Mich.). The report declared, "the United States, as it approaches its 200th anniversary, lags behind other enlightened and indeed some newly emerging countries in the role ascribed to women."

In addition to the new guidelines, the task force recommended establishment of a permanent office of women's rights and responsibilities; a 1970 White House conference on women's rights; and new legislation providing better enforcement of federal bans against sex discrimination, liberalizing Social Security and income tax laws applying to women employes and their husbands and providing child-care assistance for working mothers.

To implement the new ban on sex discrimination by employers with government contracts, the Nixon Administration said July 31 it would require contractors to set goals and timetable to increase employment of women. Labor Secretary James D. Hodgson said in a statement: "The federal government is convinced that the under-utilization in employment throughout the nation constitutes a waste of national resources and talent." He noted that the goals and timetables concept was the method used to curb racial discrimination by government contractors.

(In the first federal suit charging job bias against both blacks and women, the department asked a federal court in East St. Louis, Ill. to enjoin discrimination by the Obear-Nester Glass Co., the Wall Street Journal reported Sept. 9, 1971.)

Hodgson Dec. 2, 1971 ordered federal contractors and subcontractors to take "affirmative action" to end the "under-utilization of women" in all areas of employment. The order required federal contractors to consider the supply of women in the local work force, their skill levels, and the training necessary if skills were lacking, in determining whether under-utilization existed.

Suit vs. LOF Glass. The Justice Department June 20, 1970 filed a suit charging job discrimination against women for the first time under provisions of the Civil Rights Act of 1964. The suit, filed in U.S. District Court in Toledo, Ohio, was against Libbey-Owens-Ford Co. Inc., a major glass manufacturer. Also named in the suit were the AFL-CIO United Glass and Ceramic Workers and its Local 9.

The suit accused the company of hiring women in only one of its five Toledo plants, of assigning them to lower-paying jobs with the least opportunity for advancement and of firing women employes first when layoffs occured. The suit said the company and union had contracts "which establish seniority systems and procedures for promotion, demotion, layoff, recall, and transfer which . . . deprive female employes of an equal opportunity to compete with their male contemporaries for the more desirable, better-paying jobs."

A spokesman for Libbey-Owens-Ford said July 21 that the company was making every effort to comply with the 1964 Civil Rights Act but was hampered by Ohio laws requiring the protection of female employes. The company employed 200 women and 5,200 men in its Toledo plants.

The case had been referred to the Justice Department by the Equal Employment Opportunity Commission (EEOC) in March. A commission spokesman said July 20 that the number of complaints about job bias against women had risen sharply in recent months, "mostly as a result of women's liberation and the publicity they have gotten." The spokesman estimated that as many as 25% of complaints currently received by the commission charged sex discrimination. He said the EEOC received 17,000 complaints in the fiscal year ending June 30, 1969, alleging sex and racial bias and other forms of job discrimination. The Justice Department said it had participated in other sex discrimination cases as a "friend of the court."

Attorney General John N. Mitchell announced Dec. 7 that the suit had been concluded successfully with the filing of a consent decree in U.S. district court in Toledo.

Under the decree, the company agreed to correct certain specific discriminatory practices charged in the suit and undertook what was described as a "continuing obligation not to discriminate on the basis of sex with regard to its future recruitment, hiring and assignment of new employes."

City Stores suit. The Labor Department Nov. 2, 1971 reported winning a suit against City Stores, Inc., a national retail chain charged with paying salesmen and male tailors more than saleswomen and female tailors. The U.S. District Court in Montgomery, Ala. ordered the firm to pay the women back wages plus interest, rejecting claims that selling and altering men's clothing were more difficult than selling and altering women's clothing.

EEOC tightens sex rules. The Equal Employment Opportunity Commission (EEOC) March 27, 1972 issued new and tighter regulations barring sex discrimination in employment practices and compensation. The rules, which did not have the force of law, were meant to single out the practices the agency might contest in court under its newly enacted enforcement powers.

Under the rules, no woman could be denied employment solely because she was pregnant, and employers would have to provide the same leave, seniority and insurance benefits for pregnancy and abortion as for other temporary dis-

Employment by Occupation Group & Sex (Annual Averages)

NUMBER EMPLOYED (thousands)

Male

Year	Total employed	White-collar workers					Blue-collar workers						Service workers			Farmworkers		
		Total	Professional and technical	Managers and administrators ex. farm	Sales workers	Clerical workers	Total	Craft and kindred workers	Operatives Total	Operatives Except transport	Operatives Transport equipment	Nonfarm laborers	Total	Private household workers	Other service workers	Total	Farmers and farm managers	Farm laborers and supervisors
1960	43,904	16,423	4,766	5,968	2,544	3,145	20,420	8,332	8,617	(²)	(²)	3,471	2,844	30	2,814	4,219	2,667	1,552
1961	43,656	16,617	4,952	6,002	2,553	3,110	20,072	8,401	8,401	(²)	(²)	3,270	2,906	44	2,862	4,061	2,578	1,483
1962	44,177	17,008	5,170	6,275	2,435	3,128	20,372	8,445	8,623	(²)	(²)	3,304	2,980	44	2,934	3,817	2,456	1,361
1963	44,657	17,059	5,309	6,180	2,453	3,117	20,956	8,675	8,974	(²)	(²)	3,307	3,095	46	3,051	3,547	2,257	1,290
1964	45,474	17,480	5,435	6,341	2,506	3,198	21,360	8,731	9,237	(²)	(²)	3,392	3,199	46	3,153	3,434	2,181	1,253
1965	46,340	17,746	5,596	6,230	2,641	3,279	22,107	8,947	9,581	(²)	(²)	3,579	3,194	40	3,154	3,295	2,107	1,188
1966	46,919	18,094	5,836	6,238	2,672	3,348	22,514	9,334	9,756	(²)	(²)	3,424	3,319	43	3,276	2,990	1,968	1,022
1967	47,479	18,527	6,183	6,318	2,622	3,406	22,683	9,560	9,706	(²)	(²)	3,417	3,334	33	3,301	2,936	1,872	1,066
1968	48,114	19,117	6,449	6,535	2,724	3,409	22,812	9,696	9,687	(²)	(²)	3,429	3,308	35	3,273	2,878	1,844	1,034
1969	48,818	19,574	6,751	6,726	2,675	3,422	23,263	9,854	9,883	(²)	(²)	3,526	3,257	39	3,218	2,723	1,764	959
1970	48,960	20,054	6,842	6,968	2,763	3,481	23,020	9,826	9,605	(²)	(²)	3,589	3,285	40	3,245	2,601	1,673	928
1971	49,245	20,138	6,737	7,182	2,911	3,308	22,579	9,792	9,015	(²)	(²)	3,772	4,034	37	3,997	2,494	1,580	914
1972	50,630	20,176	6,957	6,621	3,127	3,470	23,800	10,424	9,426	6,351	3,075	3,950	4,128	34	4,094	2,526	1,588	938
1973	51,963	20,705	7,066	7,054	3,175	3,409	24,625	10,826	9,787	6,653	3,134	4,012	4,120	23	4,097	2,513	1,561	952
1974	52,519	21,155	7,346	7,291	3,152	3,366	24,581	10,966	9,590	6,464	3,126	4,026	4,218	27	4,190	2,564	1,545	1,020
1975	51,230	21,134	7,481	7,162	3,137	3,355	23,220	10,472	8,971	5,934	3,037	3,777	4,400	30	4,370	2,476	1,492	985

Female

Year	Total employed	White-collar workers					Blue-collar workers						Service workers			Farmworkers		
		Total	Professional and technical	Managers and administrators ex. farm	Sales workers	Clerical workers	Total	Craft and kindred workers	Operatives Total	Operatives Except transport	Operatives Transport equipment	Nonfarm laborers	Total	Private household workers	Other service workers	Total	Farmers and farm managers	Farm laborers and supervisors
1960	21,874	12,099	2,703	1,099	1,680	6,617	3,637	222	3,333	(²)	(²)	82	5,179	1,943	3,236	957	109	848
1961	22,090	12,272	2,746	1,118	1,680	6,728	3,612	216	3,318	(²)	(²)	77	5,355	1,991	3,364	852	128	724
1962	22,525	12,626	2,860	1,133	1,682	6,951	3,680	223	3,371	(²)	(²)	86	5,403	1,977	3,426	815	131	684
1963	23,105	12,890	2,946	1,113	1,698	7,133	3,819	240	3,490	(²)	(²)	89	5,576	1,995	3,591	817	131	686
1964	23,831	13,381	3,107	1,108	1,730	7,436	3,982	250	3,643	(²)	(²)	88	5,694	1,995	3,699	778	132	646
1965	24,748	14,106	3,276	1,110	1,858	7,862	4,140	269	3,764	(²)	(²)	107	5,742	1,916	3,826	758	131	627
1966	25,976	14,974	3,474	1,167	1,869	8,464	4,436	255	4,073	(²)	(²)	108	5,893	1,861	4,032	676	123	553
1967	26,893	15,705	3,697	1,177	1,904	8,928	4,580	286	4,178	(²)	(²)	117	5,992	1,737	4,255	618	98	520
1968	27,807	16,435	3,877	1,241	1,923	9,394	4,712	319	4,267	(²)	(²)	126	6,072	1,689	4,383	587	82	505
1969	29,084	17,271	4,018	1,261	2,017	9,975	4,974	339	4,489	(²)	(²)	146	6,271	1,592	4,679	569	79	489
1970	29,667	17,943	4,298	1,321	2,091	10,233	4,771	332	4,303	(²)	(²)	136	6,428	1,518	4,909	525	80	445
1971	29,875	18,114	4,334	1,493	2,155	10,132	4,605	387	3,968	(²)	(²)	250	6,642	1,449	5,192	514	86	428
1972	31,072	18,915	4,502	1,410	2,226	10,777	4,776	386	4,123	3,989	134	267	6,838	1,403	5,435	543	100	443
1973	32,446	19,681	4,711	1,590	2,240	11,140	5,244	463	4,482	4,319	163	299	7,008	1,330	5,678	514	103	411
1974	33,417	20,583	4,992	1,650	2,265	11,676	5,195	511	4,331	4,164	167	354	7,156	1,201	5,955	484	98	385
1975	33,553	21,092	5,267	1,729	2,323	11,773	4,742	501	3,885	3,703	182	357	7,258	1,141	6,116	460	102	358

²Not available

From "Employment and Training Report of the President," submitted by President Ford to Congress June 1976

abilities. All fringe benefits would be equalized, with no special distinctions for heads of household, and no benefits limited to families of only male employes.

Federal employment laws, the EEOC ruled, would prevail over conflicting state laws, including any laws setting different working conditions or compensation on a sexual basis.

EEOC wins GM decree. The EEOC announced June 27, 1972 that it had filed in U.S. district court in St. Louis a suit charging the General Motors Corp. (GM) with discrimination against women at its St. Louis assembly plant.

The EEOC said GM job requirements, including a 130-pound weight minimum had the effect of excluding women. Once hired, the suit charged women faced discriminatory promotion practices.

The court action ended with the filing of a consent decree under which the company agreed to try to fill at least 20% of all new hourly rate production and assembly jobs with women at its St. Louis assembly plant, it was reported Jan. 17, 1973.

The settlement was the first reached under new EEOC court case initiation powers. GM agreed to make affirmative recruitment efforts to place women in the jobs, after laid-off employes were rehired.

EEOC sees NBC bias. The Equal Employment Opportunity Commission found that WRC-TV and WRC AM-FM, the National Broadcasting Company (NBC)-owned broadcast stations in Washington, had discriminated against women in hiring and promotion (reported Jan. 31, 1973).

EEOC upheld 27 women employes in their charge that before 1971, NBC's "word of mouth method of recruiting and/or announcing vacancies was inadequate" in informing all potential employes about new jobs as required by the 1964 Civil Rights Act. In addition, the commission ruled, the company's maternity leave and training policies discriminated against women. EEOC said it also found reasonable cause to believe the stations discriminated against blacks.

In reply, NBC claimed it employed larger proportions of women and blacks in important positions than most broadcast stations in the country. The company said the EEOC had held no hearings, heard no witnesses and allowed no cross-examination.

Federal Employment

Bias in jobs banned. The Civil Service Commission ruled May 12, 1971 that "men only" and "women only" designations must be eliminated for almost all federal jobs. Sex specifications would be permitted only if the job required that the employes sleep in common quarters or in certain institutional jobs, such as matron in a women's prison.

According to the ruling, women could no longer be excluded automatically from jobs requiring physical strength or from law enforcement jobs requiring the carrying of weapons. A spokesman for the commission said a number of complaints had been received from women turned down for federal police jobs.

(Four women were among 81 graduates of the Treasury Department's training school for sky marshals April 8. The four were the first women to be trained for the special security force created in September 1970 to guard against airliner hijackings.)

Few women in top U.S. jobs. The Democratic National Committee, in a study published May 27, 1971, said that the percentage of women in policy-level positions in the federal government had increased by only .2% in the last three years. The study said there were currently 3,854 policy-level jobs, those in the top two Civil Service grades and the major appointive jobs, and that women held 63 (1.6%) of these positions. In 1968, the study said, women held 1.4% of the top federal positions.

In a Washington news conference, Mary Lou Burg, vice chairmen of the

Employment & Unemployment by Sex & Age

[Thousands of persons 16 years of age and over; monthly data seasonally adjusted]

Year or month	Employment Total	Males Total	Males 16–19 years	Males 20 years and over	Females Total	Females 16–19 years	Females 20 years and over	Unemployment Total	Males Total	Males 16–19 years	Males 20 years and over	Females Total	Females 16–19 years	Females 20 years and over
1947	57,039	40,994	2,218	38,776	16,045	1,691	14,354	2,311	1,692	270	1,422	619	144	475
1948	58,344	41,726	2,345	39,382	16,618	1,683	14,937	2,276	1,559	255	1,305	717	152	564
1949	57,649	40,926	2,124	38,803	16,723	1,588	15,137	3,637	2,572	352	2,219	1,065	223	841
1950	58,920	41,580	2,186	39,394	17,340	1,517	15,824	3,288	2,239	318	1,922	1,049	195	854
1951	59,962	41,780	2,156	39,626	18,182	1,611	16,570	2,055	1,221	191	1,029	834	145	689
1952	60,254	41,684	2,106	39,578	18,570	1,612	16,958	1,883	1,185	205	980	698	140	559
1953 [1]	61,181	42,431	2,135	40,296	18,750	1,584	17,164	1,834	1,202	184	1,019	632	123	510
1954	60,110	41,620	1,985	39,634	18,490	1,490	17,000	3,532	2,344	310	2,035	1,188	191	997
1955	62,171	42,621	2,095	40,526	19,550	1,548	18,002	2,852	1,854	274	1,580	998	176	823
1956	63,802	43,380	2,164	41,216	20,422	1,654	18,767	2,750	1,711	269	1,442	1,039	209	832
1957	64,071	43,357	2,117	41,239	20,714	1,663	19,052	2,859	1,841	299	1,541	1,018	197	821
1958	63,036	42,423	2,012	40,411	20,613	1,570	19,043	4,602	3,098	416	2,681	1,504	262	1,242
1959	64,630	43,466	2,198	41,267	21,164	1,640	19,524	3,740	2,420	398	2,022	1,320	256	1,063
1960 [1]	65,778	43,904	2,360	41,543	21,874	1,769	20,105	3,852	2,486	425	2,060	1,366	286	1,080
1961	65,746	43,656	2,314	41,342	22,090	1,793	20,296	4,714	2,997	479	2,518	1,717	349	1,368
1962 [1]	66,702	44,177	2,362	41,815	22,525	1,833	20,693	3,911	2,423	407	2,016	1,488	313	1,175
1963	67,762	44,657	2,406	42,251	23,105	1,849	21,257	4,070	2,472	500	1,971	1,598	383	1,216
1964	69,305	45,474	2,587	42,886	23,831	1,929	21,903	3,786	2,205	487	1,718	1,581	386	1,195
1965	71,088	46,340	2,918	43,422	24,748	2,118	22,630	3,366	1,914	479	1,435	1,452	395	1,056
1966	72,895	46,919	3,252	43,668	25,976	2,469	23,510	2,875	1,551	432	1,120	1,324	404	921
1967	74,372	47,479	3,186	44,293	26,893	2,497	24,397	2,975	1,508	448	1,060	1,468	391	1,078
1968	75,920	48,114	3,255	44,859	27,807	2,525	25,281	2,817	1,419	427	993	1,397	412	985
1969	77,902	48,818	3,430	45,388	29,084	2,686	26,397	2,832	1,403	441	963	1,429	412	1,016
1970	78,627	48,960	3,407	45,553	29,667	2,734	26,933	4,088	2,235	599	1,636	1,853	506	1,347
1971	79,120	49,245	3,470	45,775	29,875	2,725	27,149	4,993	2,776	691	2,086	2,217	567	1,650
1972 [1]	81,702	50,630	3,750	46,880	31,072	2,972	28,100	4,840	2,635	707	1,928	2,205	595	1,610
1973 [1]	84,409	51,963	4,017	47,946	32,446	3,219	29,228	4,304	2,240	647	1,594	2,064	579	1,485
1974	85,936	52,519	4,074	48,445	33,417	3,329	30,088	5,076	2,668	749	1,918	2,408	660	1,748
1975	84,783	51,230	3,803	47,427	33,553	3,243	30,310	7,830	4,385	957	3,428	3,445	795	2,649
1974:														
Jan	85,865	52,881	4,207	48,674	32,984	3,357	29,627	4,536	2,340	677	1,663	2,196	631	1,565
Feb	85,948	52,755	4,164	48,591	33,193	3,376	29,817	4,631	2,441	694	1,747	2,190	614	1,576
Mar	86,033	52,671	4,154	48,517	33,362	3,373	29,989	4,516	2,344	694	1,650	2,172	617	1,555
Apr	85,990	52,573	4,116	48,457	33,417	3,343	30,074	4,482	2,385	681	1,704	2,097	546	1,551
May	86,154	52,760	4,135	48,625	33,394	3,290	30,104	4,599	2,391	710	1,681	2,208	632	1,576
June	86,167	52,606	4,075	48,531	33,561	3,344	30,217	4,827	2,522	767	1,755	2,305	673	1,632
July	86,292	52,464	4,032	48,432	33,828	3,247	30,581	5,007	2,570	746	1,824	2,437	732	1,705
Aug	86,170	52,492	4,021	48,471	33,678	3,314	30,364	4,987	2,655	705	1,950	2,332	593	1,739
Sept	86,155	52,542	4,065	48,477	33,613	3,408	30,205	5,419	2,833	824	2,009	2,586	693	1,893
Oct	86,012	52,481	4,056	48,425	33,531	3,368	30,163	5,584	3,044	803	2,241	2,540	730	1,810
Nov	85,549	52,237	3,995	48,242	33,312	3,319	29,993	6,177	3,283	844	2,439	2,894	731	2,163
Dec	85,053	51,815	3,948	47,867	33,238	3,246	29,992	6,589	3,558	852	2,706	3,031	733	2,298
1975:														
Jan	84,666	51,387	3,849	47,538	33,279	3,295	29,984	7,297	3,901	942	2,959	3,396	823	2,573
Feb	84,163	51,151	3,812	47,339	33,012	3,220	29,792	7,360	4,048	944	3,104	3,312	753	2,559
Mar	84,110	50,952	3,794	47,158	33,158	3,199	29,959	7,770	4,261	952	3,309	3,509	809	2,700
Apr	84,313	51,046	3,775	47,271	33,267	3,224	30,043	7,941	4,412	982	3,430	3,529	737	2,792
May	84,519	51,195	3,859	47,336	33,324	3,247	30,077	8,254	4,637	970	3,667	3,613	842	2,771
June	84,498	50,978	3,728	47,250	33,520	3,254	30,266	8,071	4,608	1,057	3,551	3,463	765	2,698
July	84,967	51,280	3,799	47,481	33,687	3,234	30,453	8,096	4,657	1,015	3,642	3,439	795	2,644
Aug	85,288	51,446	3,791	47,655	33,842	3,235	30,607	7,924	4,472	997	3,475	3,452	832	2,620
Sept	85,158	51,334	3,818	47,516	33,824	3,273	30,551	7,970	4,604	912	3,692	3,366	796	2,570
Oct	85,151	51,300	3,787	47,513	33,851	3,230	30,621	8,062	4,645	933	3,712	3,417	802	2,615
Nov	85,178	51,325	3,804	47,521	33,853	3,234	30,619	7,939	4,538	883	3,655	3,401	764	2,637
Dec	85,394	51,390	3,804	47,586	34,004	3,249	30,755	7,735	4,246	895	3,351	3,489	829	2,660

[1] Not strictly comparable with other data due to population adjustments

From 1976 "Economic Report of the President," submitted by President Ford to Congress Jan. 26, 1976

Democratic National Committee, said the data indicated that "the Nixon Administration is not keeping up with the dynamic movement toward equal employment opportunity for women."

Mrs. Burg said she was unimpressed by the Administration's contention that 200 women had been appointed to key positions. She said the majority of these appointments were to advisory committees "and there is some question of the impact they have on policy."

Miss Burg said that of the 200 women appointees cited by the Nixon Administration, "62 are on a single committee— the Advisory Committee on the Arts of the John F. Kennedy Center for the Performing Arts." She noted that advisory committee appointments were "part-time, unpaid" positions.

The study showed there were 36 federal agencies, with a total of 1,209 policy-making positions, that employed no women. Among these agencies were the Office of Management and Budget, the Small Business Administration, the Commission on Civil Rights, the Commerce Department, the Office of Science and Technology and the Smithsonian Institution.

Women urged for Supreme Court. The American Bar Association's Committee on Rights of Women urged President Nixon Oct. 8, 1971 to name "a qualified woman" to the Supreme Court. The panel objected to reports that the Administration was "unable to discover a woman of sufficiently distinguished legal background" and said there were many qualified women even though "the institutions of the legal profession . . . have limited the access of women to the profession and restricted their advancement."

Nixon cites women's gains—President Nixon reported April 28, 1972 that the number of women in federal policy making jobs earning over $28,000 had risen from 36 in April 1971 to 105 currently. Over 1,000 additional women held middle management positions earnings $17,-700–$24,200 a year.

In a Washington news conference the same day, Civil Service Commission Vice Chairman Jayne Baker Spain, who helped direct the Administration's recruitment effort among women, said progress had been hindered by the science or mathematics training requirements for 60% of middle and high level federal jobs.

U.S. agencies charged with bias. Charges of sex discrimination in hiring were filed against the Federal Bureau of Investigation (FBI) Aug. 4, 1971. In another case, a charge of State Department bias against a woman foreign service officer was settled in favor of the complainant Aug. 25.

The suit against the FBI, Attorney General John Mitchell and FBI Director J. Edgar Hoover was filed in federal court in Washington by Cynthia Edgar, 24, an attorney on the staff of Rep. Bella Abzug (D, N.Y.). The suit was joined by Sandra Rothenberg Nemser, 28, also a lawyer.

Miss Edgar said at a press conference that FBI agents had told her in April that women need not apply because they "do not command enough respect" and "could not handle combat situations." Her lawyer, Philip Hirschkop, commented that a woman "can tap a phone as well as the next person." The suit was backed by the American Civil Liberties Union.

In the State Department case, Alison Palmer, 39, charged that she had been denied three consecutive posts in 1965 and 1966 as political officer to Tanzania, Uganda and Ethiopia because of her sex. In arguing against her appointment in Ethiopia in 1966, U.S. Ambassador Edward M. Korry had written the State Department that a woman would not receive enough respect to carry out her duties. The statement reportedly coincided with a department policy to exclude women from certain foreign posts "for compelling reasons of foreign policy."

The case was settled in favor of Miss Palmer Aug. 25 by Deputy Undersecretary William B. Macomber Jr., who also admitted "a pattern of discrimination" against women in the foreign service. Acting on the Aug. 19 recom-

Annual Work Experience by Sex: 1950, 1960, 1970, and 1974

(Numbers in thousands. Civilian noninstitutional population 16 years and over in 1974 and 1970, 14 years and over in 1950 and 1960)

Work experience and sex	1974	1970	1960	1950	Percent change, 1950 to 1974
NUMBER WORKED DURING YEAR					
Women..........................	42,841	38,704	30,585	23,350	+83.5
Men............................	58,908	54,919	50,033	45,526	+29.4
Ratio: women/men..............	0.73	0.70	0.61	0.51	(X)
Percent Worked During Year[1]					
Women..........................	53.9	52.5	46.9	41.1	+31.1
Men............................	83.0	84.1	84.5	86.8	-4.4
Ratio: women/men[2]...........	0.65	0.62	0.56	0.47	(X)
NUMBER WORKED 50 TO 52 WEEKS AT FULL-TIME JOBS					
Women..........................	18,311	15,738	11,299	8,592	+113.1
Men	39,211	36,295	31,966	29,783	+31.7
Ratio: women/men	0.47	0.43	0.35	0.29	(X)
Percent Of Workers Who Worked 50 To 52 Weeks At Full-Time Jobs[3]					
Women..........................	42.7	40.7	36.9	36.8	+16.0
Men............................	66.6	66.1	63.9	65.4	+1.8
Ratio: women/men[2]...........	0.64	0.62	0.58	0.56	(X)

X Not applicable.
[1] Percents based on all persons.
[2] Ratios of percents.
[3] Percents based on persons who worked during the year.

Source: U.S. Department of Commerce, Bureau of the Census, Current Population Reports, Series P-50, No. 35, and unpublished data and U.S. Department of Labor, Bureau of Labor Statistics, Special Labor Force Reports, Nos. 141 and 19.

From "A Statistical Portrait of Women in the U.S.," U.S. Department of Commerce, Bureau of the Census, April 1976

mendations of Civil Service hearing examiner Andrew B. Beath, Macomber said women would no longer be excluded for the "compelling reasons" cited in Miss Palmer's case. He said she would be offered "a desirable African assignment" and her record would be amended to note that her career had been adversely affected by discrimination.

Macomber also said he would move on Beath's general recommendations for a comprehensive policy regarding women employes and an increase in the authority of the department's Equal Employment Opportunity office. Macomber said he had appointed two women foreign service officers to deal with women's problems in the department—Mary Olmsted, to be deputy director of personnel, and Gladys Rogers, to be Macomber's special assistant for women's affairs.

FBI to recruit women—L. Patrick Gray, who had become acting director of the FBI after the death of Hoover, announced May 11, 1972 that for the first time in the bureau's 48-year history it would recruit women for positions as special agents.

Gray also said that Barbara Lynn Herwig, his special assistant in the Justice Department's Civil Division, would move with him to the FBI and hold the same position as his aide. Miss Herwig was the first woman to play a major role in the FBI.

HEW bars bias. Health, Education & Welfare (HEW) Secretary Elliott L. Richardson Jan. 14, 1972 issued a report prepared by the department's Woman's Action Program. He pledged to enforce over 100 recommendations for reform of HEW's employment practices and its social programs affecting the role of women.

Richardson ordered top assistants to establish timetables for implementation. Upgrading and counseling services would be provided for female HEW employes, while part time jobs and day care arrangements would be provided for working HEW mothers.

Legislation was recommended to bar sex discrimination in vocational education supported by HEW. Currently, men were given preference in some state-run programs.

NIH sued re panel bias. Organizations representing 30,000 women scientists filed suit in U.S. District Court in Washington March 28, 1972 against Robert Marston, director of the National Institutes of Health (NIH), and HEW Secretary Elliott Richardson on charges of bias against women in appointments to NIH advisory panels controlling $2 billion annually in research and training funds.

Richardson had ordered in September 1971 that one third of all such posts be filled by women. However, according to Sylvia Roberts, attorney for the plaintiffs, the order exempted "technical panels" from the requirement. Roberts said March 28 that the proportion of women on all advisory panels had dropped from 5.4% to 4.2% between 1968 and 1971.

The plaintiffs included the Association for Women in Science, The Association of Women in Psychology, Caucus of Women Biophysicists, Sociologists for Women in Society, Association for Women in Mathematics, National Organization for Women and Women's Equity Action League.

Social Security agency sued. The 200-member Organization for Women of the Social Security Administration filed suit March 14, 1972 in U.S. court in Baltimore charging that "highly qualified women" were "ignored and discounted" by the agency, and that the agency's promotional plan was not being carried out.

The court was asked to order merit promotions for women and require that available jobs be publicized.

Woman a Nixon counselor. Mrs. Anne Armstrong, departing co-chairman of the Republican National Committee, was named Dec. 18, 1972 as a presidential counselor and "a full member" of the

Cabinet. White House Press Secretary Ronald L. Ziegler, who made the announcement, said that while Mrs. Armstrong would be a member of the Cabinet, she would not be in the line of succession to the presidency, which ran through the heads of departments.

Woman named to be HUD secretary. President Ford's appointment of a woman, Carla Anderson Hills, to his Cabinet as secretary of housing and urban development was announced Feb. 13, 1975. Hills, a lawyer, was assistant attorney general in charge of the civil division of the Justice Department. She had been appointed to that post Feb. 12, 1974.

The appointment drew an objection from Sen. William Proxmire (D, Wis.), chairman of the Senate Banking, Housing and Urban Affairs Committee, which would handle confirmation hearings on the nomination. While Mrs. Hills was "able and intelligent," Proxmire said Feb. 13, she had "absolutely no known qualifications for the job" and "this is no time for on-the-job training." Similar criticism came Feb. 13 from representatives of the National Association of Home Builders, the National League of Cities and the U.S. Conference of Mayors.

Ford's press secretary, Ron Nessen, assured reporters Feb. 13 that "sex was not a factor" in the selection and the choice was made because Mrs. Hills was "a highly competent lawyer and an extremely competent administrator."

Expressions of support for the nomination were made Feb. 14 by Sen. Alan Cranston (D, Calif.), Frances Farenthold, chairman of the National Women's Political Caucus, Ruth Clusen, president of the League of Women Voters, and Karen DeCrow, head of the National Organization for Women.

Hills' nomination, made officially Feb. 20, was confirmed by the Senate March 5.

The last woman Cabinet member was Oveta Culp Hobby, secretary of health, education and welfare 1953-55. The only other woman Cabinet member was Frances Perkins, labor secretary 1933-45.

Woman heads AEC. Dr. Dixy Lee Ray became the first woman chairman of the Atomic Energy Commission (AEC) Feb. 6, 1973. She had been confirmed as an AEC commissioner in 1972 and did not require confirmation for promotion to chairman.

Woman heads NLRB. President Ford selected Betty Southerd Murphy Jan. 8, 1975 as a member and chairman of the National Labor Relations Board. She became the first woman member of the NLRB.

Senators pay women less than men. A study published June 16, 1975 by the Capitol Hill chapter of the National Women's Political Caucus disclosed that members of the Senate paid women less than men for doing the same type of work.

Put together by a group of female Congressional employes, the study revealed that 30 of the 100 senators employed no woman making more than $18,000 a year, while every senator employed men earning this amount or more. The median salary for persons being paid more than this amount was $22,627 for women and $28,091 for men.

The report analyzed the January–July 1974 payroll data for 2,300 persons in senatorial employ and found no significant differences in pay practices between Democrats and Republicans. Because payroll data by itself did not show whether variations of experience and length of service were responsible for pay differentials, the report did not ask that Congress amend laws exempting itself from the authority of the Equal Pay Act of 1963 and Title 7 of the Civil Rights Act of 1964.

City & State Governments

N.Y.C. bans sex & age bias. Mayor John V. Lindsay of New York City Aug. 24, 1970 signed executive orders prohibiting discrimination on the basis of sex or age in city employment and in work contracted by the city. Lindsay had signed a law Aug. 10 banning sex discrimination in public places.

Texas bias suit filed. The Department of Justice filed a suit June 4, 1975 in federal district court in Fort Worth, Texas charging Wichita Falls with sex discrimination by failing to hire more women as police officers.

A department press release said the city employed 76 men and three women as police officers and that the suit was asking the court to bar the city from engaging in sex discrimination and to order Wichita Falls officials to establish goals for hiring and promoting women in the police department and to compensate women for alleged injury from unfair employment practices.

Pittsburgh bias case settled. In a consent order signed Feb. 24, 1976, the Pittsburgh Board of Education agreed to pay a total of $100,000 to 313 female janitors as compensation for higher wages paid to men for similar work between July 1973 and June 1975. The order, signed by U.S. District Court Judge Gerald J. Weber, resolved a sex discrimination suit filed by the U.S. Department of Labor. The order bound the school board, which admitted no violation of the law, to pay men and women equal wages for equal work.

Philadelphia police to hire women. In a consent order March 5, 1976, the City of Philadelphia agreed to hire 100 women as police officers by the end of 1976 and to open up to women such formerly all-male positions as sergeant and detective. As part of the agreement, which settled a sex discrimination suit brought against the city Police Department by the U.S. Department of Justice, the city said it would make a two-year study of the female officers' performance on beat patrols and report back in March 1978.

The order, signed by U.S. District Court Judge Charles Weiner, released to the police $4 million in federal Law Enforcement Assistance Administration (LEAA) funds that had been withheld because of sex discrimination in the Police Department.

Policewoman Penelope Brace, who had filed a separate discrimination suit against the department, did not participate in the agreement. Her claims for monetary damages were severed from the other issues in the case by the order. Judge Weiner had consolidated the two suits for trial.

Other terms of the consent order:

■ Changing the job titles of policeman and policewoman to police officer.

■ Allowing the 76 women currently assigned to the Juvenile Aid division to transfer within 90 days to assignments formerly open to men only.

■ Promoting women to newly created positions in formerly all-male ranks if they scored at least as high on promotion tests as the lowest-scoring man promoted in each category.

City & state bias widespread. Rep. Donald M. Fraser (D, Minn.) inserted in the Congressional Record April 28, 1976 excerpts from a book charging that there was widespread sex discrimination in city and state as well as federal government jobs. The book, a project of the Women's Action Alliance, was by Catherine Samuels and was entitled The Forgotten Five Million: Women in Public Employment—A Guide to Eliminating Sex Discrimination. According to Fraser's excerpts:

Female and male employment patterns reflect de facto job segregation. Most jobs in Government have been stereotyped as either "men's jobs" or "women's jobs." Most women work with other women.

In New York City Government, where women are 42% of the total work force, they are 94% of the nurses, 81% of the clericals and 61% of the teachers.

Men, on the other hand, hold all of the laborer and craftsmen jobs, and are 98% of the engineers, 94% of the architects, and 91% of the attorneys . . .

In California State Government, where women are 37.7% of the work force, they represent 87.6% of all clerical jobs compared to 2.3% of crafts, trades, semi-skilled and laborer jobs. Also, women hold 15.3% of administrative positions . . .

Jobs held primarily by women have more limited promotional possibilities than "men's jobs." Job Ladders for Women's jobs are often dead-ended.

In the Boston Assessing Department, where a majority of employees are female, women do not hold the job of Assistant Assessor. Because such a job is a prerequisite for promotion to higher level positions, the absence of women from that position bars them from all policy-making jobs.

In New York, there are virtually no promotional opportunities for females in custodial work. After one year's experience in the title of Custodial Assistant, women can be promoted to Senior Custodial Assistant with a raise of $150. This is the first and last promotional possibility in that job.

However, after two years experience, men can be promoted to Junior Building Custodian with a raise of $900 a year, and then to Senior Building Custodian where they receive $9,750 to $12,650 . . .

Women are almost entirely absent from the top positions in Government. Management and administration have been "men's jobs."

In New Jersey, there are no women holding Commissioner titles (which are appointed by the Governor). Of the 24 Assistant Commissioners, none are women. Of the management and middle management job categories of Commissioner, Assistant Commissioner, Director, Assistant Director, Deputy Director, and Chief, only 14% are women.

In Dallas, only 1 of the City's 35 departments is headed by a woman—the Library.

The average women worker earns less than the average male worker, even in job areas where women predominate (such as education).

In Montgomery County (Maryland), in every occupational group (including Clerical), the median pay grade for women is 1-4 grades lower than the median for men.

In California, the average monthly salary for women is $775 compared to $1,128 for men.

Women participate in fewer training programs than men. Most of the programs for women aim to improve their performance in their present job and not to prepare them for promotion.

In Boston, the only training for office workers organized by a Federal Agency (U.S. Civil Service Commission) aimed to help the secretary "to see her role as an adjunct to the management team." Courses included: "Techniques for Self-Improvement" and "Tips on Grooming and Personal Poise."

On the other hand, men in predominantly male municipal jobs (such as police, fire, paraprofessional engineers) regularly participated in educational programs that lead to bachelor's or technical associate degrees.

In New Jersey and in Boston, Executive Development programs are available only to those already in supervisory and management positions, areas where women are severely underrepresented.

Most governments have differential policies based on sex in pension, maternity, health insurance, and other fringe benefits.

In New York and New Jersey, women pay more than men (making the same salary) into the pension fund and receive back less.

In New York, health insurance (Blue Cross) usually pays full hospital costs for 21 days for surgery or a heart attack, but will only pay a total of $80 for childbirth.

In the Dallas County Clerk's Office, a woman is not allowed to return to work until six months after childbirth; also "concrete evidence" that a child is being cared for is requested before the mother is permitted to return.

State and local governments in this country are dependent upon more than five million women who make up our public work force. Representing 50% of all municipal employees and 43% of all state employees, women make an important contribution to the welfare of their states, cities and towns. In return for their contribution, women are segregated into dead-end jobs, concentrated in the lowest paying job categories, passed over for promotion, denied many of the benefits men enjoy, and even paid less for jobs requiring as much, if not more, skill than comparable jobs for men. Instead of leading the country out of the mire of sex discrimination, governments are a prime offender—and our taxes pay to subsidize discriminatory practices. . . .

However, the plight of these five million women has been largely ignored. It was not until March, 1972, when Title VII of the Civil Rights Act of 1964 was extended to cover state and local governments, that these five million women received the simple legislation protection enjoyed by their counterparts in private employment. Until now, no major efforts had been made to document or analyze the problems. No major (or even minor) thrust has been developed by antidiscrimination agencies to enforce the law. No large-scale educational campaigns have been designed to make publicly employed women aware of their rights or employers of their responsibilities. . . .

Court Decisions

Sex bias in hiring barred. The Supreme Court ruled Jan. 25, 1971 that companies could not deny employment to women with pre-school children unless the same criterion applied to men. In its first sex discrimination ruling on equal hiring provisions of the 1964 Civil Rights Act, the court said the law forbids "one hiring policy for women and another for men."

The case was an appeal by Mrs. Ida Phillips, who had been denied a job by the Martin Marietta Corp. at its Orlando, Fla. plant. Lower courts had dismissed her appeal on the ground that she had not been denied employment only because of sex but because of her sex plus the fact that she was the parent of young children. The case had gained prominence when feminists cited G. Harrold Carswell's support of the "sex plus" argument in opposing Carswell's nomination to the Supreme Court.

The Supreme Court returned the case for further evidence, contending that "the existence of such conflicting family obligations, if demonstrably more relevant to job performance for a woman than for a man, could arguably be a basis for distinction." Justice Thurgood Marshall concurred in the outcome of the case but said sex could only be a job qualification in unusual cases, such as employment of actors and fashion models.

Mrs. Phillips' appeal had been argued by the NAACP Legal Defense Fund Inc. joined by the Justice Department and the Equal Employment Opportunity Commission.

Sex bias barred in help-wanted ads. Judge Edwin J. Martin of Allegheny County (Pa.) Common Pleas Court ruled March 24, 1971 that both of Pittsburgh's daily newspapers must run their classified job advertisements under a single category rather than classifying jobs according to male help wanted and female help wanted.

Martin noted two federal court precedents in his ruling, but he said it was the first time a state court had been required to rule on the issue. A spokesman for the Pittsburgh chapter of National Organization for Women (NOW), which had filed the original complaint, said it was a "landmark case." She noted that some cities had local ordinances requiring that help wanted ads not be segregated.

Pittsburgh ordinance valid—The Supreme Court June 21, 1973 upheld a Pittsburgh ordinance barring newspapers from listing help-wanted ads according to sex.

The 5–4 majority held that employment ads were "commercial speech" that fell outside 1st Amendment guarantees of freedom of the press.

Justice Potter Stewart strongly dissented from the majority findings: "So far as I know this is the first case . . . that permits a government agency to enter a composing room of a newspaper and dictate to the publisher the layout and makeup of the newspaper's pages. This is the first such case, but I fear it may not be the last. The camel's nose is in the tent."

State job laws voided. The U.S. Court of Appeals for the 9th Circuit ruled in San Francisco June 1, 1971 that California laws permitting sex discrimination in employment violated provisions of the 1964 Civil Rights Act. The court said the federal act invalidated sections of the state labor code, which limited female working hours and forbade employment of women on jobs requiring the lifting of heavy weights.

The ruling upheld a lower court ruling in a case brought by Mrs. Leah Rosenfeld, who had been refused a job by the Southern Pacific Co. The appellate court endorsed Federal Equal Employment Opportunity Commission guidelines that persons should be considered for jobs "on the basis of individual capacity and not on the basis of any characteristics generally attributed to a group."

Similar provisions of an Ohio employment law had been declared invalid in March by a federal district court judge in Dayton, according to a New York Times report March 28. The Ohio law—challenged in suits against two divisions of the General Motors Corp., two union locals and the Ohio Department of Industrial Relations—forbade the employment of women on jobs requiring "frequent or repeated lifting of weights over 25 pounds" and limited a woman's working days and hours per day.

The plaintiffs in the suit said the law denied them opportunities available to males, such as overtime work and better paying jobs. U.S. District Court Judge Carl A. Weinman based his ruling on the 1964 Civil Rights Act.

General Electric Co. filed suit March ·26 in federal court in Cincinnati asking

Years of School Completed By Employed Persons 25 to 64 Years Old by Major Occupation Group and Sex: March 1974

Major occupation	Years of school completed									
	Elementary, 8 years or less		High school, 1 to 3 years		High school, 4 years		College, 1 to 3 years		College, 4 years or more	
	Male	Female	Male	Female	Male	Female	Male	Female	Male	Female
Total employed..........thousands..	6,280	2,630	5,823	3,640	14,368	10,908	5,531	3,187	7,778	3,549
Percent.........................	100.0	100.0	100.0	100.0	100.0	100.0	100.0	100.0	100.0	100.0
Professional, technical, and kindred workers................	0.9	1.0	1.9	1.6	6.3	7.0	17.1	22.5	54.1	71.4
Managers and administrators, except farm...................	5.5	2.9	8.8	5.2	15.5	6.3	24.2	7.7	26.3	6.8
Sales workers...................	1.3	3.7	3.4	7.4	5.9	7.8	10.6	5.0	8.3	3.0
Clerical and kindred workers.....	2.9	6.5	4.6	19.0	8.3	45.4	10.0	46.8	3.1	13.5
Craft and kindred workers........	25.4	2.7	31.8	3.0	29.4	1.9	18.7	1.2	3.9	0.5
Operatives, including transport...	29.7	35.1	28.7	27.9	19.3	11.5	8.9	4.4	1.1	1.3
Laborers, except farm............	13.4	1.4	8.3	1.5	4.2	0.7	2.2	0.7	0.4	-
Farm workers....................	10.4	4.0	4.2	1.3	3.8	1.3	1.9	0.7	1.2	0.4
Service workers.................	10.6	42.9	8.5	33.0	7.3	18.1	6.4	11.0	1.6	3.1

- Represents zero.

Source: U.S. Department of Commerce, Bureau of the Census, Current Population Reports, Series P-20, No. 274.

From "A Statistical Portrait of Women in the U.S.," U.S. Department of Commerce. Bureau of the Census. April 1976 for a clarification of conflicts in state and federal employment laws regarding women. A state appeals court in Columbus had ruled March 9 that the Ohio law regulating women employes was valid and that if it was discriminatory, "it is a discrimination in favor of female employes." Other sections of the Ohio law required suitable seats and lunchtime breaks to be provided for female employes.

A federal judge had ruled in Springfield, Ill. Aug. 20, 1970 that a 61-year Illinois law discriminated against women. The statute, similar to laws in other states which were designed to protect women employes, prohibited women from working more than eight hours a day at most jobs.

Forced early retirement invalid. The Supreme Court Nov. 9, 1971 upheld a circuit court decision ruling that company pensions requiring women to retire earlier than men were in violation of federal civil rights law. The Supreme Court's ruling applied only in Indiana, Illinois and Wisconsin, the jurisdictional territory of the 7th Circuit Court. That court had said that requiring women to retire at 62 while men would work to 65 was "tantamount to discharge" on an unfair basis of sex discrimination.

Airline stewardesses. The Supreme Court Nov. 9, 1971 let stand a decision that it was a violation of the 1964 Civil Rights Law for domestic airlines to impose a "women only" qualification for stewardess positions.

U.S. Judge Aubrey E. Robinson Jr. ruled in Washington Nov. 13, 1973 that Northwest Airlines was guilty of "willful violation" of federal discrimination laws because it favored male pursers over female stewardesses in hiring practices, pay, promotions and working conditions. It was estimated that retroactive pay increases of up to $250 a month would be required under the ruling.

Robinson said despite the fact that the jobs of purser and stewardess required "equal skill, effort and responsibility," the airline had consistently discriminated against the stewardesses, particularly on basic pay scales and work rules.

State liability. The Supreme Court ruled unanimously June 28, 1976 that states found to have violated federal bans on discrimination in employment could be held liable in court for compensatory damages (as well as court costs to the plaintiffs in bringing the discrimination suit). The decision came on a suit in which past and present male employes of the state of Connecticut contended—and the trial court agreed—that the state's retirement system was biased against them. They also claimed that female employes received certain benefits not given to men.

Academic Discrimination

University bias reported. A survey by the American Association of University Women, released Nov. 23, 1970, indicated that women did not have equal status with men in the academic world. Questionnaires were sent to 750 colleges in January, and the report was compiled from the responses of 454 of the institutions.

Dr. Mabelle G. McCullough, assistant dean of students at the University of Minnesota who headed the committee that made the survey, said there were "clear indications that there are discriminations" against women in the practices if not the policies of universities.

The summary of the survey said 90% of the schools said their faculty promotional policies were the same for both sexes; however the mean number of women department heads in all schools was less than three, and 34 coeducational schools had no women department heads. Women who chaired departments were mostly in the fields of home economics, physical education, languages, nursing and education.

The report said women made up 22% of the faculty in all ranks in the nation's

Median Annual Salary of Scientists and Engineers Employed Full Time by Field and Sex: 1974

Field	Median annual salary		Ratio: women/men
	Women	Men	
Computer specialists..........	$16,300	$18,600	0.88
Engineers.....................	15,600	19,500	0.80
Mathematical specialists......	15,600	20,000	0.78
Life scientists...............	13,500	18,100	0.75
Physical scientists...........	15,000	20,000	0.75
Environmental scientists......	14,400	20,100	0.72
Psychologists.................	17,200	19,900	0.86
Social scientists.............	16,100	20,900	0.77

Note: The determination of the field of science or engineering was based on a combination of education, employment and self-identification.

Source: National Science Foundation, Science Resources Studies Highlights, "National Sample of Scientists and Engineers: Median Annual Salaries, 1974," (NSF 75-332).

From "A Statistical Portrait of Women in the U.S." U.S. Department of Commerce, Bureau of the Census, April 1976 colleges and universities, but that the "percentage of women decreases . . . as rank increases, with less than 9% holding the rank of full professor." The report said 21% of the schools surveyed had no women trustees.

Prof. Pauli Murray of Brandeis University, in a 1971 Valparaiso University Law Review article reprinted in the Congressional Record Feb. 25, 1972, provided additional statistics on discrimination against women members of university faculties:

A nationwide study of degree-granting institutions conducted by NEA in 1966 found that women represented 18.4% of the full-time faculty, distributed as follows: 32.5% of instructors, 19.4% of assistant professors, 15.1% of associate professors and 8.7% of full professors. These figures, however, do not reveal the complete picture. Women comprise 40% of the facilities in the teachers colleges and 10% or less in the prestigious private institutions and large state universities. A report on the distribution of women faculty at ten high endowment institutions of higher education in 1960 showed that the proportion of women faculty ranged downward from 9.8% of instructors to 2.6% of full professors. Similarly, in ten high enrollment institutions, women comprised 20.4% of all instructors, 12.7% of all assistant professors, 10.1% of all associate professors and 4.3% of all professors.

Other testimony noted that more than half of all academic women are concentrated in the fields of English, fine arts, health, education and physical education; that they are more likely to teach beginning college students—freshmen and sophomores—than upperclassmen or graduate students, and that they tend to cluster in the lower non-tenured ranks. While it was suggested that "concentration in the untenured ranks may be attributed to fewer advanced degrees among women, to their youth, to the recency of appointment, or to the fact that it is not always easy to find a woman in the proper field," other testimony stressed discriminatory hiring patterns and policies of promotion as significant factors in the lower percentage and low status of women on college facilities. It was also charged that women are losing ground to men even in faculty positions at women's colleges, which traditionally have provided the best teaching opportunities for women.

Law schools, particularly, have made a poor showing in hiring women as faculty. The enrollment of women in law school has almost tripled from 1962 to 1969, when women numbered 5,000, or 6.9% of the 72,000 students enrolled in law school. The White study showed that in 1966, of 2,355 teaching faculty members in 134 accredited law schools, only 51 women were full-time teaching faculty members in 38 law schools—slightly over 2%. No appreciable change has occurred since 1966. The 1969–70 Directory of Law Teachers lists 53 women full-time faculty in 45 of a total of 144 accredited law schools.

The pattern of inequality continues in the area of academic salaries. A 1965–66 NEA survey found that the median annual salary of female faculty members was 16.6% lower than the median salary of men: $7,732 compared with $9,275. In every faculty rank women earned less than their male counterparts. The median salary for women full professors was $11,649 compared with $12,678 for male full professors. Differentials ranged from 6% among instructors to 8.8% among full professors. Dr. Muirhead concluded from these and other facts that even taking into account such factors as low expectations, lack of day care centers, or institutional practices, "the inequities are so pervasive that direct discrimination must be considered as paying a share, particularly in salaries, hiring, and promotions, especially to tenured positions."

Prejudice against hiring academic women is manifested in departmental practices as well as in the attitudes of hiring officials. The use of the informal grapevine to fill job openings almost automatically excludes women. For example, [t]he cliche opening, "Do you know a good man for the job", results in continuous but largely unconscious discrimination against women. Most of the men who use this phrase would deny vigorously that they are discriminating and would not also consider a "good woman," but the "good man" is an effective subconscious roadblock because the image we all tend to carry in our minds of a scholar is a masculine one.

Graduate faculties "receive regular requests for graduate students with all but their PhDs completed, man preferred." Professional organizations accept "male" openings. Dr. Lawrence A. Simpson discovered in his study of attitudes of hiring agents—deans, departmental chairmen and faculty—that while a statistically significant number of females were preferred over less qualified males, when men and women were equally qualified, hiring officials strongly favored the selection of males for faculty appointments. "Women should recognize," he concluded, "well in advance of their adventure into the academic marketplace, that they typically may not be selected on an equal basis with men. Prospective academic women must recognize that they should, in effect, be more highly qualified than their male competitors for higher education positions."

University of Michigan accord. A deadline was reached Nov. 5, 1970 in a dispute between the Health, Education and Welfare Department (HEW) and the University of Michigan when the university failed to produce proposals to remedy its hiring policies, which HEW contended discriminated against women. (Agreement was reached early in 1971.)

A Washington spokesman said Michigan was one of a dozen colleges and universities where HEW had found sex discrimination and had begun blocking approval of new federal contracts through the department's contract compliance division.

The Michigan contract freeze resulted from an Oct. 6 HEW staff report of discrimination.

Owen P. Kiely, HEW's director of contract compliance, said Jan. 19, 1971 that the government had negotiated an "historic" plan to end sex discrimination in employment at the University of Michigan. Kiely said the university had agreed to equalize salaries and job opportunities and to increase participation of women on employment committees. Kiely said HEW was investigating sex bias complaints against 29 other colleges and universities.

CUNY charges filed. A group of women on the City University of New York (CUNY) faculty announced June 7, 1972 that 700 woman faculty members had filed class complaints with the EEOC and the Department of Health, Education & Welfare charging discrimination in hiring, promotion, tenure, maternity leave and other areas. Some 5,000 of the university's 14,000 faculty members were women.

Academic society bias cited. The 85,000-member Phi Delta Kappa, the world's largest professional education society, suspended the Harvard University Graduate Education School chapter for allowing women to join (reported March 18, 1973). The Cornell University chapter had also been suspended, and the Rutgers University chapter faced suspension for the same reason.

. **Affirmative action program found unfair.** U.S. District Judge D. Dortch Warriner voided an affirmative action program of Virginia Commonwealth University, on the ground that it gave unfair preference to female job applicants. The May 28, 1976 ruling involved a suit by Dr. James A. Cramer, who said that VCU's department of sociology had considered only female applicants for two job vacancies. Cramer said that he had presented qualifications "equal or better than" those of female applicants.

Warriner's ruling barred the school from implementing an affirmative action program that would discriminate against either sex, and from setting employment quotas based on sex. Warriner said that the "cosmetic remedies" embodied in VCU's hiring plan did not get at the "root cause" of the disparity in numbers of male and female employes. He identified this as "a paucity of available females and minority applicants whose credentials are superior to those of the male applicants for similar employment."

Armed Forces

All branches of the armed forces took steps to open wider opportunities for the employment of women in the uniformed services during the first half of the 1970s.

Army to double WAC force. The director of the Women's Army Corps (WAC) said Aug. 7, 1972 that the Army planned to double the size of the WAC force by 1978 and to give it almost any type of assignment except combat.

Brig. Gen. Mildred C. Bailey, WAC director, said that the Army's intention to use more women in more roles was a move to ease the problems in achieving an all-volunteer Army by mid-1973.

Gen. Bailey told newsmen that the 13,320-WAC force would be increased to 15,900 by June 1973. By June 1978, it would reach 24,000. During World War II the corps had 100,000 members.

WACs were currently allowed to fill

only 139 of the 484 Army assignments open to men. Under the new program only 48 would be forbidden to them.

(Warrant Officer Jennie A. Vallance, the first woman graduate of the U.S. Army's Helicopter Flight School, announced June 29, 1976 that she was resigning from the Army because of sex discrimination. The pilot, assigned to a medical detachment, had been refused a job with the combat cavalry unit in which her husband flew.)

Women to see ship duty. Adm. Elmo R. Zumwalt Jr., chief of naval operations, said Aug. 8, 1972 that women in the Navy would soon be able to get assignments for general sea duty.

Zumwalt's plan to open all Navy jobs to women was disclosed in a four-page message to all ships and stations. Zumwalt said he believed the Navy "may very well have authority to utilize officer and enlisted women on board ships" in the "near future." At a news conference in Washington, Zumwalt linked such a time to ratification of the equal rights amendment.

Currently, Navy women enlistees had been allowed on board only hospital and transport ships as nurses and doctors.

Zumwalt said "the imminence of an all-volunteer force has heightened the importance of women as a vital personnel resource."

Zumwalt ordered the Navy to accept application from women officers who wanted to serve as chaplains or civil engineers, open "paths of progression to flag rank within the technical, managerial spectrum" in "essentially the same manner" as for men, assign women to "the full spectrum of challenging billets," or posts, and consider women for selection to the joint war colleges of the armed forces.

■ Transportation Secretary John A. Volpe announced Oct. 6 that women would be admitted to the Coast Guard officer candidate program in 1973 for the first time since World War II. Women would need essentially the same qualifications as men, and would become commissioned ensigns on completion of their training.

Women to be Navy pilots—The Navy announced Jan. 10, 1973 that eight women had been chosen to take naval pilot training at Pensacola, Fla. On graduation from their 18-month courses they would be the first women pilots in the Navy. Federal law prohibited combat duty for women. Although women had ferried aircraft during World War II, they had not flown in combat.

Air Force opens more jobs to women. Revising its policy to coincide with the other armed services, the Air Force said Nov. 22, 1972 that it would allow women to hold virtually any noncombatant job.

The policy change was announced by Brig. Gen. Jeanne Holm, director of Women in the Air Force (WAFs). Gen. Holm said women would not be allowed to become pilots because they would then be required to see combat duty.

Gen. Holm said the Air Force planned to more than triple the number of WAF's in the next five years from 14,200 to 44,700.

(The Air Force announced Jan. 22, 1973 that Holm, one of five women generals in the U.S. armed forces, was being promoted to major general. This made her the highest ranking woman in the services.)

Army women get rifle training. The Army said March 24, 1975 that all women joining the Army after June 30 would be required to become qualified with the M-16 rifle. Although the Army would continue to preclude women from assignments to units having direct combat missions, a spokesman said, it nonetheless believed they should be trained to help defend their supporting outfits when stationed overseas.

The Air Force had announced Aug. 11 that it had put a woman in compromising men as well as women. An Air Force spokesman said it was the first time "in any of the U.S. armed forces" that a woman had been assigned to head a mixed unit. The Air Force said Col. Norma E. Brown, 46, had taken command of the 6970th Air Base-Group at Fort Meade,

Md. The 2,000 man unit included 14 women.

AF waives pregnancy rule. The Air Force, reversing a 1971 decision, said Dec. 1, 1972 that it had waived its pregnancy rule to allow an Air Force nurse who had given birth to a baby girl out of wedlock to remain in the service.

The announcement was made five weeks after the Supreme Court said it would hear the case of Capt. Susan B. Struck, 28. Capt. Struck was challenging her dismissal from active duty on the ground that military laws providing for the discharge of pregnant servicewomen were unconstitutional.

Struck was the first Air Force officer in history to give birth while on active duty. The 9th U.S. Circuit Court of Appeals Nov. 15, 1971 had rejected her petition that she be allowed to remain in the service. Denying her plea, the court said Struck could be discharged because of "a compelling public interest in not having pregnant female soldiers in the military establishment."

Struck had given birth to a daughter out of wedlock in December 1970.

Pregnant military can stay. The Pentagon said July 7, 1975 that pregnant members of the military forces would automatically be allowed to remain in the service instead of having to get special permission to stay.

Under the new rules, pregnant women would have the choice of remaining in the service, applying for a discharge or taking a "convalescent leave." Each situation was to be decided "on a case-by-case basis," a Pentagon spokesman said.

The Washington Post July 8 quoted from letters written by a pregnant unmarried Wave at a naval air station in Maryland to Rep. Gilbert Gude (R, Md.) which it said had helped bring about the change in policy. In one letter she said that "in order for me to give my child the kind of life he has a right to, I feel that I should not only continue my service tour but advance and specialize as quickly and efficiently as is possible." In another she declared: "My current marital situation does not constitute any more of a burden on the service than a divorced serviceman having custody of his children or a widower facing the recent loss of his wife."

National Guard to get women. The New Jersey Department of Defense said Feb. 10, 1973 that it would admit women into four of its National Guard units in a test of plans to sexually integrate all New Jersey guard units. The units were transportation, administration, public information and band companies.

Equal benefits for women. The Supreme Court May 14, 1973 ruled, 8–1, that female members of the armed services were entitled to the same dependency benefits for their husbands as were servicemen for their dependent wives. Justice William H. Rehnquist dissented.

The court struck down a law dating from World War II requiring servicewomen to prove their spouses were dependent on them. There was no equivalent requirement for men.

The court majority stopped short of deciding the critical issue of whether discrimination based on sex was Constitutionally offensive. That vote was 4–4.

Justice Lewis F. Powell Jr. said the court should allow the states to make the ultimate decision whether sex discrimination, like racism, was inherently suspect. This was being done as the states considered the equal rights amendment, he said.

The ruling involved Air Force Lt. Sharron Frontiero, whose husband was a full-time student at a college near the base at which she was stationed.

■ The court June 4 affirmed a ruling upholding the Navy's right to discharge a Wave lieutenant who had been commissioned for 13 years but was not on a promotion list. She charged discrimination, although equivalent discharge provisions existed for male naval officers.

■ In a decision announced Jan. 15, 1975, the court, by a 5–4 vote, reversed a lower federal court ruling that the Navy's discharge policy favoring women over men was unconstitutional. At issue was a

Defense Department regulation guaranteeing female officers 13 years of commissioned service, but requiring involuntary discharge of male officers after nine years if they were twice passed over for promotions.

The majority held that the needs of a combat-ready service and the Navy's desire to compensate women for past discrimination justified a mustering-out policy favorable to women.

Service academies to admit women. Under legislation signed by President Ford Oct. 8, 1975 (it was passed by the House Sept. 24, 1975 and the Senate Sept. 28), the nation's three military academies—at West Point (Army), Annapolis (Navy) and Colorado Springs (Air Force)—began to admit women appointees in June 1976.

Sen. Jacob K. Javits (R, N.Y.) had nominated Barbara Jo Brimmer to the U.S. Naval Academy at Annapolis in February 1972. Navy Secretary John H. Chafee rejected the nomination later the same month although, as Javits told the Senate March 28, Chafee "was opening Naval ROTC to women for the first time." Javits had said in his press conference announcing Brimmer's nomination:

First, I wish to emphasize that the step I am taking today is not designed to compel the Navy to use women officers in any Naval career to which women are now not already assigned.

It may well be that the Navy *ought* to expand the scope of permissible activity for women officers—I suspect that that is the case. But that is not what *this* nomination seeks to accomplish.

At this point, I seek only to have the Academy conform to the Navy itself. Some 3.6 percent of Naval Officers are women. Shouldn't a similar percentage of Annapolis entering class and graduates also be women? Shouldn't there be at least *one*?

There are now women Naval officers serving in a broad range of Naval careers. I have examined the recruiting literature which the Navy uses, no doubt at considerable expense to itself, to recruit women Naval officers. The colorful brochures published by the Navy tell the potential women recruit "side by side with them (men) in *every kind of Naval activity ashore*, we do our part to see that these goals (the Navy's goals) are achieved. *Our assignments cover the widest possible range of interests.*"

What are these assignments? The Navy's brochure tells the prospective woman recruit that she may work in meteorology, electronic data processing, purchasing, expediting material and equipment from private industry for Navy use, as an instructor in one of the Navy's specialized schools, as an information and education officer, in the field of office administration, as a member of the Medical Service Corps, as a public affairs officers, as a personnel officer, and in innumerable other professional capacities now open to both men and women officers, and for which the Navy is *now actively recruiting women to seek careers as Naval officers.*

That is what the Navy wants women officers for. Now if one examines the Departments and majors in the Academy catalog, it is easy to see how very appropriate Academy training would be for a woman who could be outstanding in a career—for which the Navy is already seeking women officer recruits.

For example, the Navy seeks women officers to work in meteorology; and the Academy offers a whole Department of Environmental Sciences.

The Navy seeks women officers to work in electronic data processing, and the Academy offers a whole Department of Computer Science.

The Navy seeks women to serve in such office-oriented fields as office administration, personnel, and public affairs, and the Academy offers a major in general management.

The Academy offers a major in Naval Achitecture—hardly a career for which men alone can qualify (certainly the many highly-qualified women architects already practicing their profession in this country could testify to that).

None of these specialties is limited to "general line" combat officers, and thus women should be permitted to prepare for these careers as they are taught at the Naval Academy.

Indeed, the Navy's own recruiting brochure includes a full-page picture of one Lieutenant Roberta Hazard, who is the Project Manager for the Computer Assisted Research Project at the Naval Academy! How can we accept that she is good enough to *manage* projects at the Academy, but not to go there as a Midshipman? How can she be good enough to instruct at the Academy, but not good enough to learn there?

In short, the Academy's tradition is to train officers for the Navy who are highly skilled and motivated to rise to top leadership positions in the service—in any of the many careers which Naval officers pursue. Many of those careers are already open to women for which the Navy already recruits women officers. But the Academy—the best training available, for the best officers—is still closed to women officers. That is unfair to women. And it is *not* in the best interests of the Navy—the *only* Service which has no women in "flag grade" (Admiral, General) positions.

It was just over a year ago that I announced

my appointment of the first female Page to serve in the United States Senate.

The precedent I confronted there was just as old and established as the all-male precedent at the Academy.

Then, as now, it was argued by some that the work involved was not appropriate for females. Then, as now, I was confronted by the argument that the ambiguous law on the subject (in that instance, the Senate's own Rules) precluded such an appointment. Then, as now, I argued that no such legal prohibition existed.

Then, as now, I had the power to "nominate", but the actual appointive power is elsewhere (in the Sergeant at Arms, and the Rules Committee). After making the nomination, I was denied the appointment by the appointive power, but the Senate as a whole sustained such a nomination. Since then, we have seen a half-dozen girls from all corners of the nation serving as Senate Pages—and serving every bit as successfully as the boys.

Federal Judge Oliver Gasch ruled in Washington June 19, 1974 that since law and custom forbade women's participation in combat roles, a "legitimate government interest" was served by the refusal of the Air Force and Naval Academies to admit women. Gasch noted that military officials had described the primary purpose of the service academies as preparation of combat officers.

The ruling came in a suit filed by two women who had been nominated to the schools and Reps. Jerome Waldie and Don Edwards (both D, Calif.).

In a related development, women were admitted for the first time July 16 to the Merchant Marine Academy. Fifteen women joined 985 men at the school.

Pregnancy

Guidelines of the Equal Employment Opportunity Commission bar discrimination against an employe or job applicant because of pregnancy. Under the guidelines, disabilities caused or contributed to by pregnancy, miscarriage, abortion or childbirth and recovery should be treated as temporary disabilities *under any health or temporary disability-insurance or sick-leave plan of the employer. The accrual of seniority, reinstatement and payment under a sick-leave plan or temporary disability insurance was to be applied to disability due to pregnancy or childbirth. If an employer had no leave policy, he was required to consider childbearing as justification for leave of absence for a reasonable period. After childbirth, and on the employe's signifying that she intended to return within a reasonable time, she was to have the right of reinstatement to her original job or to one of like status and pay without loss of service credits.*

Court voids pregnancy rule. District Court Judge Richard W. McLaren July 10, 1972 voided a Chicago Board of Education rule that required pregnant teachers to take six months unpaid leave after their fifth month of pregnancy.

McLaren said the rule violated the Illinois and U.S. constitutions, and ordered the board to allow teachers to remain at their jobs as long as their physicians permit.

California disability bar upheld. The Supreme Court ruled June 17, 1974 that a California job disability insurance program did not unconstitutionally discriminate against women because it did not include benefits for normal pregnancies.

The California program, which excluded "any injury or illness caused by or arising in connection with pregnancy and for a period of 28 days thereafter," was contested by four women no longer able to work because of pregnancy. Financed by deductions from the wages of its participants, the California program was mandatory for all employes not covered by private disability programs certified by the state.

In its 6 3 decision, the court reasoned that in excluding benefits for normal pregnancies, California was not discriminating against anyone eligible for insurance protection, but that it had decided against insuring all employment disability risks.

Justice Potter Stewart, author of the court's majority opinion, said that nothing in the Constitution required a state "to subordinate or compromise its legitimate interests solely to create a more comprehensive social insurance program than it already has."

Stewart also noted that inclusion of pregnancy-related benefits would cause a substantial boost in the program's cost, a point to be considered since California had a "legitimate interest" in keeping its program self-supporting. Another "legitimate concern" was keeping the employe contribution rate low enough as not to place an unfair burden on low income earners, who might be most in need of the disability insurance.

The dissenting justices—William O. Douglas, William J. Brennan Jr. and Thurgood Marshall—asserted that California had created a "double standard" by "singling out for less favorable treatment a gender-linked disability peculiar to women."

Utah jobless pay ban voided. The Supreme Court Nov. 17, 1975 invalidated a Utah law denying unemployment benefits to women in their third trimester of pregnancy on the ground they were automatically presumed to be unable to work.

The court, in a short, unsigned opinion, said that this presumption was often incorrect. "It cannot be doubted that a substantial number of women are fully capable of working well into their last trimester of pregnancy and resuming employment shortly after childbirth," the court wrote. Moreover, the court said, the state law was in violation of the constitutional guarantee of due process, which required that eligibility for unemployment benefits be based on individual capacity for work and not a blanket "conclusive presumption" that pregnancy removed women from the potential work force.

Mary Ann Turner of Salt Lake City had challenged the law after her jobless benefits had been terminated when she entered her seventh month of pregnancy. The Utah Supreme Court sustained the law Feb. 4, stating that Turner should have applied to the "Great Creator," not the courts. "Should a man be unable to work because he was pregnant, the statute would apply to him equally as it does to her. What she should do is work for the repeal of the biological law of nature. She should get it amended so that men share

equally with women in bearing children," the Utah high court said.

Other pregnancy-case rulings. U.S. District Court Judge Robert R. Merhige ruled in Richmond, Va. April 14, 1974 that the General Electric Co. (GE) had practiced sexual discrimination in denying disability benefits to pregnant employes.

Merhige rejected company arguments that denial of benefits was justified because pregnancy was a "voluntary" disability, noting that similar standards were not applied to male employes incurring disabilities which might also be deemed voluntary.

The ruling came in a suit filed by seven workers in Virginia on behalf of all of GE's female workers.

The ruling was upheld by the Circuit Court of Appeals in June 1975.

The New York State Division of Human Rights found the Rochester plant of the Stromberg Carlson Corp. guilty of denying pregnant workers disability benefits and of setting mandatory periods of maternity leave without regard to the ability to keep working, the Wall Street Journal reported Aug. 4, 1975.

The Supreme Court Nov. 17, 1975 declined to hear an appeal by the Goodyear Tire & Rubber Co. against a decision by a labor arbitrator, who ruled that the company must pay accident and sickness benefits to employes on maternity leaves. The arbitrator's finding that the benefits were required under guidelines promulgated by the Equal Employment Opportunity Commission, Goodyear unsuccessfully argued, illegally superseded a collective bargaining agreement between Goodyear and the United Rubber Workers Union. The Ohio Supreme Court ruled earlier that the arbitrator had acted within his powers.

Discrimination Cases

Magazine jobs. Newsweek magazine Aug. 26, 1970 signed an accord to speed the recruitment and promotion of women. The document had been worked out in negotiations with representatives of

46 women employes, who had filed a sex discrimination complaint in March with the U.S. Equal Employment Opportunity Commission (EEOC).

But 50 women editorial workers at Newsweek May 16, 1972 filed a complaint at the EEOC's New York office charging that the magazine had made only "token alterations" in hiring and promotion practices.

The 1972 complaint said only 4 of 41 writers and 12 of 71 correspondents were women while 33 of 40 researchers, the "lowest editorial position," were women. Newsweek issued a statement May 16 charging that the women had demanded quotas, and cited its own proposals "to hasten the expanded employment, training and advancement of women."

Time Inc., publisher of four major magazines, had agreed with more than 140 female employes Feb. 6, 1971 to open all jobs in the company to qualified candidates regardless of sex or marital status.

In complaints to the New York attorney general's office, the women charged that they were limited to jobs as researchers at Time, Life, Fortune and Sports Illustrated. New York Attorney General Louis J. Lefkowitz worked out the agreement, and the State Division of Human Rights was to review periodically salaries of men and women in the same job category at the magazines. In addition, the editors agreed to masthead changes that would "reflect more adequately the significant contributions being made by women."

Stock exchange. The American Stock Exchange (Amex) in New York announced Jan. 15, 1973 that it would prepare an "affirmative action" program to recruit and upgrade women and minority-group members at Amex. It urged the Securities & Exchange Commission to develop equal employment programs in the entire securities industry.

The SEC Jan. 14, 1974 refused requests by various organizations that it require "affirmative action" programs against race and sex discrimination in the securities industry.

The SEC said the groups' contention that women and nonwhites were often confined to low-level jobs might be historically accurate. But the commission cited recent changes in employment patterns as indications of improvement. Acknowledging that it had the authority to impose antidiscrimination rules, the SEC suggested that the Equal Employment Opportunity Commission would be the appropriate agency to handle such complaints.

Night differentials barred. The Supreme Court June 3, 1974 ruled, 5 to 3, that an employer's retention of some traditional night shift pay differentials favoring male employes over women was a violation of the Equal Pay Act.

The ruling involved two Corning Glass Works plants, in Corning, N.Y. and Wellsboro, Pa., in which male night shift inspectors had been paid more than female day shift inspectors doing the same work. This policy was changed in 1966 when Corning opened night shift jobs to women and again in 1969, when the company decided to pay all subsequently hired workers at the same base rate, regardless of sex or shift worked. Employes hired before 1969 continued to receive a higher night differential.

Finding that the company's pre-1966 employment practices violated the Equal Pay Act, the court decided that Corning failed to "cure" its violation, despite opening the night shift to women. Moreover, the 1969 company decision to abolish shift differentials still did not end the violation because those hired previously continued to receive the higher night shift rates.

Corning had not proved, the court said, that the pre-1966 night shift pay differential was added compensation for night work. There was substantial evidence that it reflected the fact that men would not work for the low wages paid day shift women workers, the court said.

Sex-segregated union locals voided. Overruling one of its hearing examiners, the National Labor Relations Board ruled that separate locals for men and women within the same union at the same plant violated the National Labor Relations

Act (reported June 14, 1974). The board ordered the merger of two locals of the Glass Bottle Blowers Association representing workers at an Owens-Illinois Inc. plant.

Although the examiner had ruled that separation was not injurious to a female plaintiff because rights and benefits in the two locals were the same, the board ruled that "separate but equal treatment on the basis of sex is as self-contradictory as separate but equal on the basis of race. In both areas separation in and of itself creates inequalities."

A woman member of a Glass Bottle Blowers Association local in Columbus, Ohio had sued to have a work grievance handled by the male local. The examiner noted that the locals had the same pay scale and a single seniority list, and were both represented in contract bargaining.

The plaintiff said she had initiated the action because "a group of us thought we ought to belong to one union." The president of the women's local, however, said the women wanted to retain their separate identity to keep their "clout," since men outnumbered women by over 2-1 at the plant.

Sex bias settlement at Bank of America. The U.S. district court in San Francisco gave approval July 24, 1974 to a settlement of class action sex discrimination suits brought against the Bank of America, the world's largest private bank.

The consent decree, which the bank accepted without admitting guilt, was praised by both the bank and plaintiffs as a breakthrough in women's rights.

Rather than the back-pay provisions that had become the norm in settlements negotiated in disputes at other companies, the agreement provided that the bank would pay $3.75 million over five years into trust funds which would give incentives for female employes to undertake management training, educational and other "self-development" programs leading to management-level promotions.

The agreement set hiring and promotion goals under which the proportion of women officers would be increased from the current 31% to 40% by December 1978, with the sharpest percentage in-

creases to occur in the higher management levels. (About 73% of the bank's 54,000 employes were women.)

Before approving the agreement, the court inserted language to insure that reverse discrimination would not be practiced and that promotion policies would be based on ability as well as percentage guidelines.

Employment Status

Wage gap narrowing? Department of Labor statistics, reported by the Washington Post May 15, 1971, gave indications that the gap between women's and men's wages in the U.S. began to narrow in 1968 and 1969. The median annual wage for women, as compared to men, had reached a low of 57.8% in 1967, representing a decline since the mid-1950s when women earned 64% as much as men.

The Labor Department said that in 1969, however, working women earned a median wage of $4,977, 60.5% of the male median wage of $8,227. In 1968 women earned 58.2% of the male median wage. The department said some of the difference in wages earned by men and women was due to the lower average educational level attained by women and because of a larger concentration of women in lower-paying, lower-skilled jobs.

Citing data on specific job categories, the department said women who were full professors at universities had a median salary of $11,649 compared with the male median of $12,768 in 1965-66, the latest data available. In 1968, median salaries for women scientists were $1,700-$4,500 lower than for all scientists in their respective fields.

The Post quoted a study by the Women's Division of the Wage and Labor Standards Administration concluding that federal legislation prohibiting sex discrimination "has not been enough to date to close the gap between the earnings of women and men. . . . In addition to enforcement of these laws, it is also imperative for employers to review their

Median Earnings of Year-Round Full-Time Civilian Workers 14 Years Old and Over With Earnings by Sex: 1960 to 1974

(Medians in current dollars)

Year	Median earnings		Ratio: women/men
	Women	Men	
1974	$6,772	$11,835	0.57
1973	6,335	11,186	0.57
1972	5,903	10,202	0.58
1971	5,593	9,399	0.60
1970	5,323	8,966	0.59
1969	4,977	8,455	0.59
1968	4,457	7,664	0.58
1967	4,134	7,174	0.58
1966	3,946	6,856	0.58
1965	3,828	6,388	0.60
1964	3,669	6,203	0.59
1963	3,525	5,980	0.59
1962	3,412	5,754	0.59
1961	3,315	5,595	0.59
1960	3,257	5,368	0.61

Source: U.S. Department of Commerce, Bureau of the Census, Current Population Reports, Series P-60, Nos. 99, 93, 90, 85, 80, 75, 66, 60, 53, 51, 47, 43, 41, 39, and 37.

From "A Statistical Portrait of Women in the U.S.." U.S. Department of Commerce. Bureau of the Census. April 1976 recruitment, on-the-job training, and promotion policies to give well-qualified women the opportunity to move into more of the better paying jobs than they now hold."

Based on later statistics, a Women's Bureau report (made public Aug. 26, 1972) confirmed that even though the proportion of women in professional, managerial and other high status jobs had increased slightly between 1968 and 1971, average salaries for women had declined as a percentage of men's salaries over a longer period, between 1955 and 1970.

Women, who constituted 38% of the work force, increased their share of professional-technical and managerial jobs by about 1.5% over the period, rising to 39% in the first category and 17% in the second.

But in 1970, the bureau reported, the average woman earned only 59% as much as a man in the same job, down from 64% in 1955. The gap was narrowest in professional jobs, where women earned 67%, but greatest in sales jobs, where they were paid only 43% of male salaries. Only 1% of female managers on salary were paid $25,000 or more in 1970, compared with about 10% of male managers.

Somewhat similar findings were made public by another federal source early in 1973.

In an unprecedented special section on the economic role of women, the President's Economic Report to Congress, released Jan. 30, charged that women had not made much progress in achieving job equality or equal pay since 1956.

Although 43.8% of women of working age were in the work force, constituting 37.4% of the total work force, there had been only a "very small change" in "the extent of occupational segregation by sex" since 1950, perpetuating the concentration of women in lower paying jobs, the report noted. However, women had made gains in recent years in some job categories, including accountants, radio operators and editors and reporters. The report listed the proportion of women in over 250 job classifications.

Within the various job classifications, the report said, "the low representation of women in positions of responsibility is striking."

Among women who worked at all during 1971, average earnings were about 40% as large as those of men, in part a reflection of the larger number of part-time women workers. With adjustments made for the varying work hours, women still averaged only 66% of male earnings.

Part of the difference was attributed to lower experience levels of women, which in turn was said to be caused largely by the fact that women did not remain in the work force as continuously as men. But even taking these factors into account, the report claimed, the average rose to only 80%. Among men and women holding the same type of job at the same company, however, earnings were found to be equal.

Black women heads of households who worked all year had average earnings of $5,227, the report said, compared with $6,527 for white women. But the gap disappeared among women with higher education.

The report did not attempt to determine to what extent the inequality resulted from direct discrimination or cultural factors, including the choice of many women of "a life divided between home responsibilities and work." But it claimed "some of the hesitancy of women to enter or to stay in the labor force is undoubtedly the result of societally determined factors that restrict the possibilities open to them," including different career orientations beginning in the first years of school.

The report was prepared by the Council of Economic Advisers, including Marina Von Neumann Whitman, appointed in 1972.

In 1973, in a series of job and earnings reports, the Census Bureau said that while some U.S. women had made gains in getting jobs and more wives outearned their husbands than in the past, average earnings for working women with either a college or high school education were still scarcely more than half the earnings of similarly educated males.

The Census Bureau said March 9 that full-time women workers 25-64 years old with a high school diploma earned $5,067 in 1969, 56% of the $9,067 earned by males, while full-time women workers

Median Income of Year-Round Full-Time Civilian Workers 25 Years Old and Over With Income by Educational Attainment and Sex: 1970 and 1974

(Medians in current dollars. Age as of March of the following year)

Educational attainment and sex	Median income		Ratio: women/men	
	1974	1970	1974	1970
WOMEN				
Total, 25 years and over.........	$7,370	$5,616	0.58	0.59
Elementary: Less than 8 years......	5,022	3,798	0.63	0.63
8 years................	5,606	4,181	0.57	0.55
High school: 1 to 3 years...........	5,919	4,655	0.53	0.55
4 years................	7,150	5,580	0.57	0.58
College: 1 to 3 years...........	8,072	6,604	0.59	0.59
4 years or more...........	10,357	8,719	0.60	0.63
MEN				
Total, 25 years and over.........	$12,786	$9,521	(X)	(X)
Elementary: Less than 8 years......	7,912	6,043	(X)	(X)
8 years................	9,891	7,535	(X)	(X)
High school: 1 to 3 years...........	11,225	8,514	(X)	(X)
4 years................	12,642	9,567	(X)	(X)
College: 1 to 3 years...........	13,718	11,183	(X)	(X)
4 years or more...........	17,188	13,871	(X)	(X)

X Not applicable.

Source: U.S. Department of Commerce, Bureau of the Census, Current Population Reports, Series P-60, Nos. 99 and 80.

From "A Statistical Portrait of Women in the U.S.," U.S. Department of Commerce, Bureau of the Census, April 1976

with four years of college earned $7,238 that year, or 55% of the $13,103 male figure. Among blacks, the discrepancy was somewhat less.

The differential varied widely in different professions. Women domestics with four years of high school earned only 37% of their male counterparts, while women computer specialists earned 75% of males' salaries in similar jobs.

A Census Bureau analysis reported Feb. 11 that women accounted for 65.3% of the increase in jobs between 1960 and 1970, when they held 37.8% of the 76.6 million jobs. The largest gains by women were in the clerical, service, sales and operatives categories, while only 43.7% of new professional and technical workers and 28.6% of new managers were women.

The bureau reported March 18 that 3.2 million wives had incomes greater than their husbands in 1970, or 7.4% of the 44 million husband-wife households, up from 5.7% in 1960.

Few women among top executives. Fortune magazine reported in April 1973 that only 11 of some 6,500 top-ranking American corporate officers were women. Wyndham Robertson wrote in the Fortune article: ... Most of them began their careers thirty to forty years ago and—with only two exceptions—were helped along by a family connection, by marriage, or by the fact that they helped to create the organizations they now preside over. In short, most of them did not have to deal with at least two problems that have over the years held back even the most able and qualified women: they did not start out in their companies in jobs with limited futures, and they did not have to work their way through a corporate hierarchy that discriminated against them.

Three were cofounders of corporations, together with their husbands. They are Olive Ann Beech, chairman of Beech Aircraft; Ruth Handler, president of Mattel; and Vera Neumann, president of the Vera Companies, now a subsidiary of Manhattan Industries. A fourth, Tillie Lewis, founded, virtually single-handedly, a tomato-canning company that is now a subsidiary of Ogden Corp.

Four others are members of families owning big blocks of stock in the companies where they work. Dorothy Chandler, director and assistant to the chairman of the Times Mirror Co. in Los Angeles, and Katherine Graham, the president of the Washington Post Co., are two of the most powerful figures in publishing. Bernice Lavin, secretary-treasurer of Alberto-Culver, is married to Leonard Lavin, president of the company and the owner of 28 percent of its stock. Mala Rubinstein, an executive vice president of Helena Rubinstein, Inc., is the late Mrs. Rubinstein's niece.

None of these women, obviously, *has* to work, and in fact some of them wouldn't have—or wouldn't have had careers—without the family tie-in. Yet each of them plays an effective and important role within her corporation—an impressive bit of evidence that other female executive talent is going to waste.

The only women who made it to the top the way most men do—i.e., by moving up in an existing corporate hierarchy without family sponsorship—are Stella Russell and Catherine Cleary. Mrs. Russell is vice president and director of Norton Simon, and Miss Cleary is president of First Wisconsin Trust Co. The trust company is owned by a bank-holding company, First Wisconsin Bankshares, of which Miss Cleary is a director.

Study finds bias against women Ph.Ds. Women with doctorates were discriminated against in salary and promotion opportunities in favor of men, and this disparity increased with years of experience, according to an Educational Testing Service study released Jan. 5, 1975. Based on a sample of 3,658 doctorate recipients in 1950, 1960 and 1968, the report said men averaged $18,700 five to six years after receiving degrees and $27,100 after 22 or 23 years, compared with $16,400 and $21,800 for women.

The report noted recent signs of improvement for women Ph.Ds in status and pay, but added, "Whether current changes are the beginning of a trend or tokenism, as some claim, remains to be seen."

Marriage and motherhood were cited as obstacles to professional advancement of the women. More than 25% of women doctorate recipients became divorced or separated, compared with 10% of the men, the report said, indicating that "doctoral work itself or the ensuing professional commitment undoubtedly created conflicts."

Recession cut women's jobs. Sen. Harrison A. Williams (D, N.J.) told the Senate March 13, 1975 that "American working women ... are among the hardest hit by

Employment Status and Major Occupation Group of All Women and Women of Spanish Origin 16 Years Old and Over by Type of Spanish Origin: March 1974

(Noninstitutional population)

Employment status and occupation	Total women	Women of Spanish origin			
		Total	Mexican	Puerto Rican	Other[1]
Total women, 16 years and over...............thousands..	78,108	3,325	1,877	483	965
In civilian labor force.thousands..	35,321	1,400	757	163	480
Percent unemployed..............	6.0	9.8	9.7	9.8	9.9
Employed.............thousands..	33,200	1,262	683	147	433
Percent..............	100.0	100.0	100.0	100.0	100.0
White-collar workers..............	62.0	41.2	37.6	42.1	46.0
Professional, technical, and kindred workers..............	15.5	6.0	4.5	8.8	7.6
Managers and administrators, except farm..............	4.9	2.9	1.6	4.8	4.2
Sales workers..............	6.7	4.0	4.0	2.0	4.4
Clerical and kindred workers..............	34.9	28.3	27.5	26.5	29.8
Blue-collar workers..............	15.5	33.4	32.1	44.3	32.2
Craft and kindred workers..............	1.7	2.1	1.6	4.8	2.1
Operatives, including transport..............	12.9	30.2	29.3	38.1	28.9
Laborers, excluding farm..............	0.9	1.1	1.2	1.4	1.2
Farm workers..............	1.3	2.6	4.2	2.0	0.2
Farmers and farm managers..............	0.3	-	-	-	-
Farm laborers and supervisors..............	1.0	2.6	4.2	2.0	0.2
Service workers..............	21.2	22.9	26.1	10.9	21.7

- Represents zero or rounds to zero.
[1] Includes Cuban, Central or South American, and other Spanish origin.

Source: U.S. Department of Commerce, Bureau of the Census, Current Population Reports, Series P-20, No. 280.

From "A Statistical Portrait of Women in the U.S.," U.S. Department of Commerce. Bureau of the Census. April 1976 the recessionary impact." Williams, noting recent Bureau of Labor Statistics data, said:

The February 1975 statistics show that there are presently 29,700,000 American working women. In the third quarter of last year, just 5 short months ago, there were 30,500,000 working women. This is a decrease of 800,000 women in the working force; 800,000 more women who are out of work. And women are continuing to lose jobs at an alarming rate. During the month of January 1975 alone the number of working women dropped by 213,00.

The unemployment rate for women remains at a record high. This February, the rate was 7.6 percent for white women. Last February, this rate was only 4.7 percent. The unemployment rate for black and other minority women is a staggering 10.9 percent, up from 7.9 percent for February of last year.

As depressing as these figures are, they do not show the staggering loss of potential and opportunity among American working women. Wages for women are still low. In 1973, the median wage for women workers, including college-educated working women, was a mere $6,335 a year. This contrasts to a 1973 median wage for men of $11,186. In addition, the gap between men's and women's wages appears to be widening, not decreasing. In 1955 when the Department of Labor first started compiling these statistics, women's wages averaged 63.9 percent of men's wages. In 1973, women's median earnings were 56.6 percent of men's median earnings. This is the lowest percentage level since 1955.

Coupled with the increase in unemployment among women is an increase in sex-based discrimination complaints.

The number of actionable charges filed with the Equal Employment Opportunity Commission alleging sex discrimination in employment has risen from 15,505 charges in 1973 to 18,664 charges in 1974. Since the Equal Employment Opportunity Commission received 50,879 actionable charges in 1974, this means that almost a third of the charges filed complained of sex discrimination in employment.

In addition, as the recession cuts deeper into the fabric of our society, women workers often find themselves the first ones let go. Many women are seeing their

recently made employment gains in traditionally male occupations reduced or eliminated by the recession. For example, the construction trade, which many women have been attempting to break into, now has an unemployment rate of 15.9 percent. The unemployment rate in manufacturing, where 30 percent of the work force is female, showed its ninth consecutive increase and currently stands at a record 11 percent. Even those in a traditional women's field—clerical work, where 78 percent of the work force is female—are suffering a staggering setback. Between January 1975 and February 1975, 213,000 clerical workers lost their jobs. Clearly, the problem among women workers is a serious one.

Women span all categories of the unemployed. They are among the job losers laid off due to a decrease in the work demand. They are job entrants, entering the labor force for the first time, yet unable to find a job. They are job re-entrants—women who reentered the work force by the present economic trend of recession and inflation and who now cannot find a job.

Women workers rarely work for pin money. In fact, it is doubtful that a large percentage of working women ever did. Congressional documentation of exploitation of women workers is not a new phenomenon. Congress enacted legislation to protect working women from unscrupulous employers in the first part of this century. Exploitation of working women still exists, although the method of combating the problem has changed. Women workers no longer seek separate status or separate protective legislation. They now seek what is justly due them: Equalization of their status with their male counterparts—equal job opportunities, equal pay, and equal responsibility.

Gains & problems. In a speech before the National Council of Negro Women Nov. 12, 1975, Rep. Bella Abzug (D, N.Y.) summarized some of the recent gains and problems of working women and the women's movement:

Among the main goals of the women's movement are the achievement of equal pay for equal work, and equal job opportunities. And I think it is significant that black women have made some gains in these areas. For instance, since 1960 the percentage of black women in professional and technical jobs increased from six percent to 11 percent. The number of architects increased from zero to 107, the number of attorneys from 222 to 497, and the number of physicians from 487 to 1,855.

Black women in clerical jobs increased from nine percent to 22 percent, and the percentage of black women in private household work decreased from 35% to 17%.

Black women are still at the bottom of the wage earning level, but they are narrowing the wage gap with their white women counterparts. Their wages are still far too low. But the median wage for fulltime black women workers increased from $2,372 in 1969 to $4,464 in 1970, and they went from 70 percent of the wage earned by white women to 85%, and from 63% of the wage earned by minority men to 71%.

But now we are deep in a recession, the worst since the 1930's, and this is going to create problems for the women's movement. I think that fear of women taking jobs away from men was one of the hidden factors in the unfavorable ERA vote in New York. The employment gains made by minorities and women are being seriously jeopardized by the worsening economic situation.

Women and blacks, who have only recently gained access to many jobs, are too often among the first fired. Affirmative action programs are just beginning to correct the imbalance between white and black and male and female workers. As job opportunities decrease, competition for available positions more intense.

Health hazards block women workers.

The Wall Street Journal reported June 17, 1976 that "women of child-bearing age face a new form of job discrimination because employers don't want to expose them to health and safety hazards." The article was based on a joint report of the University of California's Labor Occupational Health Program and the Health Research Group, which Ralph Nader's Public Citizen organization finances. According to the Wall Street Journal article:

The companies fear that substances used on the job can cause birth defects and miscarriages. . . .
The report said job exposures can result in infertility, in genetic damage in men and women that can be passed on to offspring, damage by chemicals reaching the fetus or damage to a newborn baby caused by chemicals in a mother's breast-milk. . . .
Citing possible work hazards, the report said that exposure to lead is associated with stillbirths and miscarriages in women and with sperm abnormalities in men, and that vinyl chloride causes cancer in the offspring of exposed pregnant rats and "is linked to stillbirths and miscarriages in the wives of workers exposed to it."

Anesthetic gases have been linked to cancer, birth defects and miscarriages in exposed female operating room personnel and to miscarriages in wives of dental surgeons and birth defects in wives of exposed male operating room personnel, the study said. Carbon disulfide used in the manufacture of viscose rayon can cause miscarriages and sperm abnormalities. And exposure to high levels of estrogens can cause female menstrual difficulties and male impotence, the report warned. . . .

The report said women in Idaho, Pennsylvania and Canada have been refused jobs in hazardous areas of plants unless they can prove that they are no longer able to bear children.

In one instance, fertile women at an Idaho lead smelter were transferred to safer jobs, some at lower rates of pay. And a mother of four working in a Canadian lead storage battery plant had herself sterilized in order to keep her job.

Bias in pensions.

Rep. Shirley Chisholm (D, N.Y.) told the House Feb. 28, 1974 that "if you are low-paid, female, a minority or a parttime worker, the chances of [your] ever getting a [private industry] pension are very poor. If . . . you are a well-paid, white, male professional, you have a pretty good chance of receiving a decent pension." Chisholm cited the following data compiled by the Labor, the Health, Education & Welfare and the Treasury Departments and printed in a publication entitled "Coverage and Vesting of Full-time Employees Under Private Retirement Plans: Findings From the April 1972 Survey":

The proportion of men covered by a private pension or deferred profit-sharing plan was 45% greater than that for women and the rate for whites was almost 25% greater than that for persons of all other races.
Coverage rates rose sharply with earnings. Although only a fourth of the men earning less than $5,000 a year were covered, about ⅗ths of those earning more had coverage.
Vesting rates varied little by industry. Occupational differences were greater, however: professional and technical workers, managers, officers and craftsmen had the highest vesting rates.
Only 30% of the workers under 25 and 40% of the workers over 60 were covered vs. about ½ of those aged 25–59 who were covered.
Men were more likely to be covered than

women (52% and 36% respectively), and whites were more apt to be covered than were persons of all other races (48% and 39% respectively.)

Most of the difference between the coverage rates stems from factors not associated with either age or tenure. Men have much higher coverage rates—usually by at least 10%—than women of the same age and the same length of service.

Elective Office & Politics

Blacks Win Elections

Traditionally, few high prestige jobs had been open to American blacks, especially in the South. Among posts virtually closed to Negroes had been government jobs that could be obtained only by public election. The civil rights movement of the 1950s–60s, the new rights legislation and the black voter-registration drives resulted by the early 1970s in election victories for a growing number of black candidates in every part of the country.

Blacks in elective jobs. A nationwide survey by two private organizations released March 30, 1970 indicated that nearly 1,500 Negroes held elective public office in the U.S. The survey was conducted jointly by the Metropolitan Applied Research Center, Inc., of New York and Washington, D.C. and the Voter Education Project of the Southern Regional Council in Atlanta. It was the first time a complete list of black officeholders had been compiled.

According to the survey, there were 48 mayors, 575 other city officials, 362 school board members, 168 legislators, 114 judges and 99 law enforcement officials. Despite increases in the past several years, the survey indicated that black elected officials comprised less than 1% of more than 500,000 elected officials in the U.S. Negroes comprised about 11% of the U.S. population.

The findings showed that 38% of the black elected officials were in the 11 Southern states.

Elected blacks up in South—The private, Atlanta-based Voter Education Project (VEP) reported Feb. 12, 1973 that the number of black elected officials in 11 Southern states had reached 1,144 in 1972, with a net increase of 241 as a result of the November elections. The total was more than ten times the number of black officeholders in 1965, before passage of the federal Voting Rights Act.

The largest group was in Mississippi, with 145 officials, followed by Alabama with 144, an increase of 61 during the year. Arkansas gained 49 black officeholders, including a state senator and two state representatives, who integrated the last all-white Southern legislature and brought the state's total to

140.

Louisiana had 127 black officials (including a state appeals court judge, the highest elected black judge in the region), North Carolina 108, Georgia 104, Texas and South Carolina 98 each, Tennessee 69, Virginia 60 and Florida 51.

The officials included two Congressmen, six state senators, 55 state representatives, 126 county officials, 38 mayors, 14 vice mayors, 441 other municipal officials, 198 law enforcement officials (nine of them judges) and 268 education officials.

VEP had reported Feb. 3 that 598 blacks had won election to office in the 11 states during 1972 out of 1,276 black candidates, both record figures.

Total grows—The National Roster of Black Elected Officials (Volume 3), published in May 1973, listed 2,621 black elected officials in public office in 44 states and the District of Columbia. This was an increase of 121% since the roster was first published in 1969. Some 1,179 of the total (45%) were in the South. Sen. William Proxmire (D, Wis.), citing these statistics, noted in a statement printed in the Congressional Record April 1, 1974 that Sen. Edward Brooke (R, Mass.) was "the first black man ever to be elected and reelected to the Senate ... by popular vote." Proxmire added:

In the House there are now 16 black Members, a significant increase over previous years when the total was 2 or 3.

And 238 blacks hold seats in the legislatures of 41 States and black elected county officials increased by 20 percent in 1973 over 1972 to a total of 211.

The number of black mayors in the major cities of the United States is an area where there has been great change in recent years. Los Angeles, Newark, Cleveland, Gary, and a host of others have elected blacks to be their chief executives.

This situation, while greatly improved and one of which we can be proud in particular, still leaves much to be desired. The 2,627 black elected officials still represents only five-tenths of 1 percent—.005—of all the 521,760 elected officials in the country. Nevertheless, there have been some spectacular gains in which we can all take pride.

Black & Female Gains

Congressional election victors. A record nine black candidates—including six incumbents—had been elected to the House of Representatives Nov. 5, 1968. The previous record—seven—had been elected during the Reconstruction years 1873-74. The newcomers included Mrs. Shirley Chisholm of New York and William L. Clay of St. Louis, the first black to be elected to Congress from Missouri. The November 1970 election increased the black membership of the House of 12.

The Rev. Walter E. Fauntroy, a black Baptist clergyman, was elected March 23, 1971 as the District of Columbia's first non-voting delegate to Congress (he was to sit in the House) in a century.

The 1972 election increased the number of black faces in the House to 16, all of them Democrats. The newcomers included two more black women—Barbara Jordan of Texas and Yvonne Brathwaite Burke of California. Jordan and the Rev. Andrew Young of Georgia were the first blacks to be elected to Congress from the South in the 20th century.

Mrs. Cardiss Robertson Collins was elected to Congress June 5, 1973 from the 7th Congressional District in Illinois, the seat left vacant when her husband, George, was killed in an airplane crash in December 1972. Mrs. Collins became the state's first black congresswoman.

Sixteen black nominees were elected to the House Nov. 5, 1974.

Six more women were elected to the House—Democrats Martha Keys of Kansas, Helen Meyner of New Jersey, Marilyn Lloyd of Tennessee and Gladys Spellman of Maryland, plus Republicans Millicent Fenwick of New Jersey and Virginia Smith of Nebraska. With four women in the House retiring, the net gain of two raised the total number of women representatives to 18, two short of the record 20 women in the House in 1963-64.

Blacks & women elected mayors. Howard Lee, 34, was elected May 6, 1969 as the first Negro mayor of Chapel Hill, N.C., an 80%-white town. Lee defeated Roland

Giduz, 43, white and a 12-year veteran of the town's Board of Aldermen, by a 2,567-to-2,167 vote. Lee, director of employe relations at Duke University, said his race was not a major factor in the campaign, which was "settled on the issues, and a lot of credit is due to my opponent." The job was a part-time one (salary $100 a month); Chapel Hill (12,400 residents) was run by a town manager under the guidance of the mayor and aldermen.

City Councilman Douglas F. Dollarhide became the first black mayor of Compton, Calif. by winning a run-off June 4, 1969 against Dr. Walter Tucker, also a Negro. The town's population of 78,000 was about 65% Negro and 10% Mexican-American.

In Cleveland, Ohio, Mayor Carl B. Stokes (D), who became the first Negro to be elected mayor of a major American city in 1967, won re-election in a close race Nov. 4 with Cuyahoga County Auditor Ralph J. Perk (R). Negro mayoral candidates also ran but lost in Dayton, Ohio; Detroit, Mich.; Hartford and Waterbury, Conn.; and Buffalo, N.Y. In Detroit, the black nominee, County Auditor Richard H. Austin, lost by a 7,000-vote margin out of 509,000 votes cast. The victor was County Sheriff Roman S. Gribbs, 43, a white. Both were Democrats. The election was nonpartisan. The major issues were crime and race, but Gribbs did not stress the race issue. Austin did so on the ground his race was pertinent to his campaign.

Among other Nov. 4, 1969 results:

William S. Hart (D) became the first Negro mayor of a major New Jersey municipality, East Orange.

In Dayton, Ohio, Negro mayoral candidate Lawrence Nelson lost by a 3-1 margin to incumbent Mayor Dave Hall in a nonpartisan vote.

James H. McGee, was sworn in July 15, 1970 as the first black mayor of Dayton, Ohio. The Ohio city, with a population of 250,000 including 70,000 Negroes, was the fourth largest city in the U.S.—behind Cleveland, Washington, D.C. and Newark, N.J.—to have a black as mayor. McGee, who had filed civil suits on behalf of the National Association for the Advancement of Colored People (NAACP), was appointed by fellow members of the Dayton City Commission to succeed Dave Hall, who resigned May 13 for health reasons. McGee's selection ended a three-month impasse during which two other commission members sought the post. (McGee was reelected Nov. 6, 1973.)

Richard G. Hatcher, black candidate who was first elected mayor of Gary, Ind. Nov. 7, 1967, was reelected in 1971 and again in 1975.

Two black candidates were elected in September 1972 as the first black mayors of Alabama towns that were not all black. John Ford, a black businessman, was voted mayor of Tuskegee, an 80% black town of 11,000. A. J. Cooper, 28, a civil rights lawyer, was elected in a Sept. 13 runoff in Prichard, a blue-collar Mobile suburb, whose 41,000 residents were 52% black. Cooper was sworn in Oct. 2.

The two new mayors raised the number of black Alabama mayors to seven.

City Councilman Theodore M. Berry, a lawyer, became the first black mayor of Cincinnati Dec. 1, 1972 through an agreement by Democratic and City Charter party council members to divide the two-year term between Berry and a Democrat. Berry had served on the council a total of 10 years. The council Dec. 1, 1973 elected Berry to a second one-year mayoral term and chose another black, William Chenault, as vice mayor.

Maynard Jackson, a black lawyer, was elected mayor of Atlanta Oct. 16, 1973. He beat white incumbent Sam Massell in a nonpartisan election. Racial acrimony had marred the final weeks of the campaign. On his inauguration, Jackson became the first black mayor of a major Southern city. He gained control over a city in which blacks were a majority of the population and also controlled the city council and the board of education. Jackson had been an unsuccessful candidate for the Senate in 1968.

Thomas Bradley was elected mayor of Los Angeles in a nonpartisan election May 29, 1973 over incumbent Sam Yorty. Bradley took office July 1 as the first black mayor of a city whose black population was about 15% to 18%. Bradley had lost to Yorty in 1969.

Number of Women Candidates For Public Office and Women Elected Officials: 1972 and 1974

Public office	1974	1972	Percent change, 1972 to 1974
WOMEN CANDIDATES FOR PUBLIC OFFICE[1]			
Federal Government, total..............	47	34	38.2
U.S. Senate.......................	3	2	50.0
U.S. House of Representatives..........	44	32	37.5
State Government, total...............	1,177	870	35.3
Governor..........................	3	-	(X)
House..............................	989	741	33.5
Senate.............................	137	101	35.6
State-wide offices (excluding governor)....	48	28	71.4
WOMEN ELECTED OFFICIALS[2]			
Federal Congressional office............	18	16	12.5
State governor's office..............	1	-	(X)
State legislature office...............	596	441	35.1

- Represents zero.
X Not applicable.
[1]Restricted to candidates of the two major political parties.
[2]Incumbents and those elected in 1974.

Source: U.S. Department of Labor, Women's Bureau.

From "A Statistical Portrait of Women in the U.S.," U.S. Department of Commerce, Bureau of the Census, April 1976

Blacks and women scored further gains in mayoral elections Nov. 5, 1974:

In the Nov. 6, 1973 elections:

Voters of Raleigh, N.C., with a 30% black population, elected a black mortician, Clarence E. Lightner, mayor in a nonpartisan election.

In Miami, Maurice Ferre, a Puerto Rico-born millionaire, defeated six rivals in the mayoral race.

The Rev. Lyman Parks, black minister who had been appointed mayor of Grand Rapids, Mich. in 1971, was reelected.

In the District of Columbia, Walter E. Washington became the first elected mayor of the nation's capital in this century. Washington, black, had been appointed mayor by President Lyndon B. Johnson in 1967 and reappointed by President Richard M. Nixon.

Janet Gray Hayes (D) was elected mayor of San Jose, Calif. She became the first woman mayor of a city with more than 500,000 population.

Margaret Hance was elected mayor of Phoenix, Ariz.

Others elected. Five blacks were elected Aug. 8, 1972 to the 10-member city council in Selma, Ala., scene of violent civil rights confrontations in the 1960s. It was the first time a black had been elected to the body. Under a new state law, the elections were by wards instead of at large.

S. Howard Woodson, a 57-year old Baptist minister, was unanimously chosen speaker of the New Jersey State Assembly Dec. 10, 1973. He became the first black to hold a major position in a state legislature.

A record number of blacks and women ran for office in the Nov. 5, 1974 elections:

Rep. Ella T. Grasso (D), Connecticut's gubernatorial victor, became the **first woman elected governor of a Northeastern state and the first woman governor who did not inherit the office from her husband.***

New Yorkers elected State Sen. Mary

* Women who had succeeded their husbands as governor were Nellie Ross, elected in 1925 from Wyoming; Miriam Ferguson, elected in 1925 and 1933 from Texas; and Lurleen Wallace, elected in 1967 from Alabama.

Ann Krupsak (D) as their state's first woman lieutenant governor. Two blacks were also elected as state lieutenant governors—State Sen. Mervyn Dymally (D) in California and State Sen. George L. Brown (D) in Colorado.

Women gubernatorial candidates, both Republicans, were defeated in races in Maryland and Nevada, as were women candidates for the Senate in Maryland (a Democrat) and South Carolina (a Republican). Two Democratic women seeking House seats in California and Ohio also lost. Women candidates for lieutenant governor in Arkansas, Nevada and Rhode Island failed to gain election.

North Carolina voters elevated Susie Sharp, associate justice of the state's supreme court, to chief justice, making her the first popularly elected woman to hold such a position in any state.

In Mississippi Nov. 4, 1975, State Insurance Commissioner Evelyn Gandy was elected as the state's first woman lieutenant governor.

Thelma Stoval (D), currently secretary of state for Kentucky, was elected the state's first women lieutenant governor.

Blacks Organize

Black officials confer. Scores of elected black officials gathered in Washington, D.C. Sept. 11–14, 1969 to inaugurate the Institute of Black Elected Officials, the first national attempt to organize the 1,200 Negroes in elective office. The conference was sponsored by the Metropolitan Applied Research Center, Inc. of Washington and New York.

President Nixon greeted about 150 of the officials, most of them Democrats, at the White House Sept. 11, but there was no formal discussion of the issues that brought them to Washington.

At the first general session Sept. 12, black officeholders assailed the Nixon Administration's "new federalism." They warned that more money and authority vested in the hands of state governments could lead to a return of "tyranny" against minority groups.

The officials ended the conference

Sept. 14 with charges that the Nixon Administration had failed to adopt a positive civil rights policy.

Woodrow Wilson, a Republican assemblyman from Nevada, announced that the institute would establish a permanent headquarters in Washington.

National convention. Some 3,300 voting delegates and 5,000 observers met in Gary, Ind. March 10–12, 1972 as the first National Black Political Convention and voted to set up a permanent representative body to set the direction for black political and social actions. However, the convention failed to resolve strategy differences between those who favored working within the traditional two-party structure and those favoring separatist action.

The proposed National Black Assembly would have 427 delegates chosen from the District of Columbia and the 43 states represented in Gary. While the functions of the assembly, which was authorized by a 2,404–405 vote March 12, were left largely undefined, Imamu Amiri Baraka (formerly known as LeRoi Jones), one of the three convention co-chairmen, said it "could endorse candidates, support candidates, run national voter education and registration drives, lobby for black issues, assess black progress, make recommendations to the national convention" (which itself would be convened every four years) and "be a chief brokerage operation for dealing with the white power political institutions."

Although most speakers emphasized unity of all blacks, major differences surfaced over political cooperation with whites and other issues. Those present included elected officeholders, delegates chosen at local conventions, representatives of organizations ranging from the Black Panthers to the old-line civil rights groups, labor leaders, businessmen and members of the Nixon Administration.

A proposed political agenda drafted at Howard University in Washington prior to the convention by several black professionals, with a preamble prepared by Washington's non-voting representa-

tive to the House Walter E. Fauntroy and Illinois State Sen. Richard Newhouse, was adopted without floor debate at the close of the convention. The preamble was termed "unacceptable" because of its separatist implications March 9 by John A. Morsell, assistant executive director of the National Association for the Advancement of Colored People (NAACP). Newhouse himself said March 12 he was "shocked and dismayed" that the delegates as a whole were not given the opportunity to discuss or amend the document.

The preamble called for "an independent black political movement," since "white America moves toward the abyss created by its own racist arrogance, misplaced priorities, rampant materialism and ethical bankruptcy."

The agenda proposed a constitutional amendment to guarantee black Congressional representation in proportion to population, with 66 representatives and 15 senators, and demanded home rule for the District of Columbia. Local control of police and schools, and a bill of rights for black prisoners was also proposed.

Black Assembly meets. About 300 delegates attended the first meeting of the National Black Assembly in Chicago Oct. 21–22, 1972 and set up a permanent organizational structure, as mandated by the Gary convention.

Rep. Charles C. Diggs Jr. (D. Mich.) was chosen assembly president, Gary Mayor Richard G. Hatcher was voted chairman of the 54-member National Political Council, which would handle ongoing operations, and Imamu Amiri Baraka was elected secretary-general of the assembly and the council.

Party Platforms

1972 pledges. Both political parties, during their 1972 presidential election conventions, adopted platforms with extensive pledges to right the wrongs suffered by women and minorities.

Republican platform—The 1972 Republican charter endorsed the Equal Rights Amendment as well as promises calling for the appointment of women to top-level positions in the government, equal pay for equal work and elimination of discrimination against women at all levels in federal government.

The platform made these statements and proposals on the issue of discrimination in employment:

Equal Rights for Women

The Republican Party recognizes the great contributions women have made to our society as homemakers and mothers, as contributors to the community through volunteer work, and as members of the labor force in careers outside the home. We fully endorse the principle of equal rights, equal opportunities, and equal responsibilities for women, and believe that progress in these areas is needed to achieve the full realization of the potentials of American women both in the home and outside the home.

We reaffirm the President's pledge earlier this year: "The Administration will . . . continue its strong efforts to open equal opportunities for women, recognizing clearly that women are often denied such opportunities today. While every woman may not want a career outside the home, every woman should have the freedom to choose whatever career she wishes—and an equal chance to pursue it."

This Administration has done more than any before it to help women of America achieve equality of opportunity.

Because of its efforts, more top-level and middle-management positions in the Federal government are held by women than ever before. The President has appointed a woman as his special assistant in the White House, specifically charged with the recruitment of women for policy-making jobs in the United States government. Women have also been named to high positions in the Civil Service Commission and the Department of Labor to ensure equal opportunities for employment and advancement at all levels of the Federal service.

In addition we have:

■ Significantly increased resources devoted to enforcement of the Fair Labor Standards Act, providing equal pay for equal work.

■ Required all firms doing business with the government to have affirmative action plans for the hiring and promotion of women.

■ Requested Congress to expand the jurisdiction of the Commission on Civil Rights to cover sex discrimination.

■ Recommended and supported passage of Title IX of the Higher Education Act opposing discrimination against women in educational institutions.

■ Supported the Equal Employment Opportunity Act of 1972 giving the Equal Employment Opportunity Commission enforcement power in sex discrimination cases.

■ Continued our support of the Equal Rights Amendment to the Constitution, our party being the first national party to back this amendment.

Other factors beyond outright employer discrimination—the lack of child care facilities, for example—can limit job opportunities for women. For lower and middle income families, the President supported and signed into law a new tax provision which makes many child care expenses deductible for working parents. Part of the President's recent welfare reform proposal would provide comprehensive day care services so that women on welfare can work.

We believe the primary responsibility for a child's care and upbringing lies with the family. However, we recognize that for economic and many other reasons many parents require assistance in the care of their children.

To help meet this need, we favor the development of publicly or privately run, voluntary, comprehensive, quality day care services, locally controlled but federally assisted, with the requirement that the recipients of these services will pay their fair share of the costs according to their ability.

We oppose ill-considered proposals, incapable of being administered effectively, which would heavily engage the Federal government in this area.

To continue progress for women's rights, we will work toward:

■ Ratification of the Equal Rights Amendment.

■ Appointment of women to highest level positions in the Federal government, including the Cabinet and the Supreme Court.

■ Equal pay for equal work.

■ Elimination of discrimination against women at all levels in Federal government.

■ Elimination of discrimination against women in the criminal justice system, in sentencing, rehabilitation and prison facilities.

■ Increased opportunities for the part-time employment of women, and expanded training programs for women who want to re-enter the labor force. . . .

We pledge vigorous enforcement of all Federal statutes and executive orders barring job discrimination on the basis of sex.

We are proud of the contributions made by women to better government. We regard the active involvement of women on all levels of the political process, from precinct to national status, as of great importance to our country. The Republican Party welcomes and encourages their maximum participation.

Older Americans

We believe our nation must develop a new awareness of the attitudes and needs of our older citizens. Elderly Americans are far too often the forgotten Americans, relegated to lives of idleness and isolation by a society bemused with the concerns of other groups. We are distressed by the tendency of many Americans to ignore the heartbreak and hardship resulting from the generation gap which separates so many of our people from those who have reached the age of retirement. We deplore what is tantamount to cruel discrimination—age discrimination in employment, and the discrimination of neglect and indifference, perhaps the cruelest of all.

We commit ourselves to helping older Americans achieve greater self-reliance and greater opportunities for direct participation in the activities of our society. We believe that the later years should be, not isolated years, not years of dependency, but years of fulfillment and dignity. We believe our older people are not to be regarded as a burden but rather should be valuable participants in our society. We believe their judgment, their experience, and their talents are immensely valuable to our country. . . .

The valuable counsel of older people has been sought directly through the White House Conference on Aging. The President has appointed high level advisers on the problems of the aging to his personal staff.

We have urged upon the opposition Congress— again, typically, to no avail—numerous additional programs of benefit to the elderly. We will continue pressing for these new initiatives to:

■ Increase the amount of money a person can earn without losing Social Security benefits.

■ Increase widow, widower, and delayed retirement benefits. . . .

■ Strengthen private pension plans through tax deductions to encourage their expansion, improved vesting, and protection of the investments in these funds.

■ Reform our tax system so that persons 65 or over will receive increased tax-free income.

■ Encourage volunteer service activities for older Americans, such as the Retired Senior Volunteer Program and the Foster Grandparents Program.

■ Give special attention to bringing full government services within the reach of the elderly in rural areas who are often unable to share fully in their deserved benefits because of geographic inaccessibility.

■ Upgrade other Federal activities important to the elderly including programs for nutrition, housing and nursing homes, transportation, consumer protection, and elimination of age discrimination in government and private employment. . . .

Working Men and Women

. . .

We pledge further modernization of the Federal Civil Service System, including emphasis on executive development. We rededicate ourselves to promotion on merit, equal opportunity, and the setting of clear incentives for higher productivity. We will give continuing close attention to the evolving labor-management relationship in the Federal service.

We pledge realistic programs of education and training so that all Americans able to do so can make their own way, on their own ability, receiving an equal and fair chance to advance themselves. . . .

Ending Discrimination

From its beginning, our party has led the way for equal rights and equal opportunity. This great tradition has been carried forward by the Nixon Administration. . . .

Additionally, we have strengthened Federal enforcement of equal opportunity laws. Spending for civil rights enforcement has been increased from $75 million to $602 million—concrete evidence of our commitment to equal justice for all. The President

also supported and signed into law the Equal Employment Opportunity Act of 1972, which makes the Equal Employment Opportunity Commission a much more powerful body.

Working closely with leaders of construction unions, we have initiated 50 "hometown" plans which call for more than 35,000 additional minority hirings in the building trades during the next four years. We will continue to search out new employment opportunities for minorities in other fields as well. We believe such new jobs can and should be created without displacing those already at work. We will give special consideration to minority Americans who live and make their way in the rural regions of our country—Americans too often bypassed in the advances of the general society. . . .

We pledge to carry forward our efforts to place minority citizens in responsible positions—efforts we feel are already well under way. During the last four years the percentage of minority Federal employes has risen to a record high of almost 20% and, perhaps more important, the quality of jobs for minority Americans has improved. We have recruited more minority citizens for top managerial posts in Civil Service than ever before. We will see that our progress in this area will continue and grow. . . .

Spanish-Speaking Americans

In recognition of the significant contributions to our country by our proud and independent Spanish-speaking citizens, we have developed a comprehensive program to help achieve equal opportunity.

During the last four years Spanish-speaking Americans have achieved a greater role in national affairs. More than 30 have been appointed to high federal positions.

To provide the same learning opportunities enjoyed by other American children, we have increased bilingual education programs almost sixfold since 1969. We initiated a 16-point employment program to help Spanish-speaking workers, created the National Economic Development Association to promote Spanish-speaking business development and expanded economic development opportunities in Spanish-speaking communities. . . .

Indians, Alaska Natives and Hawaiians

. . .

We will continue the policies of Indian preference in hiring and promotion and apply it to all levels, including management and supervisory positions, in those agencies with programs affecting Indian peoples. . . .

Democratic platform—The 1972 Democratic charter called for:

Recognition of the "cultural identity and pride" of blacks, Indians, Spanish- and Asian-Americans and white ethnic groups, and implementation of antibias laws. Recognition of individuals' rights "to make their own choice of lifestyles and private habits without being subject to discrimination or prosecution." (The latter provision had been intended as a non-controversial endorsement of civil rights for homosexuals.)

Appointment of women to federal posts, including the Cabinet and Supreme Court, "to achieve" an equitable ratio of women and men.

The platform said:

The Right to be Different. The new democratic Administration can help lead America to celebrate the magnificence of the diversity within its population, the racial, national, linguistic and religious groups which have contributed so much to the vitality and richness of our national life. As things are, official policy too often forces people into a mold of artificial homogeneity.

Recognition and support of the cultural identity and pride of black people are generations overdue. The American Indians, the Spanish-speaking, the Asian Americans—the cultural and linguistic heritage of these groups is too often ignored in schools and communities. So, too, are the backgrounds, traditions and contributions of white national, ethnic, religious and regional communities ignored. All official discrimination on the basis of sex, age, race, language, political belief, religion, region or national origin must end. No American should be subject to discrimination in employment or restriction in business because of ethnic background or religious practice. Americans should be free to make their own choice of lifestyles and private habits without being subject to discrimination or prosecution. We believe official policy can encourage diversity while continuing to place full emphasis on equal opportunity and integration.

Rights of Women

Women historically have been denied a full voice in the evolution of the political and social institutions of this country and are therefore allied with all under-represented groups in a common desire to form a more humane and compassionate society. The Democratic Party pledges the following:

■ A priority effort to ratify the Equal Rights Amendment;

■ Elimination of discrimination against women in public accommodations and public facilities, public education and in all federally-assisted programs and federally-contracted employment;

■ Extension of the jurisdiction of the Civil Rights Commission to include denial of civil rights on the basis of sex;

■ Full enforcement of all federal statutes and executive laws barring job discrimination on the basis of sex, giving the Equal Employment Opportunities Commission adequate staff and resources and power to issue cease-and-desist orders promptly; . . .

■ Increased efforts to open educational opportunities at all levels, eliminating discrimination against women in access to education, tenure, promotion and salary;

■ Guarantee that all training programs are made more equitable, both in terms of the numbers of women involved and the job opportunities provided; jobs must be available on the basis of skill, not sex;

■ Availability of maternity benefits to all working women; . . .

■ Amendment of the Social Security Act to provide equitable retirement benefits for families with working wives, widows, women heads of households and their children;

■ Amendment of the Internal Revenue Code to permit working families to deduct from gross income as a business expense, housekeeping and child care costs; . . .

■ Extension of the Equal Pay Act to all workers, with amendment to read "equal pay for comparable work;"

■ Appointment of women to positions of top responsibility in all branches of the federal government to achieve an equitable ratio of women and men. Such positions include Cabinet members, agency and division heads and Supreme Court Justices; inclusion of women advisors in equitable ratios on all government studies, commissions and hearings; and

■ Laws authorizing federal grants on a matching basis for financing State Commissions of the Status of Women. . . .

Rights of American Indians

We support rights of American Indians to full rights of citizenship. The federal government should commit all necessary funds to improve the lives of Indians, with no division between reservation and non-reservation Indians. . . .

Rights of the Physically Disabled

The physically disabled have the right to pursue meaningful employment and education, outside a hospital environment, free from unnecessary discrimination, living in adequate housing, with access to public mass transportation and regular medical care. Equal opportunity employment practices should be used by the government in considering their application for federal jobs and equal access to education from pre-school to the college level guaranteed. The physically disabled like all disadvantaged peoples, should be represented in any group making decisions affecting their lives.

Rights of the Mentally Retarded

The mentally retarded must be given employment and educational opportunities that promote their dignity as individuals and ensure their civil rights. Educational and treatment facilities must guarantee that these rights always will be recognized and protected. In addition, to assure these citizens a more meaningful life, emphasis must be placed on programs of treatment that respect their right to life in a non-institutional environment.

Rights of the Elderly

Growing old in America for too many means neglect, sickness, despair and, all too often, poverty. We have failed to discharge the basic obligation of a civilized people to respect and assure the security of our senior citizens. The Democratic Party pledges, as a final step to economic security for all, to end poverty—as measured by official standards—among the retired, the blind and the disabled. Our general program of economic and social justice will benefit the elderly directly. In addition, a Democratic Administration should: . . .

■ Support legislation which allows beneficiaries to earn more income, without reduction of social security payments;

■ Protect individual's pension rights by pension re-insurance and early vesting;

■ Lower retirement eligibility age to 60 in all goverment pension programs; . . .

■ Encourage development of local programs by which senior citizens can serve their community in providing education, recreation, counseling and other services to the rest of the population; . . .

The Democratic Party pledges itself to adopt rules to give those over 60 years old representation on all Party committees and agencies as nearly as possible in proportion to their percentage in the total population.

1976 charters. Considerable space was devoted to women and minorities in the 1976 party platforms as well.

Democratic platform—The 1976 Democratic platform included the following statements:

Full Employment Policies

Special problems faced by young people, especially minorities, entering the labor force persist regardless of the state of the economy. To meet the needs of youth, we should consolidate existing youth employment programs; improve training, apprenticeship, internship and job-counseling programs at the high school and college levels; and permit youth participation in public employment projects.

There are people who will be especially difficult to employ. Special means for training and locating jobs for these people in the private sector, and, to the extent required, in public employment, should be established. Every effort should be made to create jobs in the private sector. Clearly, useful public jobs are far superior to welfare and unemployment payments. The federal government has the responsibility to ensure that all Americans able, willing and seeking work are provided opportunities for useful jobs.

Equal Employment Opportunity

We must be absolutely certain that no person is excluded from the fullest opportunity for economic and social participation in our society on the basis of sex, age, color, religion or national origin. Minority unemployment has historically been at least double the aggregate unemployment rate, with incomes at two-thirds the national average. Special emphasis must be placed on closing this gap.

Accordingly, we reaffirm this Party's commitment to full and vigorous enforcement of all equal opportunities laws and affirmative action. The principal agencies charged with anti-discrimination enforcement in jobs—the Equal Employment Opportunity Commission, the Department of Labor, and the Justice Department—are locked into such overlapping and uncoordinated strategies that a greatly improved government-wide system for the delivery of equal job and promotion opportunities must be developed and adequate funding committed to that end. New remedies to provide equal opportunities need exploration. . . .

Civil & Political Rights

To achieve a just and healthy society and enhance respect and trust in our institutions, we must insure that all citizens are treated equally before the law and given the opportunity, regardless of race, color, sex, religion, age, language or national origin, to participate fully in the economic, social and political processes and to vindicate their legal and constitutional rights.

In reaffirmation of this principle, an historic commitment of the Democratic Party, we pledge vigorous federal programs and policies of compensatory opportunity to remedy for many Americans the generations of injustice and deprivation; and full funding of programs to secure the implementation and enforcement of civil rights.

We seek ratification of the Equal Rights Amendment, to insure that sex discrimination in all its forms will be ended, implementation of Title IX, and elimination of discrimination against women in all federal programs. . . .

Older Citizens

The Democratic Party has always emphasized that adequate income and health care for senior citizens are basic federal government responsibilities. The recent failure of government to reduce unemployment and alleviate the impact of the rising costs of food, housing and energy have placed a heavy burden on those who live on fixed and limited incomes, especially the elderly. Our other platform proposals in these areas are designed to help achieve an adequate income level for the elderly. . . .

Democrats strongly support employment programs and the liberalization of the allowable earnings limitation under Social Security for older Americans who wish to continue working and living as productive citizens. . . .

Republican platform—Among statements made in the 1976 Republican platform:

Equal Rights and Ending Discrimination

Roadblocks must be removed that may prevent Americans from realizing their full potential in society. Unfair discrimination is a burden that intolerably weighs morally, economically and politically upon a free nation. . . .

There must be vigorous enforcement of laws to assure equal treatment in job recruitment, hiring, promotion, pay, credit, mortgage access and housing. The way to end discrimination, however, is not by resurrecting the much discredited quota system and attempting to cloak it in an aura of new respectability. Rather, we must provide alternative means of assisting the victims of past discrimination to realize their full worth as American citizens.

Wiping out past discrimination requires continued emphasis on providing educational opportunities for minority citizens, increasing direct and guaranteed loans to minority business enterprises, and affording qualified minority persons equal opportunities for government positions at all levels.

Women. Women, who comprise a numerical majority of the population, have been denied a just portion of our nation's rights and opportunities. We reaffirm our pledge to work to eliminate discrimination in all areas for reasons of race, color, national origin, age, creed or sex and to enforce vigorously laws guaranteeing women equal rights.

The Republican Party reaffirms its support for ratification of the Equal Rights Amendment. Our party was the first national party to endorse the E.R.A. in 1940. We continue to believe its ratification is essential to insure equal rights for all Americans. In our 1972 platform, the Republican Party recognized the great contributions women have made to society as homemakers and mothers, as contributors to the community through volunteer work, and as members of the labor force in careers. The platform stated then, and repeats now, that the Republican Party "fully endorses the principle of equal rights, equal opportunities and equal responsibilities for women." The Equal Rights Amendment is the embodiment of this principle and . . . we support its swift ratification. . . .

Handicapped Citizens

Handicapped persons must be admitted into the mainstream of our society.

Too often the handicapped population of the nation—over 30 million men, women and children—has been denied the rights taken for granted by other citizens. Time after time, the paths are closed to the handicapped in education, employment, transportation, health care, housing, recreation, insurance, polling booths and due process of law. National involvement is necessary to correct discrimination in these areas. Individual incentive alone cannot do it.

We pledge continued attention to the problems caused by barriers in architecture, communication, transportation and attitudes. In addition, we realize that to deny education and employment simply because of an existing disability runs counter to our accepted belief in the free enterprise system and forces the handicapped to be overly dependent on others. . . .

Older Americans

Older Americans constitute one of our most valuable resources. . . .

Along with loneliness and ill health, older Americans are deeply threatened by inflation. The costs of the basic necessities of life—food, shelter, clothing, health care—have risen so drastically as to reduce the ability of many older persons to subsist with any measure of dignity. In addition to our program for protecting against excessive costs of long-term illness, nothing will be as beneficial to the elderly as the effect of this platform's proposals on curbing inflation.

The Social Security benefits are of inestimable importance to the well-being and financial peace-of-mind of most older Americans. We will not let the Social Security system fail. We will work to make the Social Security system actuarially sound. . . .

· · · We will work for an increase in the earned-income ceiling or its elimination so that, as people live longer, there will not be the present penalty on work. · · · We favor the abolition of arbitrary age levels for mandatory retirement. . . .

Education

Teacher Integration Pressed

The long, highly publicized campaign for integrating black and white students in the nation's schools largely overshadowed a parallel movement to desegregate school faculties. But the integration of schools was resulting in a reduction in the number of teachers needed and in the loss of jobs by black teachers, according to early reports. Federal insistence on "affirmative action"— the requirement that schools recruit and promote minority teachers and women—led to charges of "quotas," "reverse discrimination" and unfairness to white male teachers.

Montgomery court ruling. The Supreme Court ruled unanimously June 2, 1969 that the Montgomery, Ala. school system was required to move toward racial balance in its faculty and staff assignments. The decision, written by Justice Hugo L. Black, ordered the school system to aim at a ratio of three white to two Negro teachers in each school—the same ratio in the school district as a whole—as recommended by Federal District Judge Frank M. Johnson Jr. Black emphasized that the ratio was not a universal constitutional requirement, but only applied in the Montgomery case. It was the first time the court had approved the use of faculty ratios to achieve school desegregation.

U.S. pledges integration drive. Three of the Nixon Administration's chief civil rights officers pledged in separate statements June 25–29, 1970 that the federal government would move to force Southern school districts to comply with school desegregation orders when their schools reopened for the fall term.

One of the officials, Jerris Leonard, chief of the Justice Department's Civil Rights Division, warned that unless state and local officials worked out acceptable desegregation arrangements for their districts, the government would begin filing desegregation suits against their districts.

The first disclosure that a concerted effort was under way to force compliance was made June 25 by Elliot L. Richardson, the new secretary of health, education and welfare (HEW). Richardson warned the schools that the government was prepared to terminate federal funds to those school districts that continued to ignore desegregation orders. Richardson, speaking in Washington, D.C. at his first news conference as head of HEW, said the funds cutoffs would come where necessary. "In any case where appropriate," Richardson said, "I would take that action."

Richardson also said the government would prosecute any discrimination against black students or faculty members in otherwise desegregated schools.

Leonard's statement warning Southern school administrators that they faced possible court action was made June 26 during a week of meetings with Southern public school officials in Augusta, Ga. Leonard told the officials that no further delay would be tolerated in about 50 school districts that had avoided court scrutiny while maintaining token integration arrangements under freedom-of-choice school plans. Most of the 50 districts under government observation were reported to be in the South.

Leonard stressed that no more delays would be tolerated. "Time has run out," Leonard said. "We've gone to great lengths to bring about voluntary compliance, but the end is finally here. We are going to be disinterested in discussing it after next week."

Leonard was joined in Jackson, Miss. June 29 by J. Stanley Pottinger, head of HEW's Office of Civil Rights, to conclude negotiations with Southern school officials over desegregation orders. The two federal officials asserted that most Southerners were convinced that the Nixon Administration intended to force compliance with the law when schools reopened for the fall term. Pottinger said his office would "conduct on-site reviews" of those school districts that were reneging on desegregation orders. He said those districts that failed to comply with desegregation orders would be referred "immediately to the Justice Department for action." Pottinger said about 100 HEW staffers would supervise the monitoring in the field.

U.S. seeks to update orders. The Justice Department March 19, 1971 filed court papers to have school desegregation orders updated for three North Carolina

school systems. Included in the department's motions was a request for an order to have the districts of Anson, Halifax and Northampton increase the desegregation of their schools' faculties.

In the motion involving Anson County, filed in U.S. district court in Charlotte, the department said six of the 10 elementary and one of the two junior high schools had been assigned black teachers on a disproportionate basis. The motion said that 38%–78% of the faculties of the six elementary schools were black, compared with a 52% black faculty ratio in the rest of the Anson district. The junior highs had black faculties ranging from 30% to 60%, compared with a ratio of 40% throughout the district.

The Halifax court papers, filed in U.S. district court in Raleigh, said five elementary schools had black faculty ratios of 88%–100%, compared with a ratio of 76% in other parts of the county.

In the motion against Northampton County, also filed in U.S. district court in Raleigh, the department said the black faculty ratios ranged from 40% to 87.5% in seven elementary schools. Countywide the ratio was said to be 62%. The motion also said four high schools had black faculty ratios of 21.1%–81.8%, although 41% of all high school teachers in the Northampton system were black.

The department asked the courts for orders requiring the three districts to assign faculties to their schools on substantially the same ratio of black and white teachers and other staff members in the entire county school system.

The motions also sought an order to require nondiscrimination in employment practices and the use of nonracial objective standards for the dismissal and demotion of staff and faculty members.

Chicago gets faculty plan. Chicago School Superintendent James T. Redmond unveiled during the week of June 7, 1971 a new plan designed to broaden the integration of the city's public school teachers.

The new plan would recast the city's public school faculties so that no Chicago school would have a staff more than 75% white or 75% black.

The plan was drawn up to meet a federal demand for greater integration of the city's public school teachers. The Department of Health, Education and Welfare (HEW) had recommended a 65–35 ratio of white to black teachers in predominantly white schools and the reverse in schools with a black majority.

Redmond said the new balance would be achieved by assigning all newly appointed teachers or teachers with temporary assignments to black or white schools in a manner that would achieve the integration intended by the plan.

Integration ordered in Grand Rapids. U.S. District Court Judge Albert J. Engel July 18, 1973 ordered integration of teachers and administrators in the Grand Rapids, Mich. school system but rejected a contention by the National Association for the Advancement of Colored People (NAACP) that segregation existed among the system's 70,000 students.

Ruling in a suit filed by the NAACP in 1970, Engel also dismissed from the suit the 11 suburban districts which the NAACP had sought to have included in a metropolitan area integration plan. Grand Rapids school officials had also wanted the suburbs included in any plan to prevent the flight of city whites to the suburbs.

U.S. Court of Appeals ruled May 14, 1974 in Washington that the Department of Health, Education and Welfare (HEW) could not disburse funds to school systems with racially discriminatory teacher assignment policies. The ruling, which reversed a lower court decision, came in a suit to prevent grants totaling $20 million to systems in Baltimore, Detroit, Rochester, N.Y., Los Angeles and Richmond, Calif.

Citing Supreme Court rulings, the court said that faculties in schools receiving federal funds could not be "racially identifiable," and that the effects of racial discrimination must be removed immediately if federal funds were involved. HEW had decided the grants could be made if the school districts promised to end discriminatory practices in the future.

Black Teachers Lose Jobs

U.S. to retrain ousted teachers. The Nixon Administration announced Dec. 11, 1970 an allocation of $3.2 million to retrain Negro teachers in the South who had been displaced in the wake of accelerated school desegregation and the dismantling of dual school systems.

The announcement by the U.S. Office of Education came at the same time the agency released a study indicating that racial bias rather than inadequate training was the underlying cause for the high dismissal rate among black teachers in the South. The report had been prepared by the Race Relations Information Center of Nashville, Tenn.

According to the report, black teachers and administrative personnel were being ousted from their posts as desegregation of the South's public schools continued. The report asserted that "hundreds of them have been demoted, dismissed outright, denied new contracts or pressured into resigning, and the new teachers hired to replace them include fewer and fewer blacks."

The Nixon Administration had not challenged Southern school districts for their alleged bias in dismissing black teachers from their faculties.

The $3.2 million was to be channeled into existing Office of Education programs under which teachers who had been demoted but not dismissed could receive full-year academic fellowships in such short-staffed educational fields as the handicapped, early childhood and vocational training, and part-time training programs. For those teachers who had been dismissed, the agency planned to offer manpower training for new jobs and placement and counseling services.

The new program would reportedly

help 1,500 teachers. The agency's announcement implied that widespread desegregation was almost inevitably going to cause some job losses for black teachers. The announcement said that "school consolidation usually results in a decrease in the total number of education personnel required to serve the same number of students. . . ."

School jobs for blacks in South cut. Citing previously unpublished government statistics, the National Education Association (NEA) said March 18, 1971 that as Southern communities dismantled their dual school systems the number of black teachers and principals dropped while the number of white faculty and administrative personnel increased.

The data was given to the NEA by the government on unanalyzed computer tapes from which the organization compiled its information. The NEA made the final figures public in a friend-of-court brief supporting the Justice Department in a desegregation suit against the state of Georgia. The brief was filed with the U.S. Court of Appeals for the 5th Circuit in New Orleans.

With the brief, the NEA presented the analyzed computer data showing, district by district, how black educators had been dropped from their posts as Southern school systems desegregated. Most of the figures dealt with school systems in Alabama, Florida, Georgia, Louisiana and Mississippi. Incomplete statistics from Texas were also presented.

School districts in those six states that received federal funds were required by law to report the racial compositions of their faculty and administrative staffs to the Department of Health, Education and Welfare (HEW). Of the districts that reported, 69% said the ratio of black to white faculty members had declined the past two years. During this period, the number of black principals in those districts decreased by 20%.

In the districts that submitted figures, 1,040 black teachers were dropped while the number of white teachers rose by 4,192. The data on administrative personnel in Alabama was not complete, but in the other four states 232 black principals lost their jobs while 127 white principals were added to school staffs.

The NEA said the figures "show that black educators, particularly black principals, have borne burdens incident to desegregation in measures greatly disproportionate to any burdens borne by white educators."

(The case to which the NEA brief was attached involved the Justice Department's contention that the federal circuit court did not set strict enough standards for desegregating facilities in its December 1969 order requiring 81 Georgia school district to integrate.)

Black principals losing—Spokesman representing an association of U.S. school principals told a Senate panel June 14 that hundreds of black school principals across the South were either losing their jobs or being demoted as a result of school desegregation in the area.

Members of the National Association of Secondary School Principals told the Senate Committee on Equal Educational Opportunity that federal agencies were doing little to help the ousted black administrators. Sen. Walter F. Mondale (D, Minn.), chairman of the committee, said he would refer the witnesses' testimony to the Justice Department and Department of Health, Education and Welfare (HEW).

Sen. Sam J. Ervin Jr. (D, N.C.) said he was not surprised at what he called an unfortunate situation. He said that since the whites were a majority in the South, it was not unusual for a white principal to be chosen to run a desegregated school that combined a formerly white and a formerly black school.

Dr. Owen B. Kiernan, executive secretary of the principals' association, told the panel that the ousters of black principals and demotions represented "personal catastrophes."

According to the witnesses' figures, in 10 Southern states the number of black principals dropped over the last eight years. In Alabama, for example, the number of black principals dropped in the last three years from 250 to 50. In

Mississippi, 250 black administrators were displaced.

Schools accused. The Justice Department in 1971 charged three school districts in South Carolina, Virginia, and North Carolina with discriminating against black faculty and staff members by dismissing, reassigning and demoting them.

In the South Carolina case, the Justice Department filed a motion for supplemental relief May 28 in the U.S. district court in Columbia against the Chesterfield County school district. The motion charged the district with violating a court order by discriminatorily terminating the employment of black professional staff members at the end of the 1969–70 school year and discriminatorily reassigning and demoting black faculty members for the 1970–71 school year.

The government asked the court to order the district to reinstate, with back pay where appropriate, all professional staff members who were not offered contracts for the 1970–71 school year due to racial reasons.

In the Virginia case, the government filed a motion in the U.S. district court in Norfolk June 1 charging the Nansemond County district with reducing the black teaching staff for the 1971–72 school year and making schools racially identifiable through faculty and staff assignments. In addition, the government papers said a 1970 court-approved desegregation plan had failed to dismantle Nansemond's dual school system.

The district court was asked to order Nansemond's school board to show that its employment practices were not racially discriminatory and to draw up an effective school desegregation plan for the 1971–72 school year.

The government filed papers in Charlotte, N.C. June 1 asking the district court to order the Anson County school district to adopt non-racial employment guidelines and to reassign the county's students to schools on a non-racial basis. The Justice Department had charged the Anson County school board with hiring white teachers in preference to black applicants with better qualifications and dismissing and demoting black teachers.

30,000 black jobs lost. An NEA survey found that over 30,000 teaching jobs for blacks had been eliminated in 17 Southern and border states through desegregation and discrimination since 1954, it was reported May 10, 1972.

The proportion of teachers who were black declined in the region in 1954–70 from 21% to 19%, although the proportion of black students increased slightly. The percentage of existing or projected black teaching jobs displaced was lowest in Alabama, which the report attributed to court orders and continued segregation, and highest in Kentucky, Missouri and Delaware.

According to Samuel B. Ethridge, NEA teacher rights director, "as early as 1968 one state department of education identified 25 counties which employed one or more black teachers in 1954, and employed none in 1968."

Minority teachers fare poorly outside of South. The January 1974 issue of the American School Board Journal quoted Samuel B. Ethridge, director of the National Education Association, as asserting that minority teachers generally have "fared much worse proportionally in the East, North and West than in the South." While various Southern states had relatively favorable ratios of black teachers to black students, Ethridge said, New York "would need almost as many additional black teachers to correct its . . . ratio as would the entire 17 Southern states. . . ." (New York's black teacher-black student ratio was 1–128.) The article continued:

Among cities with unfavorable ratios, according to N.E.A., are Boston, 1–89; New York City, 1–83; Buffalo, 1–79; San Francisco, 1–61; Pittsburgh, 1–57; Oakland, Calif., 1–52, and Columbus, Ohio, 1–50.

East Baton Rouge, La., with a black teacher-student ratio of 1–26, was named by N.E.A. as having the best ratio out of a group of 37 cities from across the country. Other cities with favorable ratios (1–32 or lower) included Houston; Atlanta; Charlotte-Mecklenburg, N.C.; Richmond; Caddo Parish, La.; Washington, D.C.; and Duval County, Fla.

To bring minority educator and minority student ratios in line with the national teacher-student ratio of 1–22.5, N.E.A. says that public schools would have to hire 116,-000 black teachers; 84,500 Spanish-speaking teachers; 7,400 American Indians; and 3,000 Asian Americans.

Just to correct the disparity in black teacher-student ratios, Chicago would have to hire 4,410 black teachers, Philadelphia would have to hire 3,239, Detroit, 2,115, and New York City would need an additional 15,375 black teachers, says N.E.A. . . .

Affirmative Action, Quotas & 'Reverse Discrimination'

HEW sets guidelines. The Department of Health, Education and Welfare (HEW) issued a 17-page set of minority employment guidelines Oct. 4, 1972 for 2,-500 colleges and universities holding federal contracts. The guidelines were drawn up at the request of educators faced with the loss of federal contracts for inadequate affirmative action plans.

The guidelines ruled out quotas for women or minority groups, but said that numerical "goals and timetables" would be required. The goals would be determined by "an analysis by the contractor of its deficiencies and of what it can reasonably do to remedy them, given the availability of qualified minorities and women and the expected turnover in its work force." If "changed employment conditions" or other factors prevented the school from reaching the goal despite "good-faith effort," as determined by an investigative team, the school will be considered to have "complied with the letter and the spirit" of the executive order requiring affirmative action.

J. Stanley Pottinger, director of the HEW Office for Civil Rights, said a total of $23 million in federal contracts had been withheld in the previous two years from noncomplying schools, but all the funds were eventually released after new plans were drawn up.

Before the guidelines were officially released, civil rights groups said the rules would make the executive order "virtually meaningless." In a letter to Pottinger reported Sept. 8, Marian Edelman, writing for the Washington Research Project and also in behalf of the National Urban League, the National Association for the Advancement of Colored People, the National Urban Coalition and the National Council of Negro Women, said the guidelines would replace a "result-oriented compliance system" with a "vague process." Edelman also said the rules would place university faculties in a privileged status, strengthening "a sentiment among many blacks and whites that the poor and less well educated are left to bear the brunt of civil rights compliance."

Pottinger replied, in a Washington Post interview reported Sept. 8 that the guidelines were merely a clarification of existing policy.

Columbia plan accepted. An HEW spokesman announced in Washington Sept. 1, 1972 that the HEW Department had agreed to approve a "final affirmative action" plan submitted by Columbia University, ending a three-year dispute that had temporarily held up several million dollars in federal contracts.

HEW Dec. 4, 1971 had suspended three federal contracts with Columbia University totalling $688,000, and threatened suspension of another contract worth nearly $2 million because the university had failed to submit an affirmative action plan to eliminate discrimination against women and minority group members. Columbia was alleged to have practiced discrimination in hiring for both faculty and service staffs.

The action was taken under a 1967 executive order prohibiting discrimination by federal contractors, which HEW had been delegated to enforce for universities. Columbia had been under investigation by HEW's Civil Rights Office since 1969, and had failed to provide employment data despite repeated requests. All of its contracts could be terminated, HEW warned in a Nov. 4 letter to university president William J. McGill.

The contracts suspended included two from the Agency for International Development and one from the National

Institute on Child Health and Human Development. Federal grants and loans to Columbia and its students were not affected.

HEW's Office for Civil Rights agreed Feb. 29, 1972 to accept the university's interim report on its plan to comply with sexual and minority job rights requirements. The office then provisionally lifted its freeze on $13.8 million in federal contract funds.

Director J. Stanley Pottinger gave Columbia President William J. McGill until April 6 to present a full affirmative action plan, including data on the name, race, sex, position, salary, experience and promotions of all 10,000 faculty and service employes. Pottinger said he was confident that his office and the Labor Department's Office of Federal Contract Compliance, which had final authority over contracts, would be able to accept the full plan.

Although Columbia had been the only university currently under suspension, it was reported Feb. 10 that seven other schools had been threatened with similar action, and that college and university affirmative action plans occupied half the staff of the Office for Civil Rights. In particular, over 400 individual and class action charges had been brought by women concerning hiring, promotion or pay.

The American Council on Education had reported that women held only 22% of campus faculty posts in 1964, compared with 28% in 1940, and that their salaries averaged $1,500 less than those of their male counterparts.

But McGill warned Feb. 25 that "if we take one more step into the centralization of the hiring process, and we tell the faculty that they must consider race and sex as criteria, this place will blow sky high."

Minority quotas scored. The heads of two major Jewish civil rights organizations criticized the use of preferential quotas for admission and employment of minority group members by educational institutions. The criticism was voiced June 29, 1972 in speeches before the National Jewish Community Relations Advisory Council.

Benjamin R. Epstein, national director of the Anti-Defamation League of B'nai B'rith, asked the Department of Health, Education and Welfare to revise its guidelines and discourage "preferential treatment" for some minority groups, which Epstein said resulted in discrimination against other qualified individuals. He suggested expansion of university facilities as part of affirmative action programs to rectify past discrimination.

Naomi Levine, acting executive director of the American Jewish Congress, said universities had violated the law by setting "fixed quotas" to protect "sorely needed federal funds," while the law only required "good faith efforts" to reach attendance and employment goals. The council approved a resolution supporting "specific goals and timetables not determined by population percentages" as long as no "rigid requirements" were set.

Bias cases listed—Six national Jewish organizations sent 19 cases of alleged discrimination in hiring or admissions by colleges against white males to the Office for Civil Rights, which they urged to "prevent or eliminate preferential treatment." The action was made public Jan. 14, 1973. The six Jewish groups said the cases, which they added to 33 other examples previously submitted, usually reflected "college and university policy." They cited new guidelines issued by the Department of Health, Education and Welfare in 1971 in response to an earlier complaint as the basis for action to correct the alleged violations.

The groups were the Anti-Defamation League of B'nai B'rith, the American Jewish Committee, the American Jewish Congress, the Jewish War Veterans, the Jewish Labor Committee and Agudath Israel of America.

HEW & CUNY in agreement. The City University of New York agreed to supply the Office for Civil Rights of the Department of Health, Education and Welfare with an account of the race and sex of all employes, to avoid a threatened loss of $13 million in federal research contracts (reported June 9, 1972).

HEW agreed to allow the university to withhold individual names from the master list, but threatened to move to cut off funds if the university did not allow government access to individual files in cases of discrimination.

San Francisco plan barred. Federal Judge Samuel B. Conti ruled Nov. 4, 1972 in favor of 4,000 white teachers and administrators in the San Francisco school system and ordered the Board of Education to abandon a minority hiring plan as discriminatory.

The board had planned to appoint four minority group members for every five new administrators appointed for five years, to increase the minority share of the total number of administrators from 20% to 37.5%. Conti said "no one race or ethnic group should ever be accorded preferential treatment over another."

Antibias plans for colleges criticized. A report by the Carnegie Council on Policy Studies in Higher Education Aug. 10, 1975 said that federal affirmative action programs to end discrimination in college and university faculties were confused and sometimes in conflict with each other. "Seldom has a good cause spawned such a badly developed series of federal mechanisms," the report said.

The report proposed the creation of a federal panel to revise and coordinate regulations and guidelines currently imposed by the Labor Department, the Department of Health, Education and Welfare and the Equal Employment Opportunity Commission. The HEW secretary should be given sole authority to approve affirmative action plans and impose sanctions, it said. Moreover, graduated penalties should replace the single penalty of cancellation of all federal contracts with a school judged to be failing in affirmative action, the report recommended.

Whites sue to protect job rights. The National Education Association, which had instituted numerous court actions in Alabama to eliminate discrimination against black teachers, filed suit to force the Lowndes County Board of Education to reopen nine staff positions that had been filled by blacks on a noncompetitive basis (reported Nov. 26, 1975). The suit maintained that by failing to notify qualified whites within the system of the job openings, the board violated a 1973 federal court order barring racial discrimination in faculty hiring. Among the positions so filled were superintendent of schools and two other top administrative posts.

The court order had been issued at a time when a white minority controlled the system. Since 1973, however, political control of the county had passed to blacks.

Teacher Organizations

NEA drops Mississippi unit. The nine-member executive board of the National Education Association April 13, 1970 ordered the expulsion of the group's predominantly white Mississippi affiliate because, the board said, the unit refused to merge with a black teachers' organization. An NEA spokesman said it was the first time in the organization's history that a state affiliate had been expelled.

The board members said the Mississippi group was ousted after it had refused to comply with NEA national headquarters' orders that it merge with the predominantly black Mississippi Teachers Association (MTA). In most Southern states the NEA provided teachers with legal resources and offered protection of teacher rights. These services, the board declared, would be available in the future in Mississippi only through membership in the MTA. NEA President George D. Fischer wired the white Mississippi group that it could seek readmittance to the national body only if it successfully negotiated a merger with the MTA.

Black educators seek to protect rights. Black teachers across the South were putting together black-controlled organizations or joining established national groups working to protect the rights of black teachers, according to a New York Times report Sept. 27, 1971.

In all but two Southern states, black teachers' organizations had merged with virtually all-white groups. In those states where consolidation had taken place and no new black groups set up to replace old ones, Negro teachers were reported faring poorly.

In Alabama and Texas, where black teachers set up new groups or joined existing ones, black teachers were reported to be doing better.

Black teachers in Texas, rather than merge with a white group, dissolved and put its resources into the Texas Commission for Democracy in Education, a black-controlled organization that had spearheaded the fight for equal pay for Negro teachers in the 1940s.

Despite the merger of a black teachers' group with a white organization in Alabama, contingency planning prior to the consolidation gave black teachers considerable leeway to act outside the new organization. Five black teachers went into federal court the week of Sept. 20 challenging employment practices that require pregnant teachers to forfeit tenure. The plaintiffs were able to act on their own because, during the merger negotiations between the black and white groups, Negro teachers won the right to go to the National Education Association in the event the state association did not act on requests by teachers for legal representation.

Armed Forces

Discrimination Persists

National policy officially forbids racial discrimination in the armed forces as well as in any other aspect of public affairs. Black leaders charge, however, that, in the words of Rep. Shirley Chisholm (D, N.Y.), "blatant racism ... pervades and cripples the military of this nation."

Report charges racism. Rep. Shirley Chisholm inserted in the Congressional Record Nov. 17, 1971 a report in which her legislative assistant, Thaddeus Garrett Jr., charged that " 'subtle' racism ... has literally crippled and impaired the effectiveness of American troops in NATO countries." According to Garrett's report:

Military promotion and hiring practices are of great concern to Black servicemen. Pointing to the scarcity of Black officers and Blacks in high ranking jobs, they suggested that discrimination is prevalent among those with the authority to hire, fire, promote, and degrade. Black officers, almost all of whom are older, lack rapport with younger Blacks and are considered tokens and pawns of the military and tangible incentives and divisible rewards for Black servicemen. It is felt that they offer little help.

At Athenai Air Base in Athens, Greece, Blacks expressed a firm belief that performance reports and qualifications test scores were being purposely altered or inexplicably lost in personnel offices, giving whites priority in Base employment. They said that many Blacks assigned to positions are not given the actual power and authority that normally accompany the jobs. Blacks also feel that they are not being given jobs which provide adequate exposure to areas which give a greater base for future tests for better jobs. When they apply for jobs, Blacks noted that they are heavily scrutinized and often declared ineligible for employment, whereas whites who frequently have lesser qualifications, are reviewed somewhat superficially and given more priority.

Blacks at Mannheim, Germany, were also concerned about discrimination in employment opportunities. One serviceman said that when Blacks apply for jobs, they are often told that, "we don't have any openings," "we don't need this," "we don't need that," "we can't use you," or "we're over-strengthed." When complaints are filed about these conditions, the same excuses are given. In his Division, this serviceman reported that there is not a single Black in personnel management, processing, financing, or recording, and that whites who were no more qualified than Blacks are now holding these positions.

Another serviceman told that upon returning from leave, he found that he had been replaced at his job in the base gymnasium, even though he had the qualifications and experience necessary for the job. He was offered no explanation for his dismissal.

A related incident, at the Mannheim Compound, involved the firing of a Black who also worked in the base gymnasium. He was told that a school major in physical education was needed for his particular job. Two whites were hired in his place. One of the whites had a major in English and the other a major in industrial arts; both having minors in physical education. A Black with a physical education major and two years of teaching experience behind him, who was a member of the Division, was never considered for the job.

Relative to promotion policies, the Third Armored Division at Frankfurt, Germany, set forth that "All of the Command will be given equal opportunity and treatment irrespective of race, religion, or ethnic or national origin. Every man will be judged on the basis of his job knowledge, his job performance, his on-duty and off-duty conduct as a soldier. Every member of the Division will be given equal opportunity to compete for promotions and privileges . . ." Yet, Black servicemen revealed that they knew of

cases where Blacks had been in the service for a year or more and still had the rank with which they started. They claimed that when Blacks are up for promotion, in too many cases efficiency ratings are changed on orders from the Command by those who have access to the files. The following statistics show a clear discrepancy between what is military policy and what is actual fact.

1971 PROMOTIONS—3D ARMORED DIVISION

	Blacks		Whites	
	Number	Percent	Number	Percent
April:				
E–3 to E–4	22	11.0	182	89.0
E–4 to E–5	22	8.0	238	92.0
May:				
E–3 to E–4	49	12.5	341	[1] 87.5
E–4 to E–5	32	13.2	209	[1] 86.8

[1] Provided by 3rd Army Division, Frankfurt—General Craft.

In these two months, April and May, 1971, of 1095 promotions, the Third Armored Division, Frankfurt, only 125, or less than 11.2%, were awared to Blacks.

	Blacks		Caucasians	
	Number	Percent	Number	Percent
June:				
E–3 to E–4	7	9.3	68	90.7
E–4 to E–5	5	7.1	65	92.9
July:				
E–3 to E–4	78	16.0	408	84.0
E–4 to E–5				

1971 PROMOTIONS—AVERAGE TIME IN GRADE BEFORE PROMOTION

June	Blacks (months)	Caucasians (months)
E–3 to E–4	6.7	4.6
E–4 to E–5	17.1	[1] 8.6

[1] Ibid.

Note: These facts are self-explanatory.

ENLISTED PERSONNEL BY GRADE

[Compiled Dec. 31. 1970]

Navy	Whites	Blacks	Others	Total	Percent black
E–9	3,282	52	41	3,375	1.5
E–8	8,635	283	176	9,094	3.1
E–7	36,323	2,134	1,655	40,112	5.3
E–6	71,344	5,494	4,215	81,053	6.8
E–5	88,552	4,269	3,772	96,593	4.4
E–4	121,552	3,622	4,892	130,066	2.8
E–3	117,849	6,625	7,640	132,114	5.0
E–2	55,690	6,482	1,077	63,249	10.2
E–1	9,481	1,464	297	11,242	13.0
Total	512,708	30,425	23,765	566,898	[1] 5.4

ARMY (COMPILED DEC. 31, 1969)

	Total	Percent black
E–9	5,195	6.1
E–8	17,662	11.1
E–7	59,567	16.6
E–6	105,382	20.7
E–5	204,472	11.0
E–4	343,178	10.9
E–3	170,678	11.2
E–2	171,066	7.6
E–1	183,194	5.0
Total	1,260,394	10.7

MARINE CORPS (COMPILED DEC. 31, 1970)

	Total	Percent black
E–9	1,107	2.3
E–8	4,219	5.3
E–7	8,884	10.5
E–6	15,648	13.4
E–5	30,052	10.6
E–4	39,882	8.1
E–3	42,815	10.4
E–2	33,512	13.6
E–1	32,448	14.2
Total	208,567	[1] 11.2

AIR FORCE (COMPILED DEC. 31, 1970)

	Total	Percent black
E–9	6,413	3.0
E–8	12,842	4.4
F–7	46,470	6.2
E–6	85,345	10.1
E–5	146,296	14.7
E–4	159,555	10.7
E–3	110,148	11.8
E–2	46,959	14.8
E–1	12,794	18.3
Total	626,822	[1] 11.7

OFFICERS BY GRADE

NAVY (COMPILED DEC. 31, 1970)

	Whites	Blacks	Others	Total	Percent black
07–10	313	0	0	313	0
06	4,228	3	1	4,232	.1
05	8,319	25	20	8,364	.3
04	14,930	82	50	15,062	.5
03	20,990	123	59	21,172	.6
02	16,917	103	45	17,065	.6
01	6,875	82	28	6,985	1.2
Total	72,572	418	203	73,193	[1] .6

ARMY (COMPILED DEC. 31, 1969)

	Total	Percent black
07–10	513	0.2
06	6,319	.9
05	16,469	4.1
04	24,220	5.2
03	42,656	3.7
02	22,589	2.6
01	30,636	1.7
Total	143,402	[1] 3.7

MARINE CORPS (COMPILED DEC. 31, 1970)

	Total	Percent black
07–10	78	0
06	751	0
05	1,634	.2
04	3,534	.3
03	5,317	1.4
02	7,477	1.5
01	3,039	1.9
Total	21,830	[1] 1.2

AIR FORCE (COMPILED DEC. 31. 1970)

	Total	Percent black
07–10	429	0.2
06	6,133	.4
05	14,933	1.2
04	25,903	1.7
03	49,389	2.2
02	16,199	1.4
01	14,857	1.2
Total	127,843	[1] 1.7

[1] Provided by Office of the Chief of Naval Operations (Zumwalt)

It is rather clear from these statistics that the military practices discrimination in its promotion policy. It is the objective of the United States and therefore the United States military to ensure freedom and equality for its citizens. Yet, the military openly defies this standard. Frustration and resentment is felt by low ranking Blacks who believe that they have either been denied or not considered for jobs which have been offered to and filled by whites with similar or lesser qualifications....

Army reports rise in racial tensions. Army investigators found that "all indi-

cations point toward an increase in racial tension" on bases throughout the world, according to an official summary of a survey released to newsmen in Saigon Jan. 24, 1970. The report of the inquiry, ordered by Gen. William C. Westmoreland, Army chief of staff, had been presented to the Joint Chiefs of Staff in Washington Sept. 18, 1969 and had been sent to congressmen and to military commanders in the U.S. and abroad.

The report said that "Negro soldiers seem to have lost faith in the Army system," and the investigators predicted increased racial problems unless "aggressive command action, firm but impartial discipline and good leadership can prevent physical confrontation of racial groups." Data collected in the survey indicated that tensions were more serious on overseas bases than in the U.S. and that in Vietnam "polarization of the races" was "more obvious in those areas where groups were not in direct contact with an armed enemy."

Although the study said the Army "has a race problem because our country has a race problem," the investigators cited conditions within the Army that could contribute to unrest among black GIs. According to the report, the number of black junior officers had been decreasing although there were more black noncommissioned officers of lower rank. The survey found that on bases in Europe, where one of every eight soldiers was black, one of every four nonjudicial punishments (minor penalties fixed without trial) was imposed on a Negro GI.

■ A black Pentagon official said July 27, 1971 that nearly a dozen officers had been relieved of command, transferred to new assignments or reprimanded for failure to adequately enforce the Defense Department's guidelines for racial equality in the armed services. Frank W. Render 2nd, deputy assistant secretary of defense, declined to identify the officers beyond saying they ranged from general down to company grade.

Racism cited in Air Force. A 15-man human relations team of Air Force personnel July 26, 1971 denounced the manner in which the leadership at many Air Force training bases was dealing with racial problems.

The team, attached to the Air Training Command (ATC), submitted its finding July 26 to Lt. Gen. George B. Simler, who ordered the study. The official report was not made known until Aug. 30.

In its report, the panel said one thing "has to be taken and understood by everyone in ATC. There is discrimination and racism in the command and it is ugly."

The team's conclusions were made after a six-month study of 15 bases. The group found there was often a double standard for black and white airmen on such matters as punishment, work details, availability of post exchange products and enforcement of regulations.

The report said that "the cause of this is blatant supervisory prejudice in many cases, but for the most part it was the supervisory indifference to human needs."

The panel included seven officers and eight enlisted men. Four of the team's members were Negro and two were Mexican-Americans.

Military racism probed. Members of the Congressional Black Caucus held hearings at military installations in the U.S. Nov. 15, 1971 and in Washington Nov. 16–18 to investigate charges of racism in the armed forces. The hearings were dominated by reports that blacks were unfairly treated by the military justice system, that racial tensions had become "explosive" at some bases in the U.S. and abroad, and that the Defense Department limited the number of black servicemen stationed in some foreign countries at the request of the countries involved.

Rep. Donald V. Dellums (D, Calif.) co-chaired the hearings with Rep. Shirley Chisholm (D, N.Y.).

The inquiry had been announced Nov. 3 by Reps. Chisholm and Dellums, who pointed to a Justice Department report that blacks formed a heavily disproportionate percentage of servicemen in confinement, ranging from 16.2% in the Navy to 53.4% in the Air Force, as possible evidence of discrimination.

Secret Navy and State Department memoranda were quoted by Dellums at the Nov. 16 hearings documenting charges that the armed forces had carefully limited the number of black service personnel stationed in Iceland. According to the documents, the Iceland government in 1961 modified its former refusal to admit any black servicemen, but informal agreements sharply limiting the number of black personnel were still in effect as late as Sept. 9, 1970.

The Iceland U.N. mission in New York Nov. 18 denied that such agreements had been made. The previous day Rear Adm. John Beling, Iceland military chief, said that 40 of 3,000 American troops in his country were black, about twice as many as in 1970.

U.S. Defense Secretary Melvin Laird said Nov. 17 that no discriminatory accords were currently in effect. White House Press Secretary Ronald Ziegler the same day reported President Nixon's opinion that such accords, if they existed, would be improper.

Dellums also charged at the Nov. 16 hearing that the governments of West Germany, Greece and Turkey demanded restrictive assignment for blacks, but he was unable to provide documentation.

The conviction among black soldiers of unfair treatment by the military justice system was found to be common. At a Ft. Meade, Md. hearing conducted Nov. 15 by Rep. Parren J. Mitchell (D, Md.), Army attorney Arthur Stein said authorities frequently imprisoned soldiers who had psychological problems, and unfairly issued less than honorable discharges. Victims of both practices were disproportionately black. But several black commissioned and noncommissioned officers at the base denied the allegations, and praised the Army's efforts to counteract racism.

Nathaniel Jones, general counsel for the National Association for the Advancement of Colored People (NAACP), who had led an NAACP probe of bases in West Germany, Nov. 16 called judicial practices "the most intense problem" he uncovered. Black troops mistrust the system, he said, partly because of "the near total absence of black judges and total absence of black military lawyers."

Action Against Bias

Black defense aide named. Defense Secretary Melvin R. Laird named Donald L. Miller, a New York shipbuilding executive and former Army major, to be the Pentagon's new assistant secretary of defense for equal opportunity Nov. 19, 1971.

Miller succeeded Frank W. Render 2d, who had been forced to resign in August. Both men were black.

The Pentagon rights post was charged with the responsibility of trying to end racial discrimination in the armed forces.

Pro-black bias? Ed Reavis reported in the March 31, 1972 edition of the Stars and Stripes, a newspaper for the U.S. forces in Europe, that "the stated policy of USAREUR [U.S. Armed Forces in Europe] Commander-in-Chief Gen. Michael S. Davison—discriminating in favor of blacks—is paying off, according to the man Davison put in charge of the program, Maj. Gen. Frederic E. Davison." Reavis' article continued:

"We don't like the idea of setting goals or quotas," said Maj. Gen. Davison, "but we don't have the time or luxury to let this occur in an evolutionary manner."

The goal, says Davison, is to put minority members, blacks specifically, in key positions in proportion to their content in USAREUR.

"The decision was made here," Davison said, "to get more blacks in key staff and command positions. The question was how to get people out of a machine that is impartial."

Davison explained that since the Army's machine or machine-assisted system of making assignments is blind, USAREUR could expect no more than its normal share of the Army's black officers, despite the fact that USAREUR had been given priority by the Department of the Army. . . .

Not only does USAREUR expect to increase its percentage of black officers, Davison said, "but we have tried to draw an assignment blueprint of Europe that would give optimal distribution to these positions. In Europe we would attempt to have in every battalion or equivalent-type unit at least one black battalion commander, executive officer or company commander. We also want black NCOs in some key spots in the battalion such as sergeant major or first sergeant." . . .

Touching on the area of civilian employ, Davison said as of November 1971, there were 4,200 GS-appropriated fund employees of whom 200 were blacks. One month later that number jumped to 260.

In the nonappropriated fund area, 420 or 13 per cent of the employes were minority members. In December 1971 it rose to 16.2 per cent, Davison said.

"One point to be noted here is where we only had 19 people in the GS7 to GS11 category in November 1970, we had 30 in December 1971," Davison added. . . .

Davison stressed that the examination for teaching positions will be centralized in USAREUR because of some charges of inequity under the old decentralized system . . .

Both races claim favoritism. The Army Feb. 20, 1973 released a survey that concluded that both white and black soldiers felt that favoritism was extended to soldiers of the other color. The Human Resources Research Organization of Alexandria, Va. collected 86,297 responses from basic trainees at Ft. Ord, Calif. and Ft. Jackson, S.C. in 1971. The study questioned soldiers during their first, eighth, and sixteenth weeks of training about how they thought the Army treated minorities.

In the final survey, 23% of the whites said blacks got favored treatment. This compared with a 5% response the first week.

Of the blacks questioned during the first week, 15% said whites received better treatment. This rose to 38% in the final survey.

Panel probes Navy clashes. A special House Armed Services subcommittee held hearings Nov. 20–25, 1972 into recent racial disorders aboard the aircraft carriers Constellation and Kitty Hawk.

Chief of Naval Operations Adm. Elmo R. Zumwalt was the leadoff witness behind closed doors in Washington. Zumwalt discounted some claims by Navy officials and others that a breakdown in discipline had led to the disorders.

Zumwalt's remarks followed an opening statement by subcommittee chairman Floyd V. Hicks (D, Wash.) that the panel "cannot overlook the possibility that there may exist at this time an environment of—for lack of a better word—'permissiveness,' where all that is needed is a catalyst. Perhaps perceptions of racial relations in these cases provided that spark."

In San Diego Nov. 21, the panel heard Capt. J. D. Ward, commanding officer of the Constellation, relate how he called off maneuvers at sea and put off ship 137 crewmen to avoid open racial warfare aboard the carrier.

The Constellation's executive officer, Cmdr. John Schaub, described for the panel Nov. 22 what he called the Navy's "poorly conceived and totally unfair" system of minority recruitment. Schaub was one of several officers who testified that the racial problems could be tied to the Navy's recruiting of educationally disadvantaged black youths.

Speaking to newsmen, Schaub said he believed the Navy's program of recruiting such men was "totally unfair" because it placed them in competition with other recruits "more fortunate."

Navy condemns bias slowdown. More than 100 Navy admirals and Marine Corps generals were rebuked in Washington Nov. 10, 1972 by Secretary of the Navy John W. Warner and Chief of Naval Operations Adm. Elmo R. Zumwalt Jr. for failing to act sufficiently against racial discrimination in their services.

Warner said recent racial clashes had demonstrated a "lack of communications." Zumwalt charged that the problem stemmed from "the failure of commands to implement" equal opportunity programs "with a full heart," because of allegiance to "hallowed routine."

The officers were warned that "every effort" would be made "to seek out and

take appropriate action, either punitive or administrative, against those persons who are engaged in or condoning discriminatory practices or who have violated either the spirit or the letter of our equal opportunity policy."

Warner said a top-level Human Relations Council was being established to apply "downward pressure" through the ranks. Zumwalt said he was instituting a system of rewards and punishments for effectiveness in equal opportunity, and would give race relations the same priority as professional performance.

According to a Nov. 10 report, blacks in June 1972 comprised 5.8% of Navy enlisted men and .7% of officers.

Pentagon seminars set—The Defense Race Relations Institute (DRRI) said Oct. 30 that all 1,114 U.S. generals and 317 admirals would attend race relations seminars beginning in January 1973. The officers would attend two days of seminars a year.

The institute, located at Patrick Air Force Base in Florida, had already trained 574 field instructors, and was planning to have 1,400 instructors in the field by mid-1973 to conduct seminars for all service personnel.

Navy drops undesirables. The Navy confirmed Feb. 2, 1973 that it had discharged nearly 3,000 enlisted men whom it considered a "burden to the command." Adm. Elmo R. Zumwalt Jr. had issued the order Dec. 26, 1972. Zumwalt's order provided for voluntary-for-mutual-benefit-discharges for sailors with at least one year of service "whose records reflect marginal performance or substandard conduct." Of the number discharged, about 14% were black.

At the same time the Navy said it was tightening its standards of recruitment, with a new emphasis on education and character qualifications. According to the New York Times Feb. 2, one of every four enlistees was at level 4 of the Armed Forced Qualifications Tests during 1972, indicating a sixth grade reading level. The 1971 figure was 14%. One of every six

1972 recruits had a police record.

The Navy said the discharges would be mostly under honorable conditions, with no stigma attached. The Times said, however, that the discharges would carry code numbers, which knowledgable employers could understand to mean "undesirable" or "unsuitable" for re-enlistment."

A Navy spokesman said: "There are too many recruits—not only blacks but members of other minorities and under-privileged whites as well—who cannot cope with the technical training in the skills needed to operate our sophisticated weapons and navigational systems. As a result they are forced into menial jobs, in the laundries, in mess galleys and in deck crews. Their work performance is poor and their opportunities for advancement are very limited. This frequently produces festering resentment which may erupt violently. The blame is not the Navy's, it goes deeper into the American social system."

Navy seeks to recruit more blacks—The Navy had embarked upon a program to recruit more blacks at all levels, from neighborhood recruiting offices to the Naval Academy in Annapolis, Md., it was reported March 11.

However, the Navy admitted at the same time that its standards had been raised. It had taken many poorly educated blacks in recent years. A Navy directive said only blacks with high school diplomas or those who passed the high school equivalency test could be signed. A Navy spokesman said with regard to the Naval Academy, "We're looking for the blue chip kids."

The recruiting effort was reflected in the numbers of blacks attending the academy: the class of 1974 had 11 blacks, the class of 1975 had 34, the class of 1976 had 66, and the class of 1977 was projected to have 150 blacks.

In 1971, 518 blacks were officers in the Navy, of a total of 76,486 officers.

Manpower study criticized. A member of the Defense Manpower Commission, a civilian group that issued a report in April about the forces, told newsmen June 7, 1976 that the report had suppressed evidence of racial discrimination in all four major services.

Edward Scarborough said that a staff paper written for the commission by Kenneth J. Coffey and Frederick J. Reeg had shown that armed service recruiting policies were "racially motivated." These findings, he said, did not appear in the final report "in the kind of detail our staff study showed." The Washington Post quoted Gen. Bruce Palmer Jr., director of the commission, as remarking that day he thought it would have been "wrong to kick the services in the teeth" by including such details in the April report.

The staff paper, as quoted in the Post, declared that in fiscal 1975 Army Secretary Howard H. Callaway Jr. had enacted what commission staffers called the "Callaway shift," a move in which "the Army redistributed its recruiting force with a stated objective of achieving better geographical representation among recruits." This had the effect of reducing the number of blacks who applied as volunteers, "although the impact on black enlistments was not a stated goal of the redistribution program." The staff paper also alleged that "policies which directly limited the enlistment of blacks have been in effect in both the Navy and Marine Corps." It criticized an Air Force test of reading ability which it said was unfair to blacks.

Hasting Keith, who had resigned from the commission as a protest of the alleged coverup of abuses, told the Post June 8 that the commission had "danced around" racial quotas and other matters it was supposed to have investigated and that its work "was done exclusively under the direction of the military and by the military." He noted that Palmer, now retired, had been deputy chief of the Army.

Marine practices probed. Marine Corps recruitment and training practices were investigated in April–June 1976 by the Military Manpower Subcommittee of the House Armed Services Committee. Much of the testimony bore on the case of Lynn McClure, a recruit who had died after reportedly being beaten in training. McClure's parents asserted that their son had been mentally retarded.

Two former Marine recruiters—including Harry D. Faulkner, who had been responsible for signing McClure—told the subcommittee June 4 that they had been ordered to restrict the number of blacks and other racial minorities entering the corps. Faulkner said that during "four or five months of 1975" he was informed by an unnamed superior that "we could only put in two blacks this month."

Other Developments

Workers of Spanish Origin

Mexican-Americans, Puerto Ricans and other workers of Spanish origin have traditionally labored at low-paid, menial occupations. They have suffered from employment discrimination and an exceptionally high rate of unemployment. As the U.S. economy moved into recession, the percentage of Hispanic workers without jobs rose from 7.5% in 1973 to 8.1% in 1974 and 12.9% in 1975 (on an annual average basis).

Bias in government employment. Sen. John V. Tunney (D, Calif.) charged in the Senate Nov. 12, 1971 that Mexican-Americans (Chicanos) were virtually barred from most federal jobs in California and that La Raza Community (Spanish-surnamed persons in general) suffered a similar pattern of near exclusion from federal employment throughout the U.S.

Tunney quoted Sen. Joseph M. Montoya (D, N.M.) as telling the Coalition of Spanish-Speaking Americans Oct. 23 that "in higher government pay-grades, we are virtually ignored and underrepresented.... In grades 16 through 18 we are almost totally excluded in agency after agency.... We qualify to die for America [in war] ...

but not to rise near the top by merit in our government's Civil Service."

Tunney inserted in the Congressional Record a monograph prepared by Public Advocates, Inc., assisted by Tunney's office and sponsored by the Mexican-American Legal Defense & Education Fund, Inc. Summarizing sections of the monograph, Tunney declared:

Of the 293,770 full-time civilian Federal employees in California, only 5.6 percent—16,506—are Mexican American, as compared with 14.9 percent of the work force. This results in Mexican Americans being effectively precluded from middle-class Federal jobs or from jobs affecting the economic, employment, and housing problems of Chicanos. This de factò discrimination against Mexican Americans and their virtual exclusion from better-paying, policymaking positions has produced a form of Government apartheid.

With 70 percent of the agricultural work force in California being Mexican American, it is difficult to comprehend, for example, why none of the top 500 employees in the Department of Agriculture is Mexican American.

Tunney also said:

According to this report, 12 of the 27 largest agencies employ no Mexican Americans in even minor, bureaucratic decisionmaking positions. None of the 27 have more than 3 percent in such positions, and some employ Mexican Americans in proportion to their availability in the work force. Statewide, Anglos are 20 times more likely than Mexican Americans to be in even a minor decision-making position. . . .

Nationwide, Federal Government civilian employment shows a similar underemployment pattern for all Spanish-surnamed persons. Of 2,571,504 full-time employees, only 74,449 are Spanish surnamed. Although Spanish-surnamed persons represent 7 percent of the Nation's population, they constitute only 2.9 percent of all employees. This 2.9-percent Spanish-surnamed figure has remained constant over the last decade.

The absence of any Mexican Americans at agencies such as the U.S. Information Agency—0 of 52—and the Federal Trade Commission—0 of 59—are reflected in the failure of the Information Agency to achieve credibility in Latin America and the FTC to protect the rights of the Spanish-speaking consumer.

This ignominious record strains credulity in that Chicanos capable of leading combat missions should be capable of sufficient training to push papers.

The monograph provided the following tables on alleged employment discrimination against Spanish-surnamed persons by federal agencies in California:

CHART I.— SPANISH-SURNAMED EMPLOYEES FOR FEDERAL AGENCIES EMPLOYING 5,000, OR MORE, FULL-TIME CIVILIANS IN CALIFORNIA (RANKED IN ORDER OF DISCRIMINATION—NO. 1 IS THE GREATEST DISCRIMINATOR, ETC.)

Rank and department	Overall percent Spanish-surnamed employees	Percent Spanish-surnamed in decision-making	Overall percent de facto discrimination [1]
1. Transportation	2.1	0.7	610
2. Interior	2.4	0	525
3. Agriculture	2.9	0	380
4. Treasury	4.1	1.2	270
5. Veterans' Administration	4.5	3.2	220
6. Army	5.4	.7	180
7. Air Force	5.5	0	170
8. Navy	5.7	.4	160
9. HEW	5.8	1.2	160
10. Post Office	6.6	2.0	130
11. Defense Supply Agency	7.9	0	80

[1] Rounded off to nearest 10 percent.

Note: Discrimination percent based on comparison with 14.9 percent, the percent of the California work force that is Chicano.

CHART II.—FEDERAL AGENCIES EMPLOYING BETWEEN 100 AND 5,000 CALIFORNIANS (RANKED IN ORDER OF DISCRIMINATION—NO. 1 IS THE GREATEST DISCRIMINATOR, ETC.)

Rank and department	Overall percent Spanish-surnamed	Percent Spanish-surnamed in decision-making	Overall percent de facto discrimination
1. Federal Home Loan Bank Board	1.0	0	1,390
2. Selective Service	2.8	0	430
3. Commerce	2.9	0	380
4. Atomic Energy	3.0	0	360
5. Secretary of Defense	3.0	2.0	360
6. Aeronautics and Space Administration	3.3	.7	350
7. GAO	3.7	0	310
8. HUD	3.8	4.6	290
9. NLRB	3.9	0	280
10. State	4.8	6.3	210
11. Civil Service	5.4	0	180
12. Justice	5.6	.5	160
13. SBA	6.5	6.7	130
14. General Services	7.2	0	110
15. OEO	8.1	7.7	80
16. Labor	10.0	7.7	50

President Nixon Nov. 5, 1970 had ordered federal agencies to make efforts to achieve population parity in employing Mexican-Americans and other Spanish-surnamed workers. Nixon Aug. 5, 1971 ordered top federal officials to increase the number of Spanish-Americans in important jobs.

Sanchez & Banuelos get top federal jobs. Philip V. Sanchez was nominated Feb. 8, 1971 to be assistant director for operations in the Office of Economic Opportunity (OEO) and was confirmed by the Senate May 8. He became the highest-ranking official of Mexican-American descent in the Nixon Administration. Sanchez then moved up another notch in the government with his appointment Sept. 8 (and confirmation Nov. 17) as OEO director.

President Nixon Sept. 20, 1971 announced the nomination of Mrs. Romana Acosta Banuelos as treasurer of the U.S. He said she would be the highest-ranking Mexican-American woman in the federal government. Her nomination was confirmed by the Senate without opposition Dec. 6 despite controversy that had developed after U.S. immigration agents arrested 36 illegal Mexican aliens working at her Gardenia, Calif. food processing plant.

During the raid, the sixth in three years at the plant, about 30 other employes fled through rear exits. Those arrested were returned to Mexico the following day. The firm employed 400 low-wage workers.

Mrs. Banuelos, who built the $6 million a year business from a 1949 tortilla stand, charged Oct. 6 that the raid had been inspired by Democrats attempting to block confirmation of her appointment. George K. Rosenberg, district director of the Immigration Service, denied the charge. He said he had sent the firm a letter Aug. 8, 1969 asking them to cease hiring the aliens. Mrs. Banuelos denied knowledge of the letter.

White House Press Secretary Ronald L. Ziegler said Oct. 6 that the Administration would stand by its appointment. He noted that federal law did not require employers to check the residence status of employes, or prohibit employment of illegal entrants.

House Republican leader Gerald R. Ford (Mich.) said Oct. 6 that confirmation might depend on whether Mrs. Banuelos had known of the previous raids. But Joseph M. Montoya, (D, N.M.), the only senator of Mexican ancestry, said Oct. 7 that the nominee should not be rejected for having employed "these unfortunate people."

Mexican-American groups were divided in their reaction. The 300 delegates to the second annual Mexican-American National Issues Conference in Sacramento, Calif. Oct. 10 asked Nixon to withdraw the nomination. A resolution charged that Mrs. Banuelos had "repeatedly" exploited and degraded Mexican women and other employes. However, five Spanish-American groups, in a joint news conference Oct. 14, affirmed their support for the nomination. They were the National G.I. Forum, National League of Latin American Citizens, National Puerto Rican Forum, Association of Cuban American Organizations, and National Economic Development Association.

Maymi heads Women's Bureau. Carmen Maymi, a Puerto Rican woman, was nominated by President Nixon May 9, 1973 to be director of the Women's Bureau (of the Department of Labor). The appointment was confirmed by the Senate June 7.

Puerto Ricans charge neglect. The Puerto Rican Association for National Affairs Aug. 10, 1971 assailed Nixon's nomination of Henry M. Ramirez, a Mexican-American, as chairman of the Cabinet Committee on Opportunities for Spanish-Speaking People. Ramirez had dismissed two Puerto Rican staff members the previous day.

The association charged that the committee, formed to safeguard the interests of Spanish-Americans in federal programs and develop new programs, was not sufficiently concerned with Puerto Ricans. The charges were backed by Reps. Herman Badillo (D, N.Y.), a Puerto Rican, and Edward R. Roybal (D, Calif.), a Mexican-American.

A committee spokesman denied Sept. 6 that the staff members had been dismissed for ethnic reasons, and claimed that three of 25 current staff members as well as several prospective members were Puerto Rican.

Conference plans political action. The first major conference uniting Mexican-American, Puerto Rican and other Hispanic groups voted Oct. 24, 1971 to set up a permanent Washington office, and summoned a representative convention to determine national political strategy.

The conference, sponsored by four of the six Spanish-Americans in Congress, attracted about 2,000 participants to Washington, including state and local officials.

Puerto Rican bias. A study made for the U.S. Equal Employment Opportunity Commission by the Center for Environmental and Consumer Justice found that Puerto Rican businesses discriminated against Puerto Ricans, it was reported May 28, 1974.

The study—a survey of 45 local busi-

Employment status of the Spanish-origin, white, and black populations, by sex and age, annual averages, 1973-75

[Numbers in thousands]

Employment status	Spanish origin¹			White			Black²		
	1973	1974	1975	1973	1974	1975	1973	1974	1975
Total, 16 years and over									
Civilian noninstitutional population	5,997	6,424	6,689	129,302	131,375	133,501	14,788	15,159	15,541
Civilian labor force	3,603	3,921	4,058	78,689	80,678	82,084	8,890	9,054	9,123
Percent of population	60.1	61.0	60.7	60.9	61.4	61.5	60.1	59.7	58.7
Employment	3,333	3,604	3,561	75,278	76,620	75,713	8,061	8,112	7,782
Unemployment	270	316	497	3,411	4,057	6,371	829	942	1,341
Unemployment rate	7.5	8.1	12.2	4.3	5.0	7.8	9.3	10.4	14.7
Males, 20 years and over									
Civilian noninstitutional population	2,425	2,618	2,664	54,503	55,497	56,501	5,662	5,803	5,954
Civilian labor force	2,084	2,253	2,278	44,490	45,195	45,617	4,430	4,495	4,514
Percent of population	85.9	86.1	85.5	81.6	81.4	80.7	78.2	77.5	75.8
Employment	1,973	2,117	2,057	43,183	43,630	42,801	4,170	4,168	3,955
Unemployment	111	135	220	1,307	1,565	2,816	260	326	559
Unemployment rate	5.3	6.0	9.7	2.9	3.5	6.2	5.9	7.3	12.4
Females, 20 years and over									
Civilian noninstitutional population	2,718	2,896	3,083	61,319	62,163	63,145	7,050	7,244	7,427
Civilian labor force	1,118	1,233	1,345	26,647	27,616	28,609	3,635	3,720	3,786
Percent of population	41.1	42.6	43.6	43.5	44.4	45.3	51.6	51.4	51.0
Employment	1,038	1,138	1,189	25,494	26,222	26,459	3,325	3,397	3,328
Unemployment	81	95	156	1,153	1,394	2,149	310	322	458
Unemployment rate	7.2	7.7	11.6	4.3	5.0	7.5	8.5	8.7	12.1
Both sexes, 16 to 19 years old									
Civilian noninstitutional population	855	911	943	13,481	13,715	13,854	2,076	2,112	2,160
Civilian labor force	401	435	435	7,552	7,867	7,858	824	839	823
Percent of population	46.9	47.7	46.1	56.0	57.4	56.7	39.7	39.7	38.1
Employment	321	349	315	6,602	6,768	6,452	566	546	498
Unemployment	79	86	121	950	1,099	1,406	259	293	324
Unemployment rate	19.8	19.8	27.7	12.6	14.0	17.9	31.4	34.9	39.4

¹ Data on persons of Spanish origin are tabulated separately without regard to race, which means that they are also included in the data for white and black workers. According to the 1970 census, approximately 96 percent of their population was classified as white.

² These data refer to black workers only. At the time of the 1970 census, they comprised about 89 percent of the total "black and other" population group.

From Monthly Labor Review, Bureau of Labor Statistics, September 1976 nesses, including major companies in manufacturing, banking, retail sales, service industries, construction and transportation—found that firms gave hiring and promotion preference to U.S. continentals and Cuban immigrants over Puerto Ricans. There was also extensive discrimination against blacks and women, the study reported.

N.Y. job situation. Rep. Herman Badillo (D, N.Y.) reported in the Congressional Record Feb. 4, 1976 on the results of a study of the socioeconomic makeup of New York's Puerto Rican community. The study was made by the Bureau of Labor Statistics on Badillo's request. Badillo cited these "major findings":

In 1970, 45 percent of Puerto Rican workers residing in New York City were employed in white-collar and skilled blue-collar jobs as compared with only 27 percent in 1960. The proportion employed as unskilled laborers dropped sharply from 73 percent in 1960 to 55 percent in 1970. Despite these notable improvements, Puerto Ricans were typically found in lower paying and lower status jobs as compared with other New Yorkers.

Despite improvements in the types of jobs held, over-the-decade family income gains for Puerto Ricans—up 46 percent—lagged behind other New Yorkers—up 59 percent—resulting in a widening income gap between them. Family income for Puerto Ricans was 63 percent of the citywide median in 1959, and 58 percent in 1969.

The proportion of working-age Puerto Ricans in the labor force—working or looking for work—fell between 1960 and 1970. By 1970, less than half of working age Puerto Ricans residing in New York City were in the labor force as compared with about three-fifths of the total population. Labor force participation rates for women, aged 14 and over, fell sharply from 38 percent in 1960 to 27 percent in 1970. This was in contrast to the pattern for all New York City women, 40 percent of whom were in the labor force in 1960, and 41 percent in 1970. The rate for Puerto Rican males dropped sharply from 79 percent in 1960 to 66 percent

in 1970, as compared with a citywide decline from 79 to 71 percent.

A sharp drop in labor force participation was experienced by Puerto Rican teenagers. In 1960, Puerto Rican males aged 14 to 19, were more likely to be in the labor force than other young New Yorkers. By 1970, the participation rate for Puerto Rican male youth had fallen one-third below the rate of their counterparts through the New York area. The participation rate for Puerto Rican girls also dropped sharply....

Hispanics losing ground. Rep. Edward Roybal (D, Calif.), chairman of the National Association of Latino Democratic Officials, told the Democratic Platform Committee in May 1976 that Spanish-Americans were losing ground in employment and in general economic progress. He said:

In 1970, our median family income was 79% of that for all families.

In 1975, our median family income was only 74%. We actually lost ground.

Our unemployment rate has practically doubled in the past 5 years. In 1970, it was 6.5. In 1975, it was 12.2.

Nearly a half a million Latinos were unemployed at the end of the first quarter of 1976. The Bureau of Labor Statistics reported 453,000 Latinos out of work.

The unemployment rate for Latino young people aged 16 to 19 was a disgraceful 21.6% in the first quarter of 1976....

I trust at this late date that it is not necessary to "document" the fact of discrimination against the Latino community by citing the occupational distribution of Latino workers which indicates significant difference between the types of jobs held by Latino workers and the general workforce. Although 16% of the nationwide workforce is employed in professional and technical work (white collar) only 9% of Latino workers are so employed ...

The number of Latinos employed by the Federal government has increased seven tenths of one percent from 1966 to 1975, from 2.6 to 3.3 percent. In specific categories such as Wage Board (blue collar) we actually lost 442 positions between 1974 and 1975. In this category it took us 9 years (1966 to 1975) to "gain" a total of 905 positions.

In the very Federal agencies which play a crucial role in the solution of some of the problems we will discuss today, there is a paucity of Latinos. 1974-1975 figures for the

Federal government shows that Latinos comprise only 1.4% of the Health Services Staff
at HEW and less than 1% of the Health Resources Administration and Alcohol, Drug
Abuse and Mental Health Administration.
Even more insulting is the percentage in
the entire National Institutes of Health—
less than 0.6%.
The Bureau of the Census which plays a
vital role in providing us with the appall-
ing facts we will discuss today only had 1.4
Latinos in their total workforce, a paltry 68
out of 4,828. This 1.4% is actually a decline
from December 1974 wehn the Census workforce was 1.6% Latino....

Indians

Rights unit. The Justice Department announced Aug. 13, 1973 the creation of
an Office of Indian Rights within the department's Civil Rights Division. Assistant Attorney General J. Stanley Pottinger said the new office would coordinate most Indian matters formerly handled elsewhere in the department and
initiate litigation.

Department officials said there had
been reluctance to establish offices based
on "racial categories," but it was decided
that Indian rights were a "special area of
law" because of the complexity of federal
treaties with them.

Carl Stoiber, a civil rights division attorney, was named director of the office.
R. Dennis Ickes was named deputy director. Neither of the officials was Indian,
but Pottinger said an effort would be
made to recruit Indian attorneys.

BIA job ruling. Supreme Court Justice
Thurgood Marshall Aug. 16, 1973 stayed
a lower court ruling that had nullified employment preference for Indians in the Bureau of Indian Affairs
(BIA). He acted after a federal court
in Albuquerque, N.M. had ruled June 1
that the policy violated U.S. civil rights
laws.

Marshall issued the stay at the request
of the government, which said the bureau
was caught between conflicting court
rulings and faced contempt citations no
matter which choice was made between
Indian and non-Indian job applicants.

(Kickapoo and Pottawatomi Indians
held the local BIA office in Horton
Kan. April 9, 1975 for 12 hours and
secured the removal of Superintendent
Jack Carson and his replacement by
Robert Delaware, an Indian employed by
the bureau in Oklahoma. The action, in
which the Indians also reportedly won
government recognition for their tribal
leadership and separation from federal
funding ties with two neighboring tribes,
ended three years of efforts to replace
Carson.)

Reservation Navajo's election upheld.
The Supreme Court Feb. 19, 1974 affirmed
(by refusing to grant review) a decision
upholding the election of a Navajo Indian
as a county supervisor. Voters in the
Arizona county in which he was elected
challenged his eligibility for office on the
grounds that because he lived on a
reservation he was immune from taxes
and normal legal process.

Armed Indians occupy plants. Fairchild
Camera & Instrument Corp., a Mountain View (Calif.) based company, announced March 13, 1975 that it would
permanently close its Shiprock, N.M.
electronics plant, which had been occupied for eight days by armed members
of the American Indian Movement (AIM)
protesting the layoff of 140 Indian
workers. The plant, which made semicon-
ductors and integrated circuits for use in
computers, was located on the reservation
of the Navajo Nation and had employed
about 600 Navajos—mostly women—before Fairchild had instituted the layoff in
early February.

A Fairchild spokesman said the firm
had "been assessing the damages and
evaluating the long-term implications of
this seizure," which had ended March 3.
"Fairchild has concluded that it couldn't
be reasonably assured that future disrup-
tions wouldn't occur," the spokesman
said.

Larry Anderson, a Navajo and national
treasurer of AIM, said his group had
acted "because the little people have been
pushed around for too long and had been

exploited for cheap labor." Nonetheless, he and other AIM members agreed not to stage another take-over without first consulting the Navajo tribal council, it was reported March 17.

Highway patrolmen at Wagner, S.D. employed tear gas May 2 to drive out eight armed Indians from the Yankton Sioux Industries pork plant after they had taken over the building earlier in the day and ordered Melvin Rosenthal, the manager, to leave.

Mayor Raymond Duncanson proclaimed martial law. Greg Zephier, a local AIM leader, had been arrested the previous day for legal action in connection with the March occupation of the plant by some 40 members of the Eagle Warrior Society of the Yankton Sioux tribe, which owned 51% of the pork facility. The militants, who were "protesting poor working conditions and lack of communication between the manager of the plant and Indian people," had ended a three-day take-over of the building March 19 after reaching a labor agreement with Loren Farmer, head of the Yankton Sioux agency of the Bureau of Indian Affairs.

Religion & Bias

Black priests restive. The Rev. Rollins Lambert, a black priest in the Chicago Archdiocese, Jan. 10, 1969 scored Archbishop John Cody and "the whole white church" as "unconsciously racist." Father Lambert, reportedly regarded as a conservative, made the remarks following his appointment to the pastorate at the all-black St. Dorothy's Church on Chicago's South Side. Terming his appointment a "political move," Lambert contended that the Rev. George H. Clements, a militant Negro priest who had been assistant pastor of St. Dorothy's for six years, should have been named pastor. Lambert declared that "if Father Clements is not made a pastor immediately" and "if black pastors are not appointed in black parishes wherever possible, I will not continue to serve as pastor of St. Dorothy's Church."

The Black Catholic Clergy Caucus, an organization representing about one-half of the nation's 165 Negro priests, asked March 11 for creation of a black-operated Central Office for Black Catholicism in the U.S.A. Under the proposal, presented to a committee of three bishops in Detroit, the office would appoint Negro priests to parishes on invitation of the local bishop and clergy and would send teams to colleges with large numbers of Negro students.

Catholic women distribute Eucharist. Two Iowa Catholic women, Mrs. Cornell mann of New Vienna, became the first lay women in the U.S. permitted to distribute the Holy Eucharist, it was reported Feb. 23, 1970. They were among 49 "extraordinary ministers" named by Archbishop James J. Byrrie of Dubuque in accordance with a Vatican plan for lay participation in distributing the sacrament in the absence of regular priests.

National Council names blacks. The 250-member general board of the National Council of Churches met in Tulsa, Okla. Jan. 19–23, 1970, devoting much of its time to increasing minority representation within its organizational structure.

The council's general secretary, Dr. R. H. Edwin Espy, reported to the policy-making board Jan. 20 that three blacks would be named to the top posts of director of recruiting, associate general secretary for communications and associate general for overseas ministries. Espy said he was making the announcement to reinforce credibility in the council's intentions to increase minority representation among the council's 170 top "power" jobs to which only 12 blacks had been appointed in the past. Espy said the ultimate target was to fill at least 25% of those posts with blacks.

The appointments were linked to a staff paper which stressed that failure to "empower" blacks, women and youths would assure continued dissatisfaction among minorities and result in "confrontation rather than corporate consultations."

In related developments, black representation was increased in the election of 525 persons Jan. 19 as program chairmen, heads of standing committees and committee personnel. The election ratified the nominations of a nominating committee, headed by Theressa Hoover (a black United Methodist lay woman), which had insisted on increasing the participation of minority groups in council activities. The results defied a warning by the Rev. David R. Hunter, deputy general secretary, against risking "financial suicide" by electing more blacks to major planning posts that customarily had been filled by persons in a position to obtain funds for the council from their denominations.

The Rev. W. Sterling Carey of New York was unanimously elected president of the National Council of Churches Dec. 7, 1972 at the group's convention.

Cary, 45, the first black to hold that office, was an administrator of the United Church of Christ.

Claire Randell, 54, was elected general secretary (chief administrative officer) of the National Council Oct. 13, 1973. She succeeded Dr. R. H. Edwin Espy.

Seminary seeks more blacks & women. The board of the Union Theological Seminary voted May 31, 1972 to require that in future selections, students, faculty, staff and directors be one-third black and representatives of other minority groups and one-half be women.

Mrs. Beverly Harrison, a seminary professor and head of the planning group which proposed the change, acknowledged that the seminary would have initial difficulty in placing 50 women graduates a year.

Moslems elect woman. Zehia Kalil of Michigan became the first woman president of the Federation of Islamic Associations in the U.S. and Canada, which

represented two million Moslems, at the group's annual meeting Aug. 20, 1972.

1st woman rabbi ordained. The first woman rabbi in the U.S. and the second in the history of Judaism, Sally J. Priesand, 25, was ordained June 2, 1972 in Cincinnati.

Rabbi Alfred Gottschalk, president of the Hebrew Union College-Jewish Institute of Religion where she studied, said Miss Priesand's ordination "attests to the principle of reform Judaism long espoused—the equality of women in the congregation of the Lord."

Blacks head Presbyterians. The General Assembly of the United Presbyterian Church in the U.S.A., meeting in Omaha, Neb. May 16–23, 1973, elected the Rev. Clinton M. Marsh as the second black moderator in the history of the denomination.

The Rev. Dr. Lawrence W. Bottoms of Decatur, Ga. was elected June 16, 1974 as the first black to be moderator of the Presbyterian Church in the United States. Blacks comprised less than 1% of the membership of churches in the Southern and Border states.

United Church of Christ elects black woman. The United Church of Christ, at its biennial synod in St. Louis June 23–26, 1973, elected Margaret A. Haywood, a District of Columbia superior court judge, as moderator June 23. She was the first black woman to hold a top leadership position in a U.S. biracial denomination.

Episcopal women ordained. In rites at the Church of the Advocate in North Philadelphia July 29, 1974, four bishops of the Episcopal Church and 11 women deacons defied church law when the bishops ordained the women to the church's priesthood.

Official reaction to the ordination came July 31 when two of the women were suspended by the bishops of their dioceses, and presiding Bishop John Maury Allin, national leader of the church, called an Aug. 14 meeting of the House of Bishops to consider disciplinary action. Allin did not declare the ordination invalid since such action would be up to bishops of individual dioceses.

Episcopal women had won the right to be deacons, the lowest order in the ministry, at the 1970 triennial general convention but were denied ordination to the priesthood through a voting procedure under which women received a voting majority in the House of Bishops and House of Deputies, but which counted divided votes in a single diocese as negative.

The ordination was announced July 19 by the Right Rev. Robert L. DeWitt, former bishop of Pennsylvania; the Right Rev. Edward R. Welles II, retired bishop of west Missouri; and the Right Rev. Daniel Corrigan, a retired former vice president of the church. The Right Rev. J. Antonio Ramos, a Puerto Rican-born bishop of Costa Rica, presided with the others in the ceremony.

Bishop Allin, the bishop-presidents of eight U.S. provinces and the Rev. John B. Coburn, president of the House of Deputies, requested without result July 24 that the bishops reconsider their plans to ordain the women.

At the ceremony, Dr. Charles V. Willie, a black Episcopal layman, asserted to the congregation of 1,500 the belief "in a Christian duty to disobey unjust laws." Charles H. Osborn, executive director of the American Church Union, a conservative Episcopal group which had planned legal action reported June 26 to block the ordination, declared "the proceedings ... unlawful and schismatical, constituting a grave injury to the peace of Christ's church." The Rev. George W. Rutler of Rosement, Pa. accused the ordaining bishops of trying to "make stones into bread," a feat, he claimed, of "magic," rather than of "sacramental grace."

However, about 50 priests joined the bishops in the laying-on-of-hands, a symbolic welcome of the ordinand to the priesthood.

The new priests, whose ages ranged from 27 to 79: the Rev. Jeannette R. Piccard, the Rev. Emily Hewitt, the Rev. Marie Moorefield, the Rev. Carter Heyward, the Rev. Alison Cheek, the Rev. Betty B. Schiess, the Rev. Suzanne Hiatt, the Rev. Katrina Swanson, the Rev. Merrill Bittner, the Rev. Sister Alla Bozarth-Campbell, and the Rev. Constantine H. Wittig.

Two of the women were suspended July 30 by the bishops of their dioceses. Bittner, 27, of Webster, N.Y. was suspended by Bishop Ned Cole of central New York. Schiess, 51, of Syracuse, N.Y. was suspended by Bishop Robert R. Spears Jr. of Rochester, N.Y.

Women get posts as priests. Harvey H. Guthrie Jr., dean of the Episcopal Divinity School of Cambridge, Mass., announced Jan. 31, 1975 that Suzanne Hiatt and Carter Heyward, two of 11 Episcopal women ordained in the Philadelphia ceremony, would get faculty appointments with "all the privileges of other ordained members of the seminary faculty." Heyward would be assistant professor of theology, and Hiatt assistant professor of pastoral theology.

Alison Cheek was installed Aug. 25 as assistant priest of St. Stephen and the Incarnation. She was the first woman to be employed as a priest.

The New Hampshire Episcopal Diocese voted 129-53 to allow female ordination and urged that the national church change canon law, it was reported May 12.

No action vs. bishops. A board of inquiry declined March 26, 1975 to recommend disciplinary action against the four bishops who had ordained the women. The panel said it would not rule against the bishops on the ground that the "core of the controversy is doctrinal." Under church law, 10 bishops would have to bring formal charges and two-thirds of the House of Bishops would have to vote to bring about a heresy trial.

Bishop won't ordain men. William F. Creighton, Episcopal bishop of Washington, said April 1, 1975 that he would not ordain men to the priesthood so long as he could not also ordain women.

Creighton had sent a letter to other U.S. Episcopal bishops saying that his conscience would no longer permit him to act with "injustice" against qualified women deacons. He said, however, that he would not force his decision on other bishops and that male candidates were free to seek ordination in other dioceses.

The decision was welcomed by deacons Alison Palmer, Betty Rosenberg and Lee Wiesner, who had been certified for the priesthood by the Washington diocesan standing committee. The Washington standing committee had been vocal in its support of the women.

Creighton had refused Jan. 23 to ordain the Revs. Palmer and Wiesner until the general convention of the church, due to meet late in 1976, ruled on the question of female ordination.

Suffragan Bishop John Thomas Walker, following the orders of Creighton, his superior, refused to ordain Palmer, Rosenberg and the Rev. Lee McGee March 1, and Palmer again on Feb. 16. During the March 1 ceremony at the Emmanuel Episcopal Church in Anacostia, the congregation and the Rev. James R. Anderson, elevated that day to the priesthood, demonstrated support for the women while Bishop Walker said he supported their cause.

In Rochester, N.Y., Bishop Robert R. Spears Jr. refused Jan. 17 to regularize the ordination of the Rev. Merrill Bittner, one of the 11 women ordained in Philadelphia. Spears, like Creighton, supported the women but said he needed approval of the church.

Church courts convict Wendt & Beebe. Two Episcopal ecclesiastical courts convicted church rectors in separate trials for disobeying the "godly admonition" of their superior bishops. Each priest had allowed two women priests, whose legitimacy had been widely disputed within the church, to officiate at holy communion services.

The Rev. L. Peter Beebe was convicted unanimously June 20, 1975 by the church five-man court after a three-day trial ending May 15 in Sandusky, Ohio. The rector had permitted the Revs. Alison Cheek and Carter Heyward to celebrate communion against the wishes of Bishop John H. Burt.

The Rev. William A. Wendt was then convicted by a vote of 3-2 June 5 after a three-day trial ending May 2 for allowing Cheek to celebrate communion at St. Stephen's Episcopal Church in Washington against the wishes of Bishop William F. Creighton.

Both courts asked Burt and Creighton to administer a relatively light punishment, an admonition that the rectors refrain from similar disobedience in the future.

Meanwhile, Beebe again permitted Cheek and Heyward to celebrate communion June 22 and the vestry of Wendt's church formally invited Cheek to join their congregation "as a member and as a priest" June 23. Cheek petitioned Creighton for a formal transfer from the Virginia to the Washington diocese, but the bishop refused her request.

More Episcopal women ordained. The Rt. Rev. George W. Barrett, retired Bishop of Rochester ordained four Episcopal women as priests Sept. 7, 1975 in a ceremony at St. Stephen and the Incarnation Church in Washington, D.C.

A congregation of 1,200 attended the service and 50 priests joined in with the laying-on-of-hands. The Rev. James Wattley, executive secretary of the Apostolic Ministry, and Emile Oberholtzer, a layman, were given the floor to dispute the validity of the ordinations.

The ordained women were the Rev. Diane Tickell of Anchorage, Alaska, the Revs. Betty Rosenberg, Alison Palmer and Lee McGee, all of Washington. The four had announced the ceremony Aug. 24, along with the Rev. Phyllis Edwards of Evanston, Ill., who later canceled her participation. The five sent letters to all the bishops of the Episcopal Church Aug. 25 but were denied permission to be ordained by the Rt. Rev. William F. Creighton, bishop of Washington. Creighton said he had informed Barrett Aug. 26 that the "irregular ordinations [could] imperil the action of the General Convention," which Creighton said he hoped would be favorable to the women.

Creighton Sept. 3 called for a boycott of the ordinations and a prohibition on church hiring of the women. It was reported Sept. 13 that the Rt. Rev.

Robert C. Rusack, bishop of Los Angeles, in an apparently unprecedented move Sept. 3 had revoked Barrett's license to perform priestly functions at holy ceremonies. Barrett had retired in 1970 as Bishop of Rochester and was residing in California.

Homosexuals

Homosexual minister ordained. The Northern California conference of the United Church of Christ approved April 30, 1972 the ordination of a homosexual, by a 62–34 vote of lay and clerical delegates at San Carlos, Calif. It was believed to be the first ordination of an avowed homosexual by an established American church.

The Council for Church and Ministry of the United Church of Christ voted unanimously May 1 in Greensboro, N.C. that it could not "at this stage give categorical endorsement to the ordination of a stated homosexual," but asked that each case be considered locally on its merits.

Homosexuals as teachers. In 1972 a professed homosexual was officially authorized to teach in Pennsylvania.

Pennsylvania State Secretary of Education John C. Pittenger ruled Sept. 22 that Joseph Acanfora 3rd, an admitted homosexual, was certified to teach in the state. Acanfora had been dismissed in February as a student teacher in a University Park junior high school after bringing suit against Pennsylvania State University for alleged discrimination against homosexuals. The University Teachers Certification Council then split 3–3 on whether Acanfora met the requirement of "good moral character." Pittenger said he would not have certified Acanfora if he had ever been convicted of homosexual activities.

The Supreme Court Oct. 15, 1974 upheld the dismissal of a Maryland school teacher who had been fired for failing to list his membership in a homosexual organization in college on his job application form.

Homosexual rights bill rejected. The city council of New York City, by a vote of 22–19 May 23, 1974 killed a bill that would have banned discrimination in housing, employment and public accommodations because of "sexual orientation." The bill was the first to come to a floor vote in the council after 3½ years of controversy in committees.

Observers said a key factor in the bill's defeat was the strong opposition by the Roman Catholic Archdiocese of New York, which had editorialized in its official newspaper against employment of homosexuals in positions of "sensitive personal influence," such as teachers, counselors "and persons on the staffs of organizations that provide services ... to young boys and girls."

In other developments involving homosexual rights:

■ The Minneapolis city council approved an ordinance March 29 banning discrimination in education, public accommodations, housing and jobs on the basis of "affectional or sexual preference."

■ In a special election May 7, voters in Boulder, Colo. defeated by a 2–1 margin an amendment to the city charter which would have prevented job dismissals on grounds of homosexuality.

■ Town trustees in Alfred, N.Y. (population 3,800) approved an ordinance banning any bias against homosexuals, it was reported May 8.

■ According to the Associated Press May 8, laws banning various forms of discrimination against homosexuals had been passed in Detroit, San Francisco, Seattle and Washington, D.C.

AT&T bans homosexual bias. The American Telephone & Telegraph Co. (AT&T), the largest private employer in the U.S., banned discrimination against homosexuals in future hiring and retention of current jobs, it was reported Aug. 8, 1975.

An AT&T spokesman said the parent

company had recommended the policy to its operating subsidiaries, which had previously been allowed to deal with such issues independently. Some subsidiaries had reportedly followed stringent anti-homosexual policies.

Homosexual gets security clearance. Otis Francis Tabler Jr., an admitted homosexual, was granted a secret-level industrial security clearance by a Defense Department field examiner, it was reported Feb. 1, 1975. Tabler, a computer scientist, worked as a consultant for the Air Force on unclassified contracts.

In his ruling after a public hearing, examiner Richard S. Farr said it "was clearly consistent with the national interest" to grant the clearance. "It is concluded that the applicant's sexual activities are not likely to subject him to coercion, influence or pressure.... It is further concluded that the applicant successfully has rebutted any inference that his variant sexual practices tend to show that he is not reliable or trustworthy."

A spokesman for Tabler said it was the first such security clearance granted a homosexual.

Discrimination against homosexuals barred in Anchorage. The City Assembly of Anchorage, Alaska passed an ordinance Dec. 30, 1975 which specifically prohibited discrimination against homosexuals. Employment and various other items were among the many areas covered by the ordinance, which barred discrimination based on age, marital status, or physical handicaps, as well as that based on race, color, sex, religion, national origin and sexual preference.

Bias against homosexuals barred in many cities. Rep. Edward I. Koch inserted in the Congressional Record April 30, 1976 letters from officials of many communities that had established policies barring employment and other forms of bias against homosexuals as well as members of other minority groups. The communities with such policies included:

Detroit, Austin, Tex., Portland, Ore., Hennepin County, Minn., San Jose, Calif., St. Paul, Minn., Bloomington, Ind., the District of Columbia, Santa Barbara, Calif., Palo Alto, Calif., Mountain View, Calif., Madison, Wis., Seattle, Chapel Hill, N.C., Ann Arbor, Mich. and Berkeley, Calif.

Age

Airline workers win case. Airline workers won an age-bias case in 1972.

Pan American World Airways agreed to a damage settlement of $250,000 to 29 former employes who had been found by the Labor Department to have been laid off, retired or given inactive status solely because of age, in violation of the Age Discrimination in Employment Act, it was reported Oct. 18.

The employes, who had been between the ages of 40 and 65, had all worked for Pan American at Miami International Airport.

Greyhound loses suit. U.S. District Court Judge James B. Parsons ruled in Chicago Feb. 5, 1973 that Greyhound Lines, Inc. would have to stop refusing to hire new bus drivers simply because they were over 40.

The Labor Department, which had brought the suit, said it was the first to be brought under the Age Discrimination in Employment Act of 1967.

Parsons said the company had failed to show that all applicants over 40 were "inflexible, unadaptable and untrainable." In the future, he ruled, Greyhound would have to demonstrate in each case of refusal to hire that an individual would be more accident-prone than younger drivers or than older drivers who had been hired between the ages of 24 and 38, as had been the company's practice.

Standard Oil accord. Standard Oil Co. (California) agreed May 16, 1974 to pay $2 million in back wages to 160 persons between the ages of 40 and 65 who had been discharged and to rehire 120 of them. The workers had been employed in eight western states in Standard's Western Operations Division.

The Labor Department, which obtained the consent decree, had charged the company with using age as a criterion for dismissal over a three-year period.

The back-pay settlement was the largest under the Age Discrimination in Employment Act of 1967. The discharged employes would be also reinstated in the company's pension, insurance and stock-purchase plans without loss.

Rail system sued on age bias. The Labor Department filed a suit charging Chessie System Inc., owner of the Baltimore & Ohio and Chesapeake & Ohio railroads, with illegally dismissing, demoting or denying work to 300 supervisory employes because of age (reported June 20, 1974).

For the first time under the 1967 Age Discrimination Act, the department sought abolition of a mandatory retirement age of 62, which had been included in a revision of the company's pension plan. The department charged that while the 1967 law did not apply to "bona fide" pension plans, the Chessie retirement provision did not meet this criterion, since it was designed to discriminate rather than benefit the pension system itself.

The suit also sought rehiring of unfairly discharged workers, reinstatement of demoted employes to their original jobs and payment of back wages and interest totaling an estimated $20 million.

Government retirement policy upheld. The Supreme Court Feb. 24, 1975, by refusing review, affirmed a lower court decision upholding the federal government's right to retire its employes at age 70, over objections that the policy constituted illegal discrimination because of age.

Unemployment of elderly high. Rep. Bella Abzug (D, N.Y.) told the House March 9, 1976 that "the incidence of unemployment,

particularly long-term unemployment, ... is shockingly high among workers over the age of 40. According to Department of Labor Statistics, this group represents 26.7% of all unemployed Americans. In 1975, unemployment averaged 1.6 million for middle-age and older workers. This is the highest level in history.... Moreover, it is estimated that more than one million formerly employed men and women between the ages of 40 and 62 have given up the active search for work, because of a loss of hope for employment."

Rep. Benjamin S. Rosenthal (D, N.Y.) noted in a statement in the Congressional Record June 28, 1976 that the 1967 Age Discrimination Act protected "only people between ages 40 and 65 ... against discrimination." "According to recent polls," he said, "no fewer than seven million Americans have been dismissed against their will solely because the employment clock ran out."

Other Situations

Veteran wins ruling. The 5th U.S. Circuit Court of Appeals ruled that a municipality could not deny employment to a Vietnam veteran solely because he had not received an honorable discharge (reported Jan. 8, 1974). The court held unanimously that Plaquemine, La. violated the 14th Amendment's guarantees of due process and equal protection under the laws when it passed an ordinance barring city employment to any veteran not honorably discharged. As a result, Tommy Thompson, who as a conscientious objector had been administratively discharged as "undesirable," was fired from his job at the city power plant.

"Numerous factors which have absolutely no relationship to one's ability to work as a custodian in a power plant may lead to other than honorable discharges from the military, including security considerations, sodomy, homosexuality, financial irresponsibility and bed wetting," the court said.

"The point is not that some or all of these considerations must, as a matter of due process, be excluded from consideration of fitness to hold the position of power plant custodian. However, a general category of 'persons with other than honorable discharges' is too broad to be called 'reasonable' when it leads to automatic dismissal from any form of municipal employment."

Joseph B. DuPont Sr., Plaquemine city attorney and judge who drafted the ordinance, said the purpose of the law had been to "raise the moral character" of those in city employment. Col. Victor A. De Fiori, a Defense Department expert on the military discharge system, said it was his view that it was easy to achieve an honorable discharge with a good SPN number, the coded notation placed on a discharge card to indicate the pluses or minuses of a serviceman's record. De Fiori called an honorable discharge an "employment reference" for those who could get it.

In contrast, David Addlestone, director of the American Civil Liberties Union's effort to contest the discharge system, said that an other than honorable discharge could cause a veteran to be denied credit, certain types of licenses or insurance. He stressed the need for stricter standards of due process for administrative discharges (general and undesirable).

Arkansas court backs Marxist's appeal.
The Arkansas State Supreme Court April 7, 1975 ruled as unconstitutional a state law prohibiting state agencies from employing Communists or Fascists. The court characterized the statute as too broad and imprecise and a violation of the 1st Amendment of the U.S. Constitution.

The decision reversed a lower state court ruling that barred the University of Arkansas at Little Rock from paying the salary of Dr. Grant Cooper, a fomer associate history professor, who was also a member of the Progressive Labor Party, a Marxist organization. Originally, 22 state legislators had brought suit against the university to gain action against Cooper.

Cooper, a non-tenured faculty member, had been dismissed after the spring 1974 semester because the university said he was a poor teacher. Cooper later brought suit in federal court, charging he had been fired for his politics.

Anti-Jewish bias charged. The Anti-Defamation League of B'nai B'rith June 10, 1975 accused Arabian American Oil Co. (Aramco), the world's largest crude oil producer, and three other firms of anti-Jewish discrimination in recruiting personnel for employment in Saudi Arabia and Dubai. Complaints alleging violations of federal civil rights laws were filed with the U.S. Equal Employment Opportunity Commission, a Defamation League spokesman said.

Named in addition to Aramco were Bendix-Siyanco Co., a unit of Bendix Corp.; International School Services; and Hospital Corp. of America. Saudi Arabia owned 60% of Aramco's producing assets, but four U.S. oil firms—Exxon Corp., Texaco Inc., Standard Oil Co. of California and Mobil Oil Corp.—owned the company.

Bias against handicapped. Rep. Edward I. Koch (D, N.Y.) told the House May 4, 1976 that recently formed consumer groups created by handicapped people have charged that agencies specifically designed to help the handicapped actually practiced employment discrimination against handicapped persons. Koch said:

Recently, I attended meetings held in New York City by these consumer groups. Allegations concerning the hiring practices of the voluntary bodies for the disabled were shocking. To determine whether these allegations were in fact true, I conducted a survey of nine organizations to determine the number of handicapped employees on their staffs. Five agencies responded. Of the 382 persons employed by those 5 agencies, only 23 of them have any physical handicap. One would think that these institutions, most knowledgeable about the needs and abilities of the handicapped would have more such people on their staffs.

These newly established handicapped consumer groups have attempted to open channels of communication with the appropriate agencies, but as one leader,

Kurt Shamberg, president of People for Rehabilitating and Integrating the Disabled Through Education—PRIDE—said to me, "the agencies are not listening, they are dismissing us, their own consumers, as a radical minority." Unfortunately as a result of mutual distrust and animosity, both factions are reluctant to recognize the benefits that each could gain from the other.

The need for legislation to protect the rights of the handicapped has been discussed by this and previous Congresses. During the 92d Congress a bill was passed to extend the Vocational Rehabilitation Act. The President vetoed the bill. The 92d Congress enacted similar legislation. Again, the President vetoed the bill. Following this second veto a number of bills were introduced as compromise measures. On September 26, 1973, President Nixon signed into law as Public Law 93-112, the Rehabilitation Act of 1973.

At the request of my good friend and colleague from Connecticut, Mr. Dodd, the General Accounting Office recently undertook a study of the implementation of sections 503 and 504 of this act. Section 503 requires all Federal contractors with contracts in excess of $2,500 to take affirmative action regarding employment of the handicapped. Section 504 prohibits discrimination against an otherwise qualified handicapped individual by any recipient of Federal assistance. The report indicated that 3 years after the enactment of the act, there had been minimal enforcement of section 503 and even more reprehensible, no action to enforce section 504.

Last week, Mr. Speaker, the President ordered the Department of Health, Education, and Welfare to establish rules barring discrimination against handicapped workers in federally assisted programs. Specifically, the President instructed HEW to establish guidelines for compliance with the allocation of Federal financial assistance and to determine what constituted discriminatory practices.

Rights laws apply to whites. The Supreme Court held June 25, 1976 that two civil rights laws protected whites as well as nonwhites.

One law was the 1964 Civil Rights Act, Title VII, which prohibited discrimination by employers. Its applicability to whites as well as nonwhites was by unanimous agreement of the court.

The other law was part of the 1866 Civil Rights Act known as Section 1981, which affirmed that "all persons" shall have the "same right" to "make and enforce contracts, to sue, be parties, give evidence."

In continuing its guarantee of "the full and equal benefit of all laws and proceedings for the security of persons and property," Section 1981 added, "as is enjoyed by white citizens."

The court stressed the application of the provision to "all persons." In going back to the Senate discussion of the legislation before passage, the court found remarks that the law would apply to all persons including whites. The phrase "as is enjoyed by white citizens" was added in the House, the court said, but further debate on the bill reinforced the intent to have coverage for whites as well as nonwhites.

"The statutory structure and legislative history," the court said, "persuades us that the 39th Congress was intent upon establishing in the federal law a broader principle than would have been necessary simply to meet the particular and immediate plight of the Negro slave."

The extension of protection to whites under this provision was voted 7-2 by the court. Justices Byron White and William Rehnquist dissented. The majority opinion was written by Justice Thurgood Marshall, the court's only black member.

The case concerned two white men who claimed discrimination on the basis of race after they were fired for allegedly misappropriating company property. A third man, a black, also implicated in the matter, was not dismissed.

The case was McDonald v. Sante Fe Trail Transp. Co. (75-260).

Index

Farm work—92. Federal actions—10, 29. Federal jobs—153-4, 157-8
    Homosexuals—See under 'H'
    Indians, American—46
    Men—1, 5, 8, 58, 70, 92, 96.
Mexican Americans—153-4
    Part-time workers—9, 58. Private industry—45-6, 48, 93; see also specific industry name
    Service workers—92. Spanish Americans—46, 153-4, 156-8
    Unemployment—See under 'U'
    White-collar work—5, 46, 48, 60, 62, 92. Whites—1, 3, 5, 46, 58, 60.
    Women—1, 3, 5, 11, 58, 92, 96, 141, 156
EMPLOYMENT   Service,   U.S. (USES)—35-6
ENGEL, Judge Albert J.—137
ENGINEERS—37
ENVIRONMENTAL & Consumer Justice, Center for—155, 157
EPISCOPAL Divinity School (Cambridge, Mass.)—161
EPISCOPALIANS—160-1
EPSTEIN, Benjamin R.—141
EQUAL Employment Opportunity Act (1972)—14, 53, 129-30
EQUAL Employment Opportunity Commission (EEOC)—10-1, 18-9, 33, 36-7, 68, 72, 80, 129-31. Agency problems—19, 53-4, 57, 72-3, 91. AT&T charges—38-41. Legislation—10-1, 14. Private industry—65-6, 93. Puerto Ricans—155, 157. Reverse discrimination—52. Sex discrimination guidelines—91-2. Unions charged—36, 54, 65-6. Utilities—37. Women's employment—10-2, 93, 101, 106, 110, 112, 119
EQUAL Pay Act (1963)—13, 89, 131
EQUAL Rights Amendment (ERA)—85-8, 120, 129, 131-3
ERVIN Jr., Sen. Sam J. (D, N.C.)—24, 86, 138
ESPY, Dr. R. H. Edwin—159-60
ETHRIDGE, Samuel B.—139

F

FAIRCHILD Camera & Instrument Corp. (Mountain View, Calif.)—158
FAIRCHILD, Ala.—42-3
FAIR Labor Standards Act (1938)—13, 129
FARAH Manufacturing Co.—67
FARENTHOLD, Frances—98
FARMER, Loren—159

FARMERS' Cooperative Compress—41
FARM Labor Service—See RURAL Manpower Service
FARR, Richard S.—164
FAULKNER, Harry D.—152
FAUNTROY, Walter E.—70, 124, 128
FEDERAL Bureau of Investigation (FBI): Women—95, 97
FEDERAL Civil Rights Enforcement Effort (report)—21-2
FEDERAL Communications Commission (FCC)—39-40, 59. Blacks—44-5, 51. Broadcasting industry—44-5, 69-70
FEDERAL Contract Compliance, Office of—13, 141
FEDERAL Deposit Insurance Corp.—59
FEDERAL Home Loan Bank Board—59, 154
FEDERAL Power Commission (FPC)—37, 59
FEDERAL Reserve Board—59
FEDERAL Trade Commission (FTC)—154
FEDERATION of Islamic Associations in the U.S. & Canada—160
FENWICK, Millicent—124
FERGUSON, Miriam—127
FERRE, Maurice—127
FINANCIAL Industry—59, 112
FIREFIGHTERS—83
    Asian-Americans—53, 77-8
    Blacks—47, 77-9
    Mexican-Americans—53, 77-8. Minority quota—76; hiring preference ruling—78
    Spanish-Americans—47, 75, 77-8
    Women—77-8
FIRST Wisconsin Trust Co.—117
FISCHER, George D.—142
FLETCHER, Arthur A.—24, 28-9, 55
FLORIDA:
    Blacks: elected officials—124; police quota—53; school faculty desegregation—138; teacher-student ratio—139; union bias—54
    Rural Legal Services, Inc.—36
    Women—54; Equal Rights Amendment—86-7
    Unions—54
FOOD Industry—48
FORD, Gerald R.—109, 155
FORD 2d, Henry—45-6
FORD, John—125
FORD Foundation—77
FORD Motor Co.—65

HESBURGH, Rev. Theodore M.—21–2, 57
HEWITT, Rev. Emily—161
HEYWARD, Rev. Carter—161
HIATT, Suzanne—161
HICKS, Rep. Floyd V. (D, Wash.)—150
HIGGENBOTHAM Jr., Judge A. Leon—41
HIGHWAYS—34
HILL, Herbert—22, 29, 55, 66, 82
HILLS, Carla Anderson—98
HIRSCHKOP, Philip—95
HISPANIC Americans—See SPANISH-Americans
HODGSON, James D.—26, 32, 35–6, 43–4, 55, 90–1
HOLLAND, George—42
HOLM, Brig. Gen. Jeanne—107
HOMOSEXUALS: Private industry—163–4. Protestant minister—163. Teachers—163
HOOK, Sidney—82
HOOKS, Benjamin L.—51
HOOVER, J. Edgar—95
HOSPITAL Corp. of America—166
HOUSEHOLD Workers—7, 92
HOUSING—31, 34, 130, 132–3, 153
HOUSING & Urban Development, Department of (HUD)—47, 98, 154
HOUSTON—34. Black teacher-student ratio—139. Federal jobs—47. Minority hiring quota—25. Private industry—11, 36
HOWARD University—45
HUMAN Resources Research Organization—149
HUMAN Rights, State Division of (N.Y.)—111–2
HUNTER, Rev. David R.—160

I

ICELAND—148
ICKES, R. Dennis—158
IDAHO: Equal Rights Amendment—86. Farm workers—36
ILLINOIS: Blacks—32; school faculties desegregation—136–7. Minority hiring & training—32. Racial violence—74. Unions—112–3. Women—90–1, 103; Equal Rights Amendment—86–7
IMMIGRANTS—155
INCARNATION Church (Wash., D.C.)—162–3
INDEPENDENT Steelworkers Union—65

INDIANA: Black elected officials—124. Equal Rights Amendment—86–7. Farm workers—36. Homosexuals—164
INDIANAPOLIS: Minority hiring quota—25
INDIANS, American:
Auto industry employment—46
Bureau of Indian Affairs—158–9
Civil rights unit—158. Communications industry—45
Elected officials—158
Federal employment—50, 52. Firefighters—83
Job quotas—54–5
Policemen—77. Political platforms—130–1. Private industry—38, 45–6, 66. Protests & demonstrations—158–9
Teacher-student ratio—140
Unions—38. Utilities job plan—66
Women's rights—89
INDUSTRIAL Workers—26, 42–3, 54, 65, 91
INFORMATION Agency, U.S.—154
INSTITUTE of Black Elected Officials—127–8
INTERIOR, Department of the—59, 154. Bureau of Indian Affairs—158–9
INTERNATIONAL Association of Bridge, Structural & Ornamental Iron Workers—24, 29, 32, 63
INTERNATIONAL Association of Machinists & Trucking Employers, Inc.—38, 54
INTERNATIONAL Brotherhood of Electrical Workers—54, 65
INTERNATIONAL Brotherhood of Teamsters—38
INTERNATIONAL Development, Agency for—140
INTERNATIONAL Longshoremen's Association (ILA)—34, 65
INTERNATIONAL School Services—166
INTERNATIONAL Typographical Union—65
INTERNATIONAL Union of Electrical, Radio & Machine Workers—65
INTERNATIONAL Union of Operating Engineers—37
INTERSTATE Commerce Commission (ICC)—59
IOWA: Women—159; Equal Rights Amendment—86
IRON Workers—24, 29, 32, 63
IRWIN, Donald M.—29

platforms—131; pregnancy leaves—65, 110, 143; servicewomen—108; unemployment benefits—111

Other employment & employment gains—58, 70, 94–5, 106–10, 113, 115, 117, 119–20, 157; blue-collar workers—92, 100, 118–9; employment study pattern—10–2; firefighters—78; nonagricultural workers—8; policemen—75–8; white-collar workers—66, 92, 102, 113, 115, 119; work experience—96

Pensions & retirement benefits —100, 120–1, 131; profit sharing—120; Social Security reforms—90. Politics—88–9, 124–7, 129, 131–3. Private industry—39–41, 45, 63, 65–6, 68–70, 111, 157; divorce rate—117; executives—117; publishing industry—111–2, 117; professional & technical jobs—70, 113, 115, 117, 120; stock exchange job program—112; utilities job plan—66; see also specific industry. Puerto Ricans—157

Quota system—68–9, 77, 81–4, 106
Religious bias—159–63; Catholic —159; Protestant—160–3; Rabbis—160

Sales workers—70, 102. Seniority system—67–9, 90–1. Service workers—92, 102. Spanish-Americans—118, 157. Strike for equality march—88

Tax laws—90

Unemployment—2–4, 8, 58, 63–4, 111, 117, 119, 156; blacks—2, 4, 8, 63–4, 119, 156; recession—117, 119; blue-collar workers—119; white-collar workers—119. Universities & colleges—103, 105–6; Columbia University—141; Service academy admission—109–10

Wage earnings—7, 45, 104; doctorate holders—117; minimum wage —89; Equal Pay Act (1963)—13; equal

pay protection (back-pay)—40–1, 65, 67, 69, 89; wage inequities—91, 100, 105, 112–7, 119–20; Whites—1–4, 8; 64
WOMEN in the Air Force (WAFs)—107
WOMEN Biophysicists, Caucus of—97
WOMEN'S Action Alliance—99
WOMEN'S Army Corps (WAC)—106–7
WOMEN'S Bureau—13–4, 155
WOMEN'S Equity Action League—97
WOMEN'S Liberation—88
WOODSON, S. Howard—127
WORKERS Defense League—30
WRC AM-FM—93
WRC-TV—93
WREC-TV—65
WRIGHT, Dr. Nathan—17
WYOMING: Women—127

X

XEROX Corp.—65

Y

YANKTON, S.D.—159
YANKTON Sioux Indians—159
YANKTON Sioux Industries—159
YORTY, Sam—125
YOUNG, Rev. Andrew—124
YOUNGSTOWN Sheet & Tube Co.—68
YOUTH: Employment—94, 157. Unemployment—5, 64, 94, 156; blacks & other minorities—5, 63–4, 156; men —63–4, 156; Spanish-Americans —156–7; women—63–4, 156

Z

ZAGORIA, Sam A.—42
ZIEGLER, Ronald L.—18, 21, 98, 155
ZEPHIER, Greg—159
ZUMWALT Jr., Adm. Elmo R.—107, 149–50